# Praise for *Becoming Us*

*I haven't seen anything like* Becoming Us. *The world needs this!*
—Kent Hoffman, Co-Founder, Circle of Security

Becoming Us *is a landmark. It fills a huge and sorely overlooked gap and goes a long way to creating families that flourish, right from the beginning."*
—Jordan Paul, PhD, co-author of
*Do I Have to Give Up Me to Be Loved by You?*

Becoming Us *is a journey into parenthood. I love the ease with which it takes the reader down that inspired path.*
—Anni Daulter, author of
*Sacred Pregnancy: A Loving Guide and Journal for Expectant Moms*

*Parents need to be supported emotionally as well as practically.* Becoming Us *takes care of parents' hearts, attentively and sensitively guiding them through the seismic changes that each new child brings to their relationship.*
—Robin Grille, author of *Heart-to-Heart Parenting*

*Wonderful, worthy and needed.*
—Marcy Axness, author of *Parenting for Peace*

*So little focus is placed on the most important foundation a new baby truly needs—the solid relationship of their parents. This is why I love* Becoming Us. *It highlights issues that are commonly left unspoken, provides unique insights and is a resource for both mothers and fathers that I cannot recommend highly enough.*
—Darren Mattock, *LifeOfDad.com*

Becoming Us *is a game-changer for parents and professionals.*
—Sally Placksin, author of *Mothering the New Mother*

# Becoming Us

## The Couple's Guide to Surviving Parenthood and Growing a Family that Thrives

(The Journey Edition)

Elly Taylor

Three Turtles Press

The information in this book is not intended as a substitute for professional help. For personal concerns about yourself, partner, child, or other, please seek support from a professional counselor or qualified health practitioner. With respect, the author and others associated with this publication do not take responsibility for the effects of readers' use of the information contained within or linked to this book and will not be held liable.

First published in Australia in 2011
by HarperCollins Publishers Australia Pty Ltd

Second edition published in 2014
by Three Turtles Press, Sydney

This edition published in 2019
by Three Turtles Press, Sydney and San Francisco



Cover: Maxmart

Library of Congress Control Number: 2019907046

Library of Congress Subject Headings:
Relationships
Marriage
Parenthood
Parenting
Motherhood
Fatherhood

ISBN 978-0-9923856-1-3

For Our Family

Out beyond ideas of wrongdoing
and rightdoing, there is a field.
I'll meet you there.

—Rumi

# CONTENTS

# Before We Begin

## Your Journey So Far

If you've discovered this guidebook while you're still expecting, you're lucky. And your baby is even more so, because even if you only get through the first few sections before they join you, the reading you and your partner do now will serve all of you—and *especially* your baby—well after you've welcomed them into your arms.

If your baby has just joined you, congratulations! You leaped and you've landed. Somewhere. *Becoming Us* will help you find your feet and plan your way from here.

If you have a toddler or young child now, wow, you're right in the thick of it. This guide will help you make sense of the chaos, find new perspectives and support you in finding your way to creating the family you want.

If you're expanding your family and expecting a second or more baby, this book will help you to look back on your parenthood journey. It will help you see where you may have gone off-track and give you multiple opportunities for "do-overs." Hopefully, you'll find yourselves on a better path. One that leads you both to where you'll want to be.

Even if you have older children, you'll find help here. Especially if your parenting journey has left you feeling distant from your partner. *Becoming Us* will help you look back on the paths you have taken so far. You'll see your journey with clearer eyes—all the ways and times you travelled in different directions. There may be some sadness in this. But you'll also find new insights and understanding into yourself, your life, your relationships, your partner, their life and their relationships. You'll have the steps to find your way back to each other with hope and healing as well.

If you are a professional working with expecting, new, or not-so-new parents as a birth, health, mental health, coaching, therapy or other helping professional, this book is for you too. You'll find it a valuable guide and an essential resource for your parents and families. I'm honored that *Becoming Us* is on the recommended reading list for some of the world's leading childbirth organizations and is becoming a resource for birth professionals to give as a parting gift for new parents. This book *can* take over where their important work finishes.

No matter where you are in your parenthood journey, this guide is here for you because you may not have been aware of some of the most important aspects of the journey before now. There's a big information and support gap for most couples because few parents, and even few parenthood professionals, are aware of some of the most important changes and adjustments couples need to make after their baby's birth—and the ways these adjustments can transform their family

This very special time of transformation applies not only to first babies but also to fourth babies. It applies to traditional families and non-traditional ones; it's irrespective of age, religion, gender, sexuality or income. Becoming your new version of "us" applies to families with biological children and also those who have adopted. Families share more similarities than differences.

Becoming a family, any family, is all about growing and changing. The truth is that parenthood radically changes your life. You may move to a new house, buy a bigger car, or leave or change jobs. Daily routines are disrupted and then re-organized. Expectations, plans and goals are re-examined and renegotiated.

And while you may be aware of, and anticipate some of these changes, there are others that will likely surprise you. A new baby means a new mother, a new father or partner and an upgraded version of the family you had before. And as well as all the practical adjustments, parenthood involves mental, emotional and spiritual shifts, too.

For your baby, the months spent in the womb is their most intense period of growth. For you and your partner, it will be the months, and years, afterwards. And it doesn't end there—every new stage of your children's growth will invite *you* to and your partner to grow more, both as people, and as a couple.

And while people call it the "transition" into parenthood, this term is misleading. Becoming a parent involves *multiple* transitions for couples to manage: physical, financial, social, emotional, cultural and more. We really should start saying the "transitions" into parenthood. You'll learn about these, and how to chart a course through them, on the journey ahead.

Or, as I call *all* of the above: "Becoming Us."

# Our Journey So Far

Our family had a great start. I had a trouble-free pregnancy, loved doing prenatal yoga, and tolerated taking the vitamins. We did informative childbirth classes and we were lucky that the midwife I adored was working that night.

Noreen showed my husband how to stand behind me with his hands on my hips and do "birth circles" in early labor; it felt like we were dancing. She instructed him how to do acupressure when the pain became intense and I felt grateful for his touch. When it was time to give birth, she suggested he stand behind me in a supported squat, so I could lean into his arms. I felt literally and figuratively that he had my back. We were all set up to be the happy family we'd dreamed about for so long.

And then we had our first argument as new parents the parking lot the next day. And our second on the way home:

Me: "You're driving too fast."

Him: "Don't you trust me?" It was downhill from there.

Looking back, I can see that part of the problem was what was going on inside me. During pregnancy, and even more after the birth, I felt more complete and stronger in some ways, and yet more sensitive and vulnerable in others. I didn't have words to describe it. Added to that, I was so immersed in my new-mother self and so overwhelmed with my new-mother responsibilities, I didn't even stop to think what, if anything, was going on inside my partner.

Over the next few years, my husband and I found ourselves grappling with issues we'd been completely unprepared *for*; parenthood meant most aspects of my life and many of my closest relationships began to change. And while there were changes in my husband's life and some of his relationships too, they weren't nearly to the same degree as mine. It was hard for us to understand each other, let alone be supportive. We were both feeling anxious and depressed.

So of course, we went on to have another baby.

At the same time I switched from studying psychology to training as a relationship counselor in the hope of making sense of it all. I was looking for answers, but I found much, much more than that. I discovered this: becoming a family pulls apart the structure of a couple's partnership; the transitions tip them into a new life stage as individuals and a new relationship stage at the same time. Parenthood affects a person's sense of identity and self-esteem; it can change the balance of power between a couple and disrupt the sense of connection between them.

No wonder we were struggling!

So I started researching. As far back as the 1950's, psychologists were discovering the effects of parenthood on a relationship. A number of major long-term studies in the U.S. clearly showed having a baby mixed things up. The results were published in a handful of books written for professionals. Elizabeth Martin, a parenthood expert in the U.K., even came up with a name for it: babyshock.

Well, the statistics certainly were shocking. Researchers Cowan and Cowan found that 92% of couples reported increased disagreement and conflict in their baby's first year. Researchers Gottman and Gottman found 67% of couples experienced a decline in satisfaction with their relationship. Did you guess that the Cowans and the Gottmans are both married couples? They are—with kids. Funny about that. And that's not all: I also discovered that *a lot* of new parents were feeling anxious or depressed.

I was shocked by what I discovered, but also very relieved; my partner and I (as well as our friends and my clients) may well be stressed and struggling, but I learned *most* parents were, in one way or another. *We were normal.* And if we were normal, maybe we could find a way through it.

So, we had another baby.

And all the time I wondered: if relationship stress after having a baby is so bloody common: *why the heck is nobody preparing us for this?* I wanted answers. What happens to us when we become a family? What can be done to *really* prepare parents-to-be for parenthood? What difference can it make for us and our family when we do? I was on a mission.

No matter where you are in your parenthood journey now, you're about to embark on a new adventure. Becoming a parent is like emerging from two dimensions into a three-dimensional world. It's a journey into the unknown. You'll discover things you've never experienced before and face things you've never faced. Parenthood brings a richer perspective; you may see things in a different light, maybe with more clarity than before. You may find that you yearn for a simpler, less complicated, less busy life to make room for more meaning and deeper connections with those closest to you.

So, think of me as your Personal Parenthood Tour Guide. This is your guide about what to prepare for, how to do it and ways to support yourself and your partner and make sure you both get the help you'll need along the way.

In Part I, you'll find the skills for parenthood: loving, learning and growing. They sound deceptively simple, as you'll soon see. You'll also learn how to combine them all to thrive through the journey.

In Part II, you'll discover the stages of parenthood. These stages span the period of pregnancy (or even beginning with pre-conception) through the first few years of family. You may be surprised at all the ways parenthood tends to pull you and your partner apart and push you in different directions. I'll show you ways to pull together through the stages instead.

In Part III, you'll find extra support for some of the most challenging aspects of parenthood. You'll be more likely to avoid them through the guidance in Parts I and II. Think of Part III as alternative extreme adventure activities, like rock climbing, whitewater rafting or skydiving, which you don't plan on doing (because you have a new baby). But if you unexpectedly find yourself in formidable terrain, and realize there's no way around it, you'll at least have some idea of how to get up the mountain, down the river or on the ground.

Some words of warning before we start: you're likely to feel overwhelmed if you read too much in one go. It's like looking at a map and all the dangerous places to avoid. Some parents like to read the stages as they're going through them, others like to be prepared for them so they forge ahead.

You also might not like some of the things I have to say. You might find some things too old-fashioned for too new-fashioned for your liking. That's because there are old-fashioned and new-fashioned families and I'd like to be a guide for all.

There are times where, for your safety, I will be very blunt. You may not like me for doing that, and *I* don't necessarily like doing it, but it's part of my responsibility as your guide. Think of it as me telling you "you're getting too close to the edge." I can see the edges because I have been there with my clients. Heck, my husband and even went over a few edges ourselves a couple of times. But we learned from these experiences—did things differently. We were OK, and you will be too.

Just take your time through the sections. Practice, rest and relax in between. Parenthood is an endurance sport, not a race. Talk about the (bold) discussion points with your partner, friends and family, make notes in a journal if you need more room to explore.

And have plenty of pauses to just enjoy your baby and experience the journey of life as a family before you come back again to prepare for the next part.

You're about to learn how to work *with* the normal changes and challenges and transitions of parenthood instead of *against* them. Knowing how to do this, how to *become us,* is the difference between just surviving parenthood and thriving through it.

Get ready to embrace the journey of your lives—and each other. Are you ready? Let's go….

# PART I:

# THE SKILLS FOR PARENTHOOD

Parenthood is an adventure. There's the anticipation of expecting, then the otherworld of birth. The first few days with a newborn are a wonder, and then come the long weeks, both blissful and gritty.

Then months of new experiences—from the sublime delight of playing with tiny toes to the boring repetition of changing dirty diapers to the frustration of not getting enough done to the quiet delight of sleepy baby sighs—all around and back again, several times in a day.

You'll find there are new ways of seeing things and experiencing the world as a parent. Your inner world too. And then years and years for you and your partner to nurture your family—and all the time becoming your new version of "us."

Parenthood stretches you. Some days you'll feel so elated you could float, so protective you could kill, or so frustrated you could explode. Becoming a parent takes you closer to your deepest, darkest self. It's raw. Same for your partner too.

Becoming a family also stretches the bond you have with your partner. Normal issues of parenthood—fatigue, housework, finances, in-laws, raising kids, sex (where did that go?)—are likely to get between you. They may even take you in different directions at times. Over the next couple of years there's times when one of you may want to forge ahead and the other may want to stop and rest awhile. Sometimes you'll be hand-in-hand. Others, you'll want to push your partner out the door.

The truth is, growing a family means you will need to grow your relationship too. Next, you'll discover four skills for doing just that. You can read through them now in preparation for the stages, or you can jump right into the stages and come back to the skills later, it's up to you. They're here for you whenever you need them.

# Loving

With all the demands of family, it's easy for the bond that brought you together in the first place, so carefully created and tended in the beginning, to become neglected. You may need to begin loving in a new way to cope with the bigger range of issues that come with becoming a family.

Becoming a family can bring you closer to your partner. The wonder of growing your little person, of truly blending and merging your lives, can lead to a deeper, more loving relationship. You can become bonded in ways you may never have imagined before.

A true team.

More than that, the loving, trusting, supportive connection you create between you forms the foundation you will build your family on—the one that supports your children.

Love changes over time as it grows and matures, especially when you add children into the mix. The qualities that brought you and your partner together, and here to this point in your life's journey, will always be there, but a long-term love needs ongoing nurturing. A life-long love goes through three main stages and each of them happens for a very important reason.

## The Life Cycle of Love—Relationship Developmental Stages

### Coming Together

In this gorgeous, giddy stage, you may lose yourself in the intoxicating bliss of new togetherness. Through the alchemy of mutual attraction, sweetened with romance and spiced with sensuality, you may feel like you're a better self and living a better life because your beloved is right there in the middle of it.

This romantic first stage tends to bring out the best version of you—and this is the person your partner falls in love with. You fall in love with the best parts of them too. You might find that your early conversations center on what you have in common—all the ways you're good together.

You might think that because you're compatible, you're alike—soulmates even. Where it's a case of opposites attract, you may feel that your partner "completes" you. And in a way, they do, because in the beginning, when you're focused on the things you like about each other, your individual boundaries merge to give you a comforting sense of "being one." It's a lovely feeling. You may even expect that over time, through sharing and becoming closer, you will naturally become more alike.

Ummm, I'm sorry to be the one to break this to you….

**Romance is just the beginning**. Desire and passion, and even a little drama, create an intense emotional bond, which is a great start, but the flame will eventually burn lower, in between six months and two years' time, according to researchers.

When they get to here, some people make the mistake of thinking they have fallen out of love or that this person isn't "the one" after all. They may become attracted to someone else, and that works out great—until another year or two passes….

**Romance is a great start,** and an important part of a relationship, but it's not a strong enough foundation for "forever." Romance is based on loving the parts of each other that make you happy. So, in this "together" state you can easily take any differences from your partner personally or even feel that they are a rejection of you. Which is why it's vital for couples—and especially parent couples—to learn about the next stage of the journey.

## Growing Apart

After around two years, partners start to form what counselors call an "attachment bond." This bond forms through growing together in some ways—and growing apart in others. It's kind of like a giant relationship bungee cord. As trust develops, you can relax a bit (or a lot). Your sense of "being one" diminishes, you might find yourself doing more things independently, broadening your own personal boundaries and horizons and re-engaging with friends and activities you might not have in common. But you still feel connected to your partner.

Instead of presenting your best self to your partner, a growing sense of security means you can stop trying so hard. This same trust also allows you to become more vulnerable with each other and expose a fuller and deeper version of yourselves. This is nice.

**Some people start to freak out at the Growing Apart stage,** but it's actually good for your relationship. If you don't embrace this stage (and support your partner to), you can stay what psychologists call "enmeshed"—seeing your partner as an extension of you and your life rather than as their own person. This balance between personal growth and relationship growth allows you to become your new version of "us."

Growing Apart allows both of you to be your *whole* selves. And this is important for a relationship: because when you can be your whole self, you can love *whole-heartedly*.

**Revealing different sides of you brings more differences into your partnership.** It might not sound like it, but this is actually a good thing, too, over the long term—growing as people, revealing and sharing more of yourselves grows your relationship and keeps it fresh.

Here's where it gets tricky for parents though. Becoming a family brings a lot of new differences in a short space of time. This can send many couples into the Growing Apart stage abruptly rather than gradually—and often before their relationship is ready for it, especially if the baby is a surprise. If this is you, don't despair though, you'll see by the end of this our time together how it can all work out for the best.

**Babies bring differences because they are new and full of possibility.** A new sense of purpose is born along with a baby. You might find you feel a stronger sense of family belonging and a desire to create a good life and a good world for your child. Becoming a parent can prompt you to feel more strongly about who you are, who you want to become, where you're going, and the legacy you want to pass on. This is all part of the work for the Growing Apart stage.

**The problem most people have is that differences can create conflict.** So, rather than diminishing over time, as you might expect, emerging differences (especially at a time you thought you'd be even closer) can be a nasty surprise. But it's how you handle these types of surprises that will shape your future. And, if you already love your partner for who they are and not for how they make you feel, then you'll be less likely to find differences threatening.

It's if you feel like your partner has "changed on you" that can start to cause problems. Loving your partner for who they are, and not for how they make you feel, is good preparation for parenting. If you have a toddler already, you'll know exactly what I mean.

**You may need to start loving in a different way.** If you don't already, there are huge benefits in starting to see each other as friends as well as lovers. Good friends know each other intimately. They see and accept each other—even the quirky, odd and sometimes annoying bits. Friendship is a bridge that spans the distance between differences.

**Friendship keeps you connected**. Growing Apart can feel scary, but friendship soothes separation anxiety. Growing Apart is a normal, healthy stage and serves a very important function: *expanding your relationship so you can continue your own individual growth at the same time.* This is even more important when you will have to accommodate your children's growth too. The Growing Apart stage is like your training ground for parenting.

Because the truth is: a baby tests the bond between partners. Toddlers bounce on it and teenagers bungee jump off it. A romantic bond alone is not enough; you'll need a stronger bond of friendship too.

## Growing Together

The work doesn't stop here, but it does get easier. You have moved from dependence in the first stage through independence in the second. In this stage you'll realize your joint responsibility to each other, your *interd*ependence. As both lovers and friends, you create a passionate friendship. Here, finally, is your happy-ever-after.

**You need to trust**. In this final stage, you'll feel comfortable being together and also OK to spend time apart. The security you have created in your relationship will give you the confidence to go out into the world, find adventure and take risks, knowing you can return at the end of the day to your partner's arms.

**You need trust to love**. Security also gives you the confidence to go inwards. You can have open, honest conversations. Be both brave and vulnerable, share your darkest fears, highest hopes, wildest instincts and craziest notions. You can explore your deepest selves and share them with your partner, bringing a richness and depth that colors every dimension of "us."

You can begin to know, accept and value every aspect of each other—the good, the bad and the unlovely. Knowing that your partner loves you, even at your worst, gives you security and space to love every aspect of *yourself.*

**As well as pushing you into the second stage of Growing Apart,** having a baby also pushes you into the final stage of Growing Together. A child bonds you like never before. So becoming a mother or a father is not only a commitment to your child, it's also a recommitment to your partnership. Where before you could lead parallel lives, a child truly *intertwines* you. Becoming a family is the ultimate joint venture, the merging of your individual selves, again.

But this time it's different than from the romantic "you complete me" beginning because the trust you will have developed between you along the way means you'll be able to see that your differences are *expressions of who you each are* rather than *rejections of each other.*

**Your bond benefits your children**. The relationship you and your partner create is a security blanket—safety, trust, warmth—for your whole family. Your children will grow up with your relationship as a benchmark, a standard of what they consider "normal." The better your partnership, the better your child's "normal" will be.

This is what's here for you in the Growing Together stage. Parenthood pushes you higher and further through these stages of love because it presents you with countless opportunities to nurture your relationship and bring it into full bloom.

And all those opportunities are a good thing. A really good thing. Because in so many ways parenthood is also going to test you, test your partner and test your relationship. Over and over again.

# Learning

Before we go any farther, I'd like to give you a little history about this whole parenthood territory you've managed to find yourself in, so you can have another perspective on it.

Older cultures celebrate parenthood as a rite of passage. Traditionally, a rite of passage has three main stages:

1. Letting go of the old way of life,
2. Facing the uncertainty of the future, and
3. Emerging with new responsibilities, a higher social standing and a bigger sense of self.

For centuries, women mothered new mothers through these stages, swapped stories, shared wisdom and soothed fears. Fathers were initiated by brothers and uncles who worked side-by-side, offering advice, sharing laughter and providing a sympathetic ear for his woes.

In many traditional cultures even now, women come in to care for a new mother for a month or so after her baby's birth. The women bring food and other essentials, entertain visitors, wash and clean. This ensures a new mother gets the rest she needs, a dedicated time of recovery and a listening ear right there for all the adjustments that motherhood require.

In our First World suburbs, most of us lack the cocoon of extended kin, and so our transformation into family is not something we're ushered through.

We may use traditions to mark the parenthood rite of passage too, but have you noticed that our celebrations are much shallower? They lack the deeper significance or recognition of the depth and meaningfulness of change. Rather than approach parenthood holistically, we tend to focus on the romantic and materialistic aspects only: we mostly prepare by buying stuff.

And then after babies are born, rather than taking time to connect with and honor our life-changing transition and everything it means for us, couples often try to rush back to the way things were before. And then, if you're like me, you wonder why things start to fall apart.

And have you noticed any unhelpful myths of parenthood yet? Like being a mother, father or partner should just come naturally. That you'll bond with your baby at first sight. That parenting is easy and fun (OK, it is fun, but not all the time). That you'll just "know" what to do when your child gets a cotton ball stuck up their nose. Sure, some aspects of parenting *are* instinctive, but others have a very, very steep learning curve.

At first you might be learning the difference between a hungry cry and a tired one, and then later it might be how to manage your frustration when guiding your toddler to channel theirs. These things take time, focus and hard work. Some days you'll find it harder than others. And some learning curves are steeper than others. On all those days and all those curves, it's better when your partner is right there beside you, holding your hand.

Parenthood is on-the-job training. You will find many of your own and your partner's learning edges. Here are seven lessons of family:

**One: Sometimes becoming a family can be stressful.** Changing the diaper of a wriggling baby, dodging toast bullets from a cranky toddler or tidying a house that's trashed ten minutes later is stressful. So is carrying a wayward child and navigating a wobbly shopping cart with one hand. Ever tried driving with a screaming infant or nursing a sick child with a high fever? Not to mention being late for appointments, forgetting to put breast pads in the diaper bag, or trying to hold things together on four hours of broken sleep. I could go on….

I'll be honest: becoming a parent is likely to be incredibly stressful at times. Acknowledging this doesn't mean you're a bad person, a bad parent, or you don't love your baby. It means you're *human.* Acknowledging the stresses of parenthood is very important for two main reasons:

1. Most parents are so unaware of (and therefore don't know to prepare for) some of the biggest challenges of parenthood, that when they inevitably experience them, they can start to think they're struggling because there's something wrong with them, their partner, or their relationship, when in fact, other couples are also struggling through the same so-not-fun things, and
2. While parenting is stressful *at times,* the way you and your partner deal with these temporary stresses can become more of a *permanent* problem. More on this soon.

**Changes can be stressful—even good ones**. A new job, moving to a new home or getting married are all exciting, but they also involve some uncertainty, planning frustrations, unanticipated decisions and adjustments. Parenthood is the same.

**Of all these changes, parenthood is particularly stressful** because it involves so many changes in such a short space of time. You'll find that becoming a family involves social, mental and emotional transitions that can change many aspects of you and your partner's life—and those changes start happening literally overnight (if you're lucky enough to have a labor that lasts less than 12 hours).

**There's even a name for it: postnatal stress.** Motherhood researcher Wendy le Blanc found 88 percent of mothers identified themselves as suffering from postnatal stress. I'm sure their partners felt it too.

**Stress can be measured.** Back in 1967, researchers Holmes and Rahe developed a Life Events Scale, giving events a stress rating of up to 100 Life Change Units. To put things in perspective, death of a spouse rates 100 and divorce comes in at 73. Pregnancy and having a baby score around 40 points each. Add in changes in sleep patterns, finances and work, and the figure rises to 120. Holmes and Rahe asserted that score greater than 150 resulted in a 30% chance of a stress-related illness. Up to 300 resulted in a 50% risk, and over 300 netted an 80% likelihood. You don't want to get sick when you have a baby.

**It's more stressful for some parents than for others.** If you or someone you know has had to face infertility, been through the roller coaster of assisted reproduction to conceive, been unfortunate enough to experience a traumatic birth or the heartbreak of miscarriage, you'll know what I mean.

**Two: Some stressful changes of parenthood are more obvious.** Like adjusting to broken sleep (this can get really ugly) and new day-to-day routines, the challenges of supporting three people on one wage for a time and your first few arguments about how to raise your child (also not pretty). But you'll find other changes aren't so easy to identify, like having to adjust your expectations, finding a balance between everybody's needs, or maybe even feeling like you've lost yourself for a while. Changes that are hard to talk about can be more stressful.

**Think about this: you'd get professional support if this much change were part of your day job.** Any responsible organization going through a merger or a takeover would support you with some sort of change management process. Parenthood is supposed to be "the most important job in the world." And with a baby, you go through *both a merger and a takeover,* but you're expected to cope without any training or support at all!

**Only other parents can understand.** Have you ever found that those who don't have a baby or small child may not be sympathetic if you admit to being stressed? Challenges in any other area of life are more likely to get an understanding nod, but talking openly about the stressful aspects of parenting is somehow taboo and hard to do—especially if you don't want to be seen as complaining, risk being judged as a bad parent or have it taken as a sign that you're not coping. You're pretty sure to just get a "they grow up so fast."

**Which totally sucks** because we need to talk about all this stuff. Not being able to share our struggles means more stress and makes it harder to cope with them. Not talking about this stuff makes it harder for other parents to cope too.

**Coping with stress and change is a life skill.** Most of us weren't taught how to cope with change as children. "How to cope with change" isn't a subject taught at school, college, university or even in a prenatal class, when you really need it. **"**How to cope with change in your relationship" isn't either. If you were like me, you just assumed that love would get you through. In many ways, it does, but not always.

Having a baby may be the first real opportunity in your life to develop an awareness of how stress and change affect you and your partner—and develop the skills for coping.

So now that you know that sometimes becoming a family can be stressful, and some stresses are more obvious than others, here's the next lesson.

**Three: it's not the stress, but what you do with it, that counts.** Stress activates what's called "fight or flight," an automatic brain and body reaction that mobilizes you to make a fist or run like the wind. Originally this in-built protection helped humans survive in occasions when they had to flee a saber-toothed tiger or tussle with the hussy from the cave next door over the last bison rib.

There aren't too many sharp-toothed predators these days—only people who act like them. And yet your fight/flight reaction is still a functioning part of your physiology. These days it's more likely to be triggered by less dangerous situations like running late, losing your wallet, getting caught in traffic or being unable to sooth your crying baby.

You might even find that the stresses aren't even real ones—that you're worrying about "what if's" that may never happen. Like you're going to drop the baby or forget to pick them up from daycare. The responsibilities of parenthood are sooo huge, and the amount of worries that can come with them so great, it's little wonder that anxiety is so common for expecting and new parents.

The problem is, your body doesn't know the difference between real and imagined stresses. Worrying about things all the time creates a low-level ambient stress that's tiring because it takes up energy to remain in this state. But at the same time as being tired, you're not able to fully relax. Which is why it's so important to have stress management strategies for parents. More on that soon.

**Stress builds up inside, but there may be no natural path for its release.** Fleeing a tiger or fighting a cave hussy discharges the energy that builds up from the fight/flight reaction. These days you can still be primed to *fight*—by arguing or attacking. And you can still *flee*—by running away, burying yourself in denial or avoiding talking about things.

These reactions have been joined by two other modern-day ones: you can *freeze*—become confused or feel helpless or *fix:* jump in to seek premature solutions that don't last because you haven't taken the time to actually get to the bottom of things. Which then gets frustrating. The problem with all these reactions is that rather than discharging the stress energy, they tend to make a situation even more stressful.

Now, I'm not suggesting you thump someone on the head or run down the street waving your arms and screeching. People need—and parents *especially* need—to find effective (and socially acceptable) ways to manage stress instead. Because a buildup of stress is not good for you physically, mentally or emotionally.

And it's not good for your family. Stress has a ripple effect, especially on those closest to you. What affects one person in a family will affect you all.

## Signs of Stress

Stress can bring out the worst in you; it can make you appear selfish because when we're stressed, we tend to focus only on what we need to get through it. Stress affects thinking; you can be preoccupied or forgetful, have trouble concentrating, making decisions and remembering details. Physically, stress makes you exhausted or agitated. Emotionally, stress feels overwhelming and too much of it can be a trigger for anxiety, depression or physical illness. Some common signs of stress for new parents are:

**Competition.** How many diapers I've changed today compared to how many you have. How much time I've had off compared to you. Competition can be a way of saying, "I'm trying to hold up my end and you're not recognizing that." Keeping score is also a negative way of saying, "I need your help." Both are fuel for conflict.

**Reducing your life**. People can often try to cope with stress by focusing on only one area (e.g., work or baby) and tuning out everything else. Other normal aspects of life, like self-care, relationship or friends become neglected. This may give you a sense of being on top of that one thing, and this is normal in the early weeks of parenthood, but if it continues, it can cause further problems down the track.

**Resenting Interference ("gatekeeping").** Those with a serious single focus (e.g., baby) can resent any intrusion, even if the other person is wanting to help, trying to "protect" their domain, and in turn, their sense of being OK and on top of things. The problem here is that the "protection" is likely to exclude a partner, which can cause resentment and conflict all around. For a woman who has felt one-down in a man's world, this may be an opportunity, however unconscious, to claw her way back up again.

**Blaming.** Underneath blaming is often a shifting of responsibility, a way of saying, "I'm no coping, so I'm going to give the problem to you, and you can fix it." For as long as you continue to blame, you will just get stuck in what you can't change. And besides, most issues of parenthood are not problems to be solved: they're things to be explored and worked through as a team.

**Being too busy**. Some people can use constant activity and preoccupation with tasks—"have-to-do's"—as a way of managing stress through distraction. Busyness can also be a way of avoiding feelings or risking the vulnerability of a deeper connection with others.

Are you ready for more?

**Four: parenthood is likely to send you both away from each other.** Even if you've faced other challenges and managed to pull together through them, you'll find that the changes of parenthood have a curious ability to send you and your partner further apart, at least initially.

One of the most significant studies on this was conducted by researchers Belsky and Kelly, who found that this polarization occurred with both happy and unhappy couples. More importantly, they found that whether a couple's connection improved or declined after children, the most influential factor was the partner's ability to "reach across the differences."

So, it's not just the enormity of the changes that parents have to deal with, but the fact that the changes send mothers and fathers and even same-sex partners *in different directions.*

And, as if this weren't enough, partners experience changes at a different rate. Mothers and primary caregivers are largely transformed more radically and more rapidly than fathers or secondary caregivers. This is due, in part, to having already experienced big changes and challenges in pregnancy and during childbirth.

**Parenthood can send parents back into traditional gender roles.** Modern couples tend to share the responsibilities of paid work and unpaid household chores, until they have a baby. After the baby arrives, many parents divide the responsibilities in order to try stay on top of things. For example, fathers or partners may become the provider and mothers look after children and the home.

**Same-sex couples can also experience this shift**, based on who, if either, birthed the baby, who is taking up the primary role of baby care, who is providing financially, etc., but according to research, same-sex couples do tend to be more equitable.

**Gender roles are often unconscious—you might not even realize they're there.** You may find yourself unexpectedly having attitudes or thoughts that remind you of your own parents. Have you had the shock of sounding like your mother or father yet? Parenthood gives you a new opportunity to define gender roles for yourself. This can be both rewarding—and challenging.

**Both parents can have different focuses, priorities and stresses.** Traditionally it's mothers having more responsibility for the health and wellbeing of the children, spending a large part of their day doing menial, boring, repetitive and physical labor. And did I say repetitive? Mothers may give up careers, bodies and leisurely pastimes for a period. It can feel like you exist just to meet everybody else's needs.

And when partners become parents, they're not just working a job anymore—they're also supporting a family. In some areas there's fierce competition for employment, and the possibility that job security could be lost. Those who aren't happy in their job can be loath to risk of leaving. You can feel like you're trapped, and missing out at home at the same time.

Can you start to see why stress relief is so important for parents now?

**Five: Here's another problem: having a baby can limit your old ways of relieving stress.** With a pre-baby time frame and income, you could relieve stress in pretty much any way you chose—a day at the beach, an afternoon of shopping, an hour at the gym, a night out, a weekend away—whatever could give you a break from your day-to-day responsibilities.

After baby, both of your responsibilities have increased, and at the same time, your stress outlets have decreased. The at-home partner needs more help, so the at-work partner finds themselves rushing home to relieve them. But if there's no circuit breaker between the stresses at work and the stresses they come home to, they can bring work stresses home with them. Does this sound familiar?

Of course, every family is different. A mom might go back to work fairly soon after the baby comes, while the dad or partner becomes the primary baby caregiver. In any way your family decides to organize financial providing and family caregiving, how you normally manage stress can be dramatically affected by a new baby.

**Each of your lives post-baby can be so different.** You may each have little appreciation of your partner's pressures. You may idealize their life, eyeing their situation with envy. Out-in-the-world workers would love a day at home; in-the-home-carers would love an hour for lunch. It's easy to get into arguments about who works the hardest, longest or who does the most valuable job. Truth is, you're both working for the success of your family, just in different ways.

Seeing and naming your stresses is half way to dealing with them. So, if you can do more of that now that you've come this far, you're getting ahead of them. From here, you can start to acknowledge your own stresses and help your partner identify theirs. Then you can combine your resources and start on the path to managing them.

And this is important because remember earlier where I mentioned that dealing with a temporarily stressful situation can become a permanent problem? Well, here's how:

1. You aren't aware of, or don't recognize (because nobody prepared you for), the normal parenthood stresses, challenges or changes.
2. Rather than realizing your partner is likely to be challenged and stressed too, you can start to think there's something "wrong" with them and respond to them as if they have "changed."
3. When you change how you respond to your partner (e.g., less supportively), then they will respond differently to you in return.
4. If you both continue responding less supportively to each other, over time, your relationship is likely to change. You're likely to start becoming more distant from each other.

But here's the good news:

If you start to change the way you respond to your partner, then they will start to respond differently to you in return. If you both continue to respond positively to each other, over time, your relationship is likely to change. You'll start to become *closer* and *more connected.* Can you see how this works?

**Six: Parenthood is a time to learn.** You may have forgotten how to learn. You might undermine yourself with negative thoughts or become overwhelmed with emotions that sap your energy. You might not experiment with new behaviors even when it's clear the old ones aren't working.

You might find yourself so immersed in events of the past or anxieties about the future that you become immobilized in the present.

And yet, the desire to love and be loved provides you with motivation. If you give yourself and your partner permission to be learners and not experts, then you will have lots and lots of wiggle room to find your way in harmony.

**Learn from your baby**. An 11-month-old lets go of the coffee table long enough to teeter into her first step. She falls down, climbs back up and tries again. She does this again and again until she works out how to balance herself just so. She has patience, curiosity and perseverance. There is no shame, embarrassment or self-consciousness. She doesn't beat herself up or feel inadequate for not getting it right the first time. And she doesn't give up.

This next learning is huge.

**Seven: Parenthood is the time to expand your thinking.** One of the most difficult things that most parents aren't even aware of is the way parenthood challenges you to expand your thinking: going from thinking for one person (yourself) to thinking for two people (you and your partner) to thinking for three people (you, your partner and your baby). This is hard for some people to do. But it pays off in many, many ways.

Let's try a little experiment to show you what I mean. Imagine you'd never seen an elephant in your life. You have no idea what one is. If you were to stand in front of one and your partner were to stand behind it, and I asked you to tell me from what you can see: how would you describe an elephant?

Yes, sure, you'll both say it's big and grey, you'd agree on that. But one of you will insist an elephant has big flappy ears, warm brown eyes and a trunk that snorts on you. Your partner would insist that it has a small swishy tail that slaps you in the face if you get too close. Oh, and it dumps a giant pile of poop on your feet if you hang around too long too. You could go on for years arguing about the differences and trying to get your partner's sympathy for having elephant snot on your face or poop on your feet. Or you could agree on the parts you can both see and accept that your partner also has a different perspective and the thoughts and feelings that go with their experiences.

And then, if you can stretch yourself even further, imagine your future child is standing on one side, a little farther away from the elephant and watching you and your partner at the front and back. What would they see?

One of the massive challenges of parenthood is to start thinking in a "both/and" way instead of "either/or." So, an elephant is not either a head or a tail, it's *both* a head and a tail—and everything in between. So are most of the issues of parenthood—neither right nor wrong, just two different parent's points of view.

Learning and working through the lessons of parenthood will free you up to enjoy all the exciting, joyful and wondrous experiences even more—and thank goodness there are *plenty* of those. Parenting, especially when free from unnecessary stresses, is one of life's most joyous experiences. Seeing your baby, toddler or child responding to you or your partner when you get it right (or near enough—children are *very* forgiving) is heartwarming. It also frees you up to enjoy each other, to celebrate the bond that lead to your gorgeous baby in the first place.

How are you doing so far? I hope I have given you lots to think about and I'm guessing maybe even more than you bargained for. Take a break if you need one, have a stretch or grab a cuppa. When you're ready to come back, we're going to continue with a different type of history lesson—the history of you.

# Growing

Soon you'll be embarking on your journey through the stages of parenthood, but in this section, I'm going to ask you to look back—on your own journey of growing up.

I'm going to ask this of you because how you grew up, for better or for worse (I told you I was going to be straight with you!), is going to affect how you show up in your relationship with your partner and also how you'll be with your own children.

Let me give you a small personal example: as a kid, it took me almost an hour to get to school and back each day. Although it was only a 15 minute drive, my mother didn't have a car, so I had to walk to the local bus stop, wait for the bus to the train station, wait for (or miss) the train to the next station and then walk from there to the school. Now, even though our kids live a 15- or 20-minute walk from their schools, I have liked driving them there and back each day. When in fact, it would be healthier for them to walk.

So—and I'm going to be straight here again—if you weren't happy with some aspects of your own childhood, unless you want to just automatically do things the way your parents did (or the opposite), you're going to have to be prepared to change. There, I said it.

Change means different things to different people. It can be exciting. If you have an adventurous streak, you may happily anticipate what lies ahead. Or you may feel cautious, but still confident about coping with the unknown.

However, for most of us, change sucks. It's hard and scary and it can take too long. It's challenging. Uncertain. Stressful. Changing stretches your resources and pushes you to the edge of yourself.

But if you've already experienced big changes in your life, you may have discovered that change also brings: opportunity for those who can see it; invitations for insight; seeds for growth; windows for really knowing the fullness and truth of yourself; and the opportunity to learn valuable lessons in life and love.

Change also brings opportunities to nurture and deepen the relationships you have with those closest to you—your partner, your parents, other family members and friends. Especially when they're looking for comfort because things are changing for them too. From change, wonderful (and sometimes wholly unexpected) new things can grow.

Parenthood is a time of significant change. For many parents, it can be a time of rounding out yourself, which may be different for each partner, for instance, women embracing their inner strength and men embracing their inner softness. Imagine if we could grow a new generation who can be free to be their whole selves. You can do that for your children.

**Individual growth is important for your family**. The more life skills and knowledge you gain, the more wisdom and experience you'll have to pass on to your kids. They'll take it for granted, sure, but it's big for them.

**It's good for you both to grow new roots.** Roots that only grow out on one side of a tree cause it to tip and eventually fall. When you both grow the roots of your whole selves, it creates stability for your family tree.

When you become parents, you're stretched practically, mentally, emotionally and spiritually. And while this is more at the beginning, it's also with every new baby and with every stage of your children's growth.

There will be times you'll also need to stretch and expand your partnership to make room for a growing family. Because when you change and adapt, and your relationship doesn't, it becomes a source of anxiety and conflict instead of security and comfort.

But finding that your baby is bringing out the best in your partner is like tapping into a wellspring of love. You're so grateful when they step in and handle a crisis you're not coping with, or when they tenderly attend to cuts and scrapes without flinching or fix a broken toy or spend hours playing on the floor when you would have given up long ago. One of the things many mothers most appreciate is the softer, more sensitive side of their partner that parenthood brings out. It's like falling in love all over again.

## Becoming You— Your Personal Developmental Stages

From the time you were born until well into adulthood, you have been loving, learning and growing.

You didn't know it at the time, but you actually passed through eight stages as you grew from a baby into adulthood. Psychologist Erik Erikson is famous for identifying this. Knowing your personal stages of growth provides you with guidelines that can help you understand yourself, your partner and your child, as they grow and develop through their own stepping-stone stages.

## Childhood Stages of Becoming You

### Trust (0–18 months)

**First you trust caregivers to meet your needs**: you got fed when you were hungry; your diaper changed when it was dirty; and lots of snuggles for any old reason at all. Your needs may not have been met all the time, but for most people, they were most of the time and so you learned that you were OK, you felt secure This is how you formed a connection with your caregivers. If, for whatever reason, you couldn't count on your caregivers, you probably grew up feeling less secure. We'll get to that in just a couple of pages.

**Later you learned to trust yourself.** When you put one foot in front of the other, eventually you didn't fall down; when your tummy started rumbling, it was a signal that you were hungry or when you got hot it was time to peel off a layer. This is how you began a connection with yourself.

**Trusting is a lifelong process.** As an adult, self-trust means still listening to your inner signals. Tired? Rest. Stressed? Find ways to relieve it. To do this, you have to be aware of your thoughts and feelings and not dismiss them. You have to believe yourself. This is how you get to know yourself, what's right for you and what your limits are. Your intuition even.

**Trust supports you to grow as a parent.** You might not know how to express breast milk or negotiate a disagreement with your partner about the best stroller to purchase, but you know you can learn.

**When you trust your partner, you feel safe.** You can create a relationship where it's safe to make mistakes and try again. Safe to express yourself, to be your whole self, not just the good parts. Safe to grow, change and evolve. Trust gives you confidence to move into the next stage.

### Independence (18 months–3 years)

In this stage you become brave enough to move out of your comfort zones, move closer to your learning edge and explore the world around you. Here you have your first sense of power to control yourself and your environment, to make choices and to have influence over others.

Ideally your parents supported you by encouraging you to think and do for yourself, even if it meant mismatched socks. They were there for you when the world seemed scary and comforted you until you were ready to explore again. You learned to balance independence with dependence.

**As an adult, independence allows you to consider others as equal, but different.** You can have your own thoughts, feelings, opinions, beliefs, fears, hopes and dreams. You won't compare yourself with others, and you can make decisions that are right for you and your family, even if someone else may not approve of them. Because you trust, differences aren't alarming; you can see they're normal.

**Independence helps you step outside yourself** and see the view through another person's eyes, which is an essential skill for managing conflict. You don't have to agree with your partner, but for a healthy relationship, you do need to make an effort to see things from their perspective.

Trusting yourself and having a sense of independence means you can afford to take some risks, which leads you into the next stage….

## Initiative (3–5 years)

**Here you take your first baby steps towards something new.** Ideally your parents supported this by encouraging your efforts to use your mind and body creatively and imaginatively, without shame or self-consciousness. As your abilities increased, they encouraged you to seek growth, balancing this with appropriate discipline, showing you how to control your impulses and think things through.

**As adults, initiative helps you cope with stress and change**. You learn how to be flexible and look for new ways when the old ones aren't working.

**In relationships, initiative helps you avoid problems,** work through issues, surprise your partner romantically or spice up your sex life.

## Competence (5–12 years)

**In the final stage of childhood, competence helps you follow through** on what you've initiated. It's putting ideas into action. Competence fuels confidence, self-esteem, perseverance and self-control. It gives you a sense of inner power to shape your life.

Competence assists you to form, sustain and improve your relationships, develop parenting skills and cope with challenges. Competence is achieved through trial and error, and *lots and lots* of practice.

Watching your partner develop their own sense of competence can increase your respect, admiration and trust in them. As parents, your competence increases your children's trust in you, and then their own cycle of becoming begins—can you see it?

## Becoming You—Again

And here's the scary-exciting part: you actually get three main opportunities to grow up in your lifetime. The first, obviously, is in your childhood. The second is during adolescence, when you're faced with the same developmental and relationship issues as during your childhood, but at a more advanced level.

The third time of growing up again is—brace yourself—when you start a family. As your children pass through the stages of personal development, you'll be challenged to re-do them all over again. Your partner too.

This is one reason why becoming a parent can be both so hard and so healing. At a time when you're shouldered with the awesome responsibility of raising a child, don't be surprised if there are times you can feel (and act) like a child yourself. You feel all the frustration, anguish, helplessness or rebelliousness of the toddler or teen all over again. You can feel like the child that still exists inside of you, your "inner child," needs comfort and guidance almost as much as your kids do. This is not something to be ashamed of—it's normal.

So, you go through them all over again, sometimes just in time, to give guidance for your own child's navigation of each stage. Newborns make you focus on safety and comfort, toddlers on stretching the boundaries, taking risks and dealing with strong emotions. You get to experiment and increase your confidence as a parent as your children find their own strengths and challenges. Having kids grows you up. More.

The bad news is that these growing issues keep coming up. The good news is that they keep coming up. You'll keep getting more chances to manage them better. Your partner too. Sometimes this might not be until you have another child(ren).

We've just talked about the childhood stages of becoming you and we're going to get to the adult part of becoming you soon, but before we do, you might want to take a pause in your journey here. Especially if I have blown your mind. Put the book down and take a break if you need it. Pick up your journal if you have one or talk this through with your partner or someone else so you can process what we've been talking about up to now before we move on.

Ready? OK, good but you may want to sit down for this next part. Because if this information is new to you, and you can see how important it is, you may wonder why on earth you haven't heard it before. If you've ever visited a counselor, it's something they may have shared with you. If not, it's something most other people don't know about. You'll at least be ahead of the curve after this.

I'm giving you this information because I think all parents need to know it. Even if you don't read a single page more of this guide, knowing the following information about security can make all the difference in yourself, in your relationship, and in your child's life.

OK, let's get on with it: the way you were parented in the first few years of your life, at the Trust stage, before you were even old enough to remember, set you up with what psychologists call your "attachment style."

Your attachment style is your "default setting" of how comfortable you are with closeness or separation in your relationships—particularly your relationship with your partner. Where there was a high level of trust between you and your caregivers, you're likely to have developed a "secure" style. And then there are three kinds of not-so-secure styles, which some research indicates are becoming more common. Let's start with them and work our way to the good news.

The first is what's called a **Dismissive/Avoidant** attachment style. This may be your style if you don't feel much of a need for nurturing in your relationship, or you'd rather just hang out with your partner and shoot the breeze with other people, or you tend to be more task-oriented than people-focused, and/or you feel uncomfortable sharing deeper feelings.

When you're facing challenges, you're more likely to hide your stress and try to cope on your own. You don't like to ask for help. When faced with conflict, even harmless queries from your partner or others may feel to you like you're being interrogated. You're more likely to dismiss outright your partner's point of view without even listening to it and you'll be less aware of how this affects them.

Your partner might describe you at times as disinterested, cold or uncaring. If you think about life—and parenthood—as a journey, someone with this style might prefer to cover themselves in leather, slap on a helmet, jump on a motorcycle, and get going.

Then there's the **Anxious/Preoccupied** attachment style. If you prefer company, don't like to be alone so much and tend to depend on others, you may have this style.

Under stress you tend to over-share, saying too much, too soon. You worry about your partner's love and level of commitment. In conflict, you're more likely to become obviously distressed. You might even demand attention or comfort from others and you're likely to be more upset if you don't get it.

Your partner may describe you at times as clingy or hard to please. If this is you, your preferred mode of transport for travelling the road of life and through parenthood might be a tandem bicycle.

It's possible to want closeness and at the same time not trust that you'll get it. If you avoid intimacy for fear of rejection, you may have what's called a **Disorganized** attachment style.

Under stress, you'll want support, but you may not risk asking for it, for fear you won't get the response you hope for. In conflict, you can become confused, frozen or shut down. You'll want to reach out to your partner but have trouble finding your words and so give up.

Your partner would describe you as confusing; they never know what you want. Sometimes you'll want to be on the tandem bike but as soon as your partner stops pedaling, you'll want to jump on the motorcycle instead—and leave them to eat your dust.

Those who have a **Secure** attachment style, developed it either because they formed a trusting relationship originally in childhood with their parents or other caregivers, or they created what is called "earned secure attachment" through other supportive relationships, like with extended family, friends, or lovers. If this is you, you're more likely to be able to form lasting emotional connections with others. You'll feel comfortable in close relationships and also spending time in your own company. Under stress, you'll be more comfortable sharing your struggles and seeking reassurance or asking for help.

In conflict you're more flexible and prepared to work towards a mutually desirable win/win with your partner. You're more able to judge when to open up to your partner and when to stay silent. You're able to "hold" yourself and listen to your partner's point of view. You're more likely to accept that there're parts of the elephant that you can't see but your partner can.

On the journey of life and parenthood, you might like to travel in some sort of 4WD or even a classic VW bus. It keeps you warm and dry. You and your partner can both be up front and take turns at the wheel. There's plenty of room in the back when two grows into more. And when there's new terrain to explore, you can lock it and leave it and go see the best parts on foot. Traveling this way gives you the flexibility to go off track, climb a mountain or jump on a plane, either hand-in-hand with your partner or on your own for a time. And when you start to get tired or the weather turns, you know it's there for you to come back to.

Which style do you have? Which do you think your partner has? What might these answers mean for you both going forward when you have to think about balancing a baby on a bike too? Attachment styles don't tend to cause too many problems when life is going smoothly, but under stress and during times of vulnerability, they can flare up. Parenthood is both.

So, there are a few of things about attachment styles it's particularly important for parents to know:

1. Feeling secure in your partnership, regardless of which style you have, makes it easier for you to cope with all the normal changes and challenges of parenthood.
2. Feeling secure also reduces risks for anxiety or depression during the perinatal period (pregnancy and early parenthood) that are actually very common, and
3. Feeling bonded as partners creates the foundation for long-term stability for your whole family.

Now the good news that I'm *so* happy to share with you! Regardless of your attachment style, you and your partner will have countless opportunities to work with the style you have now and bond more securely through the stages of parenthood that you'll discover in Part II. I will guide you through the stages there and suggest some steps for you to take through them.

**Look into your future**. A secure bond between you and your partner leads to higher self-esteem, more affection, care and support, more intimacy and mutually satisfying sex (more on that later) and also a joint commitment to protect your relationship from negative influences (in-laws maybe? We'll get to that too).

**Your attachment style can predict a number of other things**, including feelings about becoming parents, your relationship, expectations of yourself and your partner, confidence in your parenting ability and risk for perinatal anxiety and depression. We'll talk more about this last one in Part III.

**Your partner's style may be different from yours**. And that's OK. Knowledge is power and if you know what your styles are, you can start to work with them (and each other) instead of against them.

**Parenthood is *the* best opportunity you'll have to become more bonded as a couple.** This is because the very same chemistry and processes in your brain and body that prime you both to bond with your gorgeous, precious baby, also prime you to bond more closely *with each other*. You'll find hundreds of ways to ditch the bikes and go on foot and hand-in-hand through the stages of *becoming us*. But for now, we're back to you growing up.

## Adult Stages of Becoming You

As adults, yes, you've guessed it; you're still growing in stages. And here's where it gets particularly tricky for parents—because becoming a parent can affect each of them.

### Identity (12–18 years)

Your search for identity—your thinking about who you are as a person—begins around adolescence when you transform from your child-self and work out who you are now and who you want to become.

**Without a sense of your own self, you're more likely live according to others' rules, standards or expectations.** You may also be wary of commitment, because commitment involves trusting, sharing yourself, making choices and sticking to them. That's hard for someone to do when they don't know themselves or have a less secure attachment style.

Figuring out who you are, and who you want to be as a parent, is so huge, it's a whole stage of parenthood. This stage can be so confusing and bring up such conflicting emotions, that it can mean a crisis for some. We'll get there later on in Part II.

### Intimacy (18–40 years)

As a young adult, there's that wonderful time in life when you meet a partner and fall in love. The key to making the most of this stage is developing the capacity for intimacy. Intimacy (think about these words: in-to-me-see) is sharing your thoughts, needs, feelings and vulnerabilities with another. This takes trust, initiative, confidence and competence in communication. Can you see how the stages build on each other? Intimacy can be so affected by parenthood it can become a major source of conflict. That's a whole stage too, also in Part II.

### Generativity (40–65 years)

Besides the desire to nurture a family, generativity is the drive and ability, as an older adult, to look beyond yourself and give for the benefit and care of others. Like through caring for others or caring for the environment.

**But here's an issue for parents: you and your partner may not go into generativity at the same time.** Sometimes it's a father or partner that reaches this stage first, but more often it's a mother's greater responsibilities in bearing and rearing children that can push her into generativity sooner.

**Don't blame each other**. If you're a mother who has moved first and more quickly sacrificed your own needs for the sake of your family, you might see your partner's preoccupation with their own personal interests as selfish and you may become resentful. Your partner, on the other hand, may see any pressure from you to reduce their personal time as controlling. This can cause conflict too.

### Integrity (65+ years)

This final stage is a time of looking back and weighing up your past, hopefully with a sense of pride or accomplishment more than regret and disappointment.

**Being a parent contributes to integrity**. Even with the challenges, having children tends to give people the most joy, sense of accomplishment and satisfaction in life. Sometimes the only regret for aging parents is that they didn't spend more time with their children or grandchildren.

These are the stages of growth that we all go through. If you didn't have a supportive childhood for any reason, you may find there's still room to grow—and parenthood will push you to do it.

**The way forward is to go backwards.** If you're not where you want to be, going back through the stages, beginning at trust, working towards becoming more secure, is the way to becoming the whole, healthy self you had the potential to be the day you were born. Growth is a process that naturally unfolds over time. Go with it. Trust the process.

## Emotional Growth

Have you ever noticed that in your grandparents' or even in your parents' generation, people were taught not to express their emotions? Expressing feelings (especially strong ones) was often considered impolite, inappropriate or a source of embarrassment.

So, while we may communicate very effectively from our heads, many of us grew up without the ways and words to express our hearts. This has huge consequences for our mental and emotional health and our relationships—because relationships, especially close ones, are fundamentally *emotional*.

Parenthood is even more emotional. Joy threatens to burst your chest. Responsibilities scare the heck out of you; you'll feel protectiveness so fierce you'd kill for your kids. There're times you feel you're going to explode; surges of loneliness can pull you under.

**You may not be comfortable with your feelings.** You may even be afraid, overwhelmed or ashamed of them. And yet it's your feelings that make you human and connect you with those you're closest to. The way feelings work is complex, so it's important to know how to work with them. We'll start here and do more in Stage Five.

**All your emotions serve a function**. Across all cultures, people have a number of basic emotions: fear, joy, disgust, anger and sadness. Each has a vital purpose that throughout history has helped us to survive.

**Joy** is best shared. Laughter and affection bonds you to others, increases their protectiveness of you and your sense of belonging.

You'll naturally feel **anger** in response to an intrusion or violation. Anger helps you mark your physical or psychological turf when someone oversteps into it. Anger, when expressed appropriately, protects you from other people taking advantage of your good nature. When expressed inappropriately, anger can cause great harm to people and relationships.

**Sadness** is a response to an emotional or physical injury and it's healthy for you to want to cry. Tears contain soothing chemicals and signal to others that you need comfort. This bonds you with people who can care for you and protect you. Hiding your hurt feelings distances you from others.

You'll feel **fear** in response to the threat of danger. Fear triggers the fight/flight/freeze response.

**Disgust** is what helps you to avoid foods that might make you ill. Disgust causes you to turn away from the sight of things that may distress you and avoid situations that endanger your safety. When you think of things that make you feel sick, that's disgust.

**All your emotions are a natural response to certain circumstances.** It used to be simple and clear-cut. But hundreds of years of intellectualizing, socializing and conditioning have clogged the natural causeway of basic emotions and sent us "modern" people very, very backwards. Now we have dozens of variations of basic emotions that most of us don't know what the heck to do with. In fact, some mental health issues we're seeing today are partly because people aren't comfortable expressing their natural emotions.

**Because here's the thing: emotions have energy.** Feelings are energy in motion (e-motion). Some feelings move you forward (lust, desire, excitement) and some move you away (fear, shame or disappointment). Others cause you to be still (confusion, anxiety or helplessness).

**You can work** with this energy or against it—with or against your own feelings; with or against your partner's; with or against your child's.

**Energy can be used positively or negatively.** Anger for example, isn't good or bad, but the way it's used can be. Feeling powerless? Anger helps you to be assertive. When anger turns into aggression, it's destructive.

**Emotions are signals.** They help you judge a situation, make a decision or alert you that you may need more skills. Confusion tells you that you need more information; helplessness that you need more resources; and frustration, to take a well-earned break.

When you're feeling depressed or anxious, it signals you to be extra gentle with yourself, find extra support, or do something relaxing and enjoyable. If you continue to ignore these signals, then anxiety and depression can become a state of being instead of just an emotion.

**Boys and girls were socialized to feel different emotions.** In a traditionally gendered Western society, little boys are often dissuaded from expressing sadness or distress, while anger is considered appropriate—"boys will be boys," after all. On the other hand, little girls are often discouraged from expressing anger (it's not "ladylike"), but they are more likely to be offered comfort if they express sadness or pain.

**This can become more of a problem as adults.** Anger turned inwards can become depression, so perhaps it's no surprise that women are twice as likely to suffer from depression than men (or maybe they just hide it better). By not harnessing the positive energy of anger, women can remain passive in their relationships, community and world.

Men tend to show aggression more than women. By not accessing and expressing their gentler emotions, men can limit themselves and others. We all miss out on the best of them.

**If you consistently block, avoid or ignore your emotions, life is likely to become more complicated.** When emotional energy builds up inside you and you don't allow it to pass through, over time your original emotions can get buried by others, like frustration, overwhelm or helplessness. Research also tells us that over time, a buildup of unexpressed emotions can also become physical effects like headaches, stomach upsets or decreased immune function and even cancer and heart disease. So, this is important.

**Let your inside out.** When you don't express yourself, you may appear wooden, cold or uncaring. It might be harder for you to show compassion or support. When you can't express strong emotions appropriately, you risk becoming abusive by dumping your anger or pain onto others.

Take a deep breath here. Feelings carried around inside you not only affect your *mood* but can also change *who you are*. Unexpressed feelings affect family relationships—whatever you're feeling, but not expressing, is sitting and waiting to be triggered by your partner or children. But there's power in recognizing this—you are the link between generations. It's up to you to learn (or unlearn) from your parents, so you become emotionally healthy role models for your children.

## Connecting to Your Emotions

**Emotions happen in layers, like an onion.** If you peel away one layer, there's another one underneath, until eventually you get to the core of yourself. You'll be able to access your upper layers of feelings the easiest, the more familiar ones are closer to the surface; it takes more time, attention and intention to access those more vulnerable feelings below.

For example, you're more likely to notice your surface feelings of frustration and anger. These are the feelings you may usually act on in conflict—they serve to protect you by pushing people away.

But if you can sit with these surface feelings for a while without acting on them (or talk them through with a good listener), you may discover there's something more like confusion or anxiety underneath. Again, if you are able to sit with these feelings or talk them through, you may feel fear or sadness—these feelings are farther down. Through expressing these farther down feelings, you can bring people in closer instead of pushing them away.

**You may be afraid that if you allow yourself to feel** your deeper emotions, you'll become overwhelmed or lose control. This is why some people choose to explore them in the safety of counseling. And then, over time, they find that the *opposite* is actually true. When you become masterful with your feelings, they pass more quickly. It's the continual *avoidance of* feeling, or bottling them up, that causes more problems in relationships.

On the other hand, expressing deeper emotions leads to healing, being whole and becoming more bonded.

**Emotions signal an underlying need.** Connection, protection, security, support and reassurance are all examples of needs. If you don't allow yourself to feel the feeling, you won't get to the need underneath. When you get to the need, you can express it and often get it met. This is the basis for coping with life's challenges and for creating loving, healthy relationships of all kinds.

**Where attention goes, energy flows, so focus on needs rather than reactions.** If you reject your partner when they're angry or depressed, they'll feel angry or depressed *and* rejected—and then there are more layers for them. Be there for your partner, and find out what they need, and this both supports them in coping and builds trust between you.

**Let me be clear here: I am talking about *feelings,* not *behavior.*** The aim is to get comfortable with surface feelings of anger or frustration long enough for them to pass. That *does not* mean tolerating angry behavior if it's destructive to person, property or spirit. Feelings of anger or frustration can be appropriate responses and arise for good reason. In Stage Seven you'll discover how these feelings can bring you and your partner closer.

**Emotional wellbeing has three steps.** According to Sue Johnson, creator of Emotionally Focused Couple Therapy (EFT), they are:

1. Tune in to your feeling, listen to it
2. Use it as a compass to guide you to what you need
3. Express this need directly and clearly to another

You may even find that acknowledging your feelings to yourself is all you need to do. When you get to the stages in Part II, you'll see the ways that you can check your emotional compass and learn how it can guide you.

Through sharing all your layers and confiding your emotions and needs with your partner, friends, family or others you feel safe with, you can heal pain, build trust and create a closer relationship.

Emotions are a main way you bond with your partner. Eventually, if you can stick with the process of managing them—confiding in your partner and supporting them to do the same—you'll find that the feeling of being connected increases with every struggle. The better the two of you get at expressing your feelings and needs appropriately, the more respect and admiration you'll have for yourself and each other. In this way, you build a relationship that will survive differences of opinion, disagreements on issues and ultimately, the test of time.

## Finding Your Voice

Expressing yourself can be hard. It takes a skill that many of us didn't learn growing up: assertiveness. Assertiveness is loving, learning and growing all rolled up into one package. It's taking the risk of revealing my inner journey to you and trusting that you will be there with me.

Assertiveness doesn't come naturally for many. We can grow up being passive, aggressive, or swing between the two. Thankfully, assertiveness is an attitude and a set of skills that can be learned. Recognizing the difference between being assertive, passive or aggressive is a great start.

**Assertiveness means valuing you both.** Passiveness means you value your partner more than you value yourself. Aggressiveness means you value yourself more than you value your partner. Assertiveness is an attitude of mutual respect—you value each other as equals.

**Assertiveness affects expectations.** Too low expectations can come from passiveness. Too high expectations can result from aggression. With assertiveness, you make sure your expectations are realistic by checking them out with your partner.

**Assertiveness affects our needs.** Passivity means you sacrifice your needs. Aggressiveness means you expect your partner to meet your needs at the expense of theirs. With assertiveness, both your needs are equally important. From here, you can negotiate them.

**Assertiveness comes from a sense of inner power.** Passiveness stems from having little or no sense of inner strength. Aggression comes from assuming power over someone else.

**With assertiveness you can speak up**—you can take what's inside and make it known to others. You can ask for help, comfort, space or advice, whatever and whenever you need. You can let others know when they've crossed the lines and lower the risk for it happening again.

**You have the right to be treated well in your relationships**, but it's your responsibility to teach others what you consider "well." Silence implies consent and leaves that part you unknown to your partner. Hostility and aggression make you adversaries. Brooding or sulking makes you strangers. Assertiveness makes you true partners—in life and in family.

**By being assertive you can avoid the hurts, misunderstandings and disappointments** that can cause distress and escalate problems in relationships. If you're able to assert your thoughts, feelings and needs, and hear those of your partner, then you can avoid blame and bitterness.

**Assertiveness begins with self-awareness, self-acceptance and self-esteem**—knowing what you want or need and acknowledging that you're worthwhile and that you have a right to your needs. You can take responsibility for yourself. The same is true for your partner.

**Assertiveness combines the stages for healthy personal development**—*trusting* that what you have to say is important and of value. Your self-esteem comes from within and is *independent* of someone else's opinion of you, taking the *initiative* to speak up and doing so in a *competent* and respectful way. This is how you build your confidence.

**Assertiveness is conveyed through tone of voice, body language and word choice.** Your tone will be assertive if it's not too soft or too loud. Assertive body language is facing the other person squarely and making eye contact. Your choice of words will reflect whether or not you're speaking to your partner as an equal, although they may be the best judge of that!

These loving, learning and growing skills enable you to pull together through all the challenges in all the years ahead. They weave together to create the platform that you build your family on. When you're going through a hard time, you can use the words "loving, learning, growing" as a mantra to remind yourself of the need to take your time, to be kind to yourself and to your partner and to go gently. These are also the skills you will pass down to your children to support them to love, learn and grow as they go through life.

# Thriving

Up until now, I hope I have put some context around the journey you're about to embark on. Here we put all that loving, learning and growing theory into action. The ways you and your partner relate to each other will directly affect your journey going forwards. This section on *thriving* is for you to roll up, put in your backpack and pull out at the times when you'll be needing it over the next year or two…or more. Think of this section as your Advanced Parenthood Survival Skills Manual.

And you'll need it. Time and time again. Because there will be times you'll feel lost, times when you'll be exhausted and not thinking properly and times you'll wonder who the heck you or your partner has turned into. There're times you'll take different paths and see different parts of the terrain—things your partner can't see or know what they mean because they haven't been there yet.

And while we're here, let's talk a little about "thriving." It's a word used a lot these days. I don't want to imply that the growth you'll develop through applying these skills will be easy or effortless. Quite the opposite. You'll be doing more loving, learning and growing than you know, and that's tiring. Exhausting even. Thriving happens when you pay attention to someone (yourself, your partner, your child), tend to them, and lovingly give them what they need—every single day. And even more frequently during times of stress when you're in the muddy trenches. This is where love flourishes most because at least you're in them together. You'll develop resilience for your whole family this way, not despite the challenges, but because of them.

Here we go….

Your relationship with your partner is unique, so it makes sense that how you relate to each other would be unique, too. Your partner knows you intimately and has the power to both hold you up or put you down like no one else. Their attitude towards you can make you wilt or bloom, their words can harm or heal. You have the same power with them. For these reasons, the effort and care you put into communicating with each other is even more important than the actual outcome. Going forward, you will want your relationship to be more important than any issue that might come between you. Your child will want the same thing.

Let's start with why talking with a partner can be so bloody hard some time.

## Understanding Your Filter

Your personal journey of loving, learning and growing up means that you have developed your very own way of taking in information, called a "filter." Your filters help you determine what information to focus on and what to ignore. Filters are a combination of attitudes learned from your parents, your attachment style and your experiences growing up in your pocket of the world and the people in it. Your filters are unique to you.

Your filters shape your personal beliefs, judgments and assumptions. Your filters can also distort your understanding. Nobody filters information in the exact same way as anyone else. This is how misunderstandings occur.

Although you usually aren't aware of it, a filter is often an "if/then" thought pattern like: "If you sound/look that way, then it must mean ." or, "if you're angry, then you don't love me," or, "if you don't listen, then you don't care."

## Understanding Your Triggers

**A trigger is something that sparks an emotional reaction**; often one that's extreme. It happens in the present but taps into feelings from your past and is likely to confuse you (and your partner), because its origin may be hidden deep in a filter.

Triggers can be a tone of voice (that you interpret as angry or blaming), a choice of words ("you always do that"), or a facial expression (a scowl or rolling the eyes). A trigger often comes from a seemingly insignificant event and sometimes you may wonder why you got so upset.

**How do you know if you are reacting to old stuff?** If you are *overreacting*. If you surprise yourself with the strength of your feelings, or can't understand why you reacted a certain way, you're likely to have tapped into some of your own ancient history.

For example, if I have an argument with my partner and he storms out of the house, I may feel upset and see myself as being abandoned *now,* but I may also feel frightened—the same way I felt as a child when a parent left *then,* and I didn't know if they were coming back.

If my partner raises their voice, I may feel anxious *now,* but their words have the power to reduce me in the same way my parents' words did *in the past.*

There are likely to be lots of triggers over the years to come because they're often related to issues of parenthood. If you don't know how to work through them with your partner, it can be like picking the scab off a wound.

On the other hand, if you can use these relating skills (either on your own or with a counselor), triggers can be explored, memories remembered and hurts healed. Understanding can be achieved and love can flourish again.

These guidelines for open, respectful and supportive communication can help you not only survive the challenges of parenthood, but thrive as a couple. I know it's an effort to learn and practice all this now, but trust me, doing so will save you *much* more time and energy as parents going forward.

## Guidelines for Intimate Communication

**Keep it private** until you can do it well (kids have superhero hearing).

**Pay attention**. Turn off the phone, TV, laptop, etc. Get comfortable and keep comfortable eye contact. Eye contact is a main way of connecting and showing your partner that you're interested.

**Be soft on the person but firm on the issue.** Separate the problem from the person. Don't degenerate into personal attacks or name-calling. Criticism and judgment kills trust and promotes ill feeling. Apologize for any personal remarks before moving on.

**Allow for silence.** If your partner falls silent, it may be because they're shifting emotional gears. Give them room to do this.

**Explain your silences.** Silence can be interpreted in different ways. If you need more time to process what's been said, ask for it. If you need the conversation to slow down, ask for it. If you don't understand what you've just heard, ask for clarification.

**Aim for win/win.** Negotiate, compromise, and provide a united front to your children so they see you working as a team to come up with options or a way forward. Even if you can't, at least with this goal, goodwill is preserved.

**Take turns.** Whoever raises an issue for discussion speaks first and in full. The other partner listens, and when they have demonstrated a full understanding of what the speaker has said, it's their turn.

**Don't go on and on.** Stick to digestible chunks—you'll get it all out more efficiently this way. Some couples like to hold an object in their hands while they are the speaker and when they've finished, pass this object to their partner. Have some fun choosing an object.

## Guidelines for the Speaker

**Choose the timing.** When you're exhausted, sleep-deprived or hungry, it's easy to become impatient and snappy. Leave important issues for a time when you're both reasonably rested.

**Make an appointment.** Let your partner know you have an issue you'd like to discuss. Arrange a time you know will be relatively uninterrupted and long enough (e.g., not when there's something coming up on TV, visitors due or the baby's about to awaken.

**Say how long you'd like to talk about it.** Maybe 10 minutes for a minor issue or 40 for a major one. Stick to it (unless you both agree to continue). An agreed-upon time limit can reduce anxiety. Many people can only concentrate for about 40 minutes before they need a break. If this isn't enough time, take a break before you continue.

**Start gently**. Renowned parenthood and relationship expert, John Gottman, PhD, predicts that the way you open up a topic for discussion determines how the conversation will progress 96 percent of the time. Discussions that start harshly can escalate quickly and are more likely to end badly.

This is tricky because if you remember, the first feelings in your awareness are the surface ones, which may be defensive. So, slow down and take time to get in touch with your own deeper feelings before you speak. If it's anger (women tend to hide this one, even from themselves), state yourself assertively, not aggressively.

**Be mindful of your tone**. If you feel anxious or uncomfortable, this is likely to come across. Your partner is likely to be sensitive to your tone of voice and a slight inflection can trigger warning bells. Manage this by revealing your struggles: "I find this difficult to talk about, so if it comes out the wrong way, let me know and I'll start again."

**Use endearments**. Words like "honey," "sweetheart," and "darling," are love language in action and can soften communication—if delivered with a loving tone of voice and not through gritted teeth.

**Use loving gestures to reassure**. Reach out to your partner as you make a statement that says "I want to connect with you." Give them a smile that says "I care about how you are hearing this."

**State your intention.** Why are you raising the issue? For what purpose? To gain understanding? To negotiate an outcome? To get an apology and heal hurt? Stating this at the outset prepares your partner to see where you're going. For example, "I'm confused about what you said yesterday, can we clear it up?" Or, "I'd like to talk about going away in May, can we talk after dinner?"

**Stay on track and help your partner to stay on track.** It's more likely to escalate if other issues, past hurts, or what your mother-in-law did four years ago are all brought up. Stay focused on what you want to resolve. One point at a time.

**Stay specific.** The words "always" or "never" are triggers that are likely to make your partner tune out or become defensive. Stick to specific incidences.

**Slow down.** Rapid-fire talk can feel like an attack.

**Be open to self-discovery.** You might find the issue shifts mid-discussion (e.g., you've discovered a hidden issue underneath). Let your partner know what's happening inside you so they can keep up with you: "I've just realized this is linked to something else—give me a minute…." This way you both get to the bottom of what's really going on and create trust and intimacy at the same time.

## Four Steps for Intimate Communication

**Step One: Create a safe space.** Let your partner know you want to have an intimate conversation where you will both be practicing your skills. Use the guidelines and go gently with each other.

**Step Two: Go inside.**
Relationships blossom when partners can confide their onion-layer thoughts, feelings and needs with each other. First, you need to be aware of them. Take time to check in with yourself and get in touch with what's going on inside and underneath, both tangible and also half-formed. Get in touch with your inner struggle, your discomfort, your mixed feelings and your needs so that you can give them a voice.

These deeper feelings are likely to cause you unease. They require you to be real and vulnerable and have a deeper relationship with yourself—and then with your partner. Yet vulnerability creates intimacy, because it invites your partner to be real and vulnerable in return.

Contrast the different responses you might get from these options: "You have to help me with the washing!" or "Honey, I really want your help with the washing. Everything's getting on top of me. If I have to fold one more thing, I'm going to scream. Can we get this done and then go for a walk?"

**Step Three: Find the words.** Speak your truth to yourself first. Try the words on for size. Wonder how your partner might hear them. Then find the words to express yourself assertively. Remember this means honoring and respecting you and your partner as equals.

Step Four: Reveal yourself by using "I" language.

Starting a conversation with the word "you," is likely to put the other person on the defensive before you've even uttered another word. The listener is triggered and will automatically prepare themselves for absolutes (never, have to, should), criticism or judgments. You're likely to trigger the fight/flight/freeze response and they're likely to either switch off or retaliate. "You" statements also imply that you know your partner better than they do themselves. This can be insulting.

"I" language bypasses this automatic response and allows your partner to remain open to what you want to say. "I" language reveals you, it says, "This is who I am."

People can only absorb the amount of information in four short-ish sentences before they lose concentration. For tired parents, it may only be two sentences, so, to make it easy, you can use something like the following formula (feel free to mix it up).

1. **I feel/I felt** *[insert the emotion you are aware of]* ___________
2. **when** *[describe the situation in objective terms]* _______________
   e.g., instead of "you left the garbage out," it would be "when I saw the garbage can in the street."
3. **because** *[describe a reason, hidden issue, how you interpreted it or what is unfolding for you]* _____________
4. **and I would really like/prefer** *[make a request, state a hope or describe a motivation]* __________.

Examples:

Instead of, "You're hopeless! You never bring in the washing." try:

> "I'm frustrated *(a feeling)* because I can see the washing is still out *(the situation),* and I don't have time to bring it in before it rains *(a reason).* Is there any way you could do it please *(a request)*?"

Or instead of, "You shouldn't have sent Grace to her room the other day. You don't know how to discipline properly. If you can't do it right, don't do it at all." try:

> "I thought we agreed about how to handle Grace *(the situation.* The other day when you sent her to her room, I thought you did it deliberately to annoy me *(how I interpreted it)* and I felt confused *(a feeling)* why you'd do that. I'd like to clear that up *(my hope)*."

Or instead of, "You never listen to me! You always interrupt. I hate it!" try:

> "When I can't finish what I'm saying, I feel frustrated *(the surface feeling)* because I think you don't care about me enough to listen *(a hidden issue)*. That really hurts *(a deeper feeling)*. I'm almost afraid to ask *(what's currently unfolding for me as I am speaking)*, and I'd appreciate it if I can finish what I'm saying before you start."

While you don't have to include all four components every time, they can help to avoid misunderstanding and improve your chances for being heard. "I" language can feel awkward at first, but it's really just sharing the inner conversations you have with yourself in a healthy and helpful way. With more practice, you'll both get more comfortable.

## Guidelines for the Listener

**Tune in to your partner.** You may find that when your partner is speaking, you're instead listening to the voice in your own head. You might not even wait for them to finish before you try to take your turn. One of the greatest needs we all share is the need to be heard—and often we're fighting simply for this right. At the same time. Take turns instead. Suspend your own assumptions, judgments, interpretations and mind-chatter so you're clear to receive the speaker's message.

**Hold your own reactions.** Own any reactions you can't control by saying something like, "Hang on, I need a moment. Would you stop for a bit? I'm having a reaction and I need to work out what's going on before I can keep listening." Then put your reaction aside and come back to it when it's your turn.

**Be curious.** Ask questions: How long have you felt this way? What does this mean to you? What happened for you when…? What about that is the problem? It seems like you're [feeling] because [reason]. Is there anything else you're feeling as well? Explore where your partner is at before moving on.

**Aim for understanding and empathy.** Intimate listening is supporting your partner through the onion layers of themselves that they're currently exploring and revealing. This allows them to trust you so they can have the confidence to go deeper into the next layer. Be prepared that they may start in with their defensive layer. Be brave and hold yourself through the process—it gets easier with practice. You want your partner to be able to safely share *all t*heir feelings with you. The ones that bring you closest are deepest.

**Recap your understanding often** of what your partner is saying so they know you "get it." Watch for non-verbal cues. If they're shaking their heads, getting frustrated or their voice is getting louder, it may be because you're on the wrong track. If they start nodding, their eyes go wide, they become more engaged, get animated (or go quiet to shift into a deeper emotion), keep it up, you're doing well.

**Be a mirror for your partner.** Keeping the focus on your partner has the effect of "holding" them while they take the risk of going deeper and revealing themselves.

**Reflective listening** is repeating back what you heard, or think you heard, your partner say, but using your own words, (not like a parrot, that's *really* annoying). As you get better at it, you'll be able to also reflect what your partner is feeling about what they're saying.

For example: Sarah (angry): "Brad, you forgot to get the milk."

Brad (defensive): "Well, you should have reminded me."

Sarah picks up her car keys and storms out. They're still annoyed with each other two hours later when Sarah's brother brings his boys for a sleepover.

Here Brad's defensiveness blocked Sarah's anger—which just left her angrier, for longer. With blocking, her feelings are more likely to build and bottle up—and explode next time the milk gets forgotten.

Compare this to Brad's reflective listening: Sarah (angry): "Brad, you forgot the milk."

Brad (bravely and non-defensively): "I've let you down."

Sarah (still angry): "Yes. And I need it for the mac and cheese. Pete's dropping the boys off soon and I wanted it finished before they got here."

Brad (prepared it will take time for Sarah to cool down): "and so now you're extra stressed."

Sarah (anxious): "That's right. I was hoping you'd watch them in the tub for half an hour while I fixed dinner and now one of us needs to go out again."

Brad: "…and now we'll be running late, is that it?"

Sarah (relieved, because she's feeling heard and understood): "Yes. And you know the later it is the more tired they all are and then they start to play up and it's hard to organize them for bed."

Brad: "How about I grab the milk and organize a rumble before a bath to tire them out?"

Sarah (grateful): "Thanks, that'd be great!"

Can you predict how this evening might go differently?

Remember, your feelings are like the layers of an onion. It takes time for one feeling to get down to the next. By being brave, holding his own reactions, holding her and reflecting back what he heard and saw in Sarah, Brad allowed Sarah's feelings to flow and dissipate as she went through her onion process uninterrupted.

### Use the Feedback Sandwich

This technique (positive, negative, positive) is useful for everyone, particularly in delicate situations. Some examples:

To an over-eager grandmother who's elbowing you out of the way: "I really appreciate your help, I think I've got this under control, I would love you to _____ instead."

Or to your partner: "Honey, I really appreciate your help. We need milk. Would you mind grabbing some?"

## More Advanced Parenthood Adventure Survival Skills

### Negotiate Before Compromise

Let me show you what I mean. While we're stopped here, consider this example. I have an orange. I only have one and let's say you and I both want it. We could argue about it, or we could do the right thing, compromise, cut the orange in half and walk away. Right?

But imagine if you squeezed your half of the orange into your mouth and then threw the rind in the compost. And then I went to the kitchen with my half and scraped the rind from it to make a cake we're going to have later: I don't need the juice. The moral of this story? Don't be too quick to find a solution. Talk about what you need first.

### Negotiate Before Problem Solving

**It's normal to have problems.** Problems don't necessarily mean there's anything wrong with either of you or your relationship. Working through your problems as a team strengthens your partnership.

**Negotiating means honestly and respectfully talking about** your hopes, concerns, thoughts and feelings about the problem (this may be most of the conversation) before moving into trying to solve it. By becoming clear about all these aspects up front, you can avoid many misunderstandings, assumptions and hidden concerns that can often sabotage problem solving efforts.

## Three Steps for Problem Solving:

1. Phrase the problem as a joint question: "How are we going to get to a movie this week?" "How are we going to get Joe to eat vegetables?" or "Where should we go for Easter?" or "What do we want to do with this last orange?"
2. Brainstorm possibilities. Chuck things in, be as creative and crazy as possible. Have fun with it; you just might surprise yourselves.
3. Find middle ground—areas of agreement or something you can both live with. One way is to list all the possibilities in order of ease or affordability. If the decision swings one way, what would compensate the other so it's fairer?

**If it gets heated:** Your issues don't have to be worked through in one go. It's much better to slow down and take the time, or even a few times, especially if it's an important topic. If a discussion gets too heated, have a break, take time and space to calm yourself and have another go.

**Make your intentions clear.** Arguments often heat up through simple misunderstandings or misinterpretations. So, if you find things starting to escalate, prepare to shift gears. Get in touch with what's going on and own it before you try again. Start by making your intentions known to your partner. Some examples:

"This has touched a nerve in me."

"I don't want to fight; I want to work on this. I understand that you're angry, but I don't understand why. Can you tell me more?"

"I feel a bit anxious talking about this because _______."

Another example:

> Kate: "When I'm trying so hard to talk to you and have you listen, it's because I have all these angry feelings inside of me. If I can get them out, then I can feel loving towards you again. When you block my attempts to talk, I just get *more* frustrated, angry and resentful. I don't want to feel this way towards you, and I need to be heard."
>
> Steven: "But when you talk to me like that, your voice gets loud and you have this wild look in your eyes. I don't want to listen to you when you're like that. I just want to walk away."
>
> Kate: "If you let me keep talking, I *will* calm down. I don't want to scare you away. I'm not even angry with you, I'm angry *at the situation,* but frustrated with you because you won't let me talk. And I guess, it's not just the words I'm saying that I want you to hear—it's that I'm upset, too. I want you to be here for me so I can be open and honest

and trust that you love me enough and care enough not to get scared and run away."

**If it gets too heated to continue,** despite your best efforts, things may still escalate. If they do, call timeout. This is an exercise in self-care as well as relationship-care. It's taking time away from each other to cool down. The steps are:

1. Whoever wants to take the time out calls it. You can't tell your partner they need time out—this is likely to just inflame them. Take responsibility for yourself if you're overwhelmed.
2. Check in after 20 minutes and see if either of you need more time.
3. Commit to another try at talking about the issue as soon as you have both cooled down. It may have to be the next day if you find you're just pressing the same buttons all over again.

If you mess up, it's OK. It's good practice, and you can do better next time. Apologize to your partner if the situation warrants it. This shows respect to them and for yourself. Repeat the steps as often as necessary. It gets easier.

## The Healing Apology

Hurtful words can cut deeply and leave scars, so it's important to apologize well when you say something that results in harm. Apologizing doesn't mean that you're backing down on an important issue, don't believe what you were saying is true, are admitting defeat or letting the other person "win." It's acknowledging that the *way* you said something led to an injury. Saying, "I'm sorry, I shouldn't have said that, can we try again?" gets you back on track.

It's important to apologize, not just for what you said or did, that you now feel regretful about, but what you said or did that led to *the other person* feeling bad (these might be different things). Healthy relationships aren't so much about always being in harmony with each other—they're more about stretching (and sometimes snapping) the connection between you and restoring it again. It's when repair is not attempted or successful that relationships suffer.

The steps to do a restoration and to feel close again:

1. Hear your partner's pain.
2. Acknowledge what you said or did that led to it.
3. Ask them what they need to heal.
4. Do it.

Your partner will be giving you valuable information that you'll want to be mindful of, so you're less likely to trigger their hurt the same way again.

These parenthood survival skills are high level. It may feel easier to blame your partner, throw up your hands and walk away every time an elephant issue comes between you. But think of the benefits of sticking with the process. Eventually you won't waste time and energy arguing. Instead you'll be able to work through your issues, feel proud of yourself and your partner and strengthen your relationship at the same time.

You're also passing on the most important life lessons ever: self-care, couple-care, stress relief and conflict navigation to your kids. Children learn through watching their parents. The very best thing for them is to have parents *w*ho learn, grow and *show love* to each other.

That's the end of your orientation. I hope it was informative and helpful for you. Here's our jeep to take us to the starting point of our journey. Buckle up, there may be a few bumps on the road ahead.

# PART II:

# THE STAGES OF PARENTHOOD

We've been talking a lot about the challenges of parenthood for you, so while we're driving along here, I thought it only fair to share mine.

I was lost—at a time when I was supposed to be a guide. This may not inspire confidence in you now as you're heading into uncharted territory, but stay with me…

I was starting my career as a relationship counselor and one of the first questions we ask a couple is "when did things start to change between you?" Inevitably, after some gentle exploration, clients would say it was after the birth of their first child.

I was shocked. I didn't want to hear that—because I was a new mother myself and I could sense that things were changing between my husband and me, too—in a big way. In a *not-good* big way!

And yet here I was. Trying to guide my clients. I knew what I *should* be doing, where we *should* be heading, but my personal struggles kept getting in the way—like roadblocks. Every session with my clients just made me more aware of my own distress. It was painful, lonely and confusing. How on earth was I supposed to help my clients, when I wasn't even sure how to help *us?* I felt like a failure.

But I persevered. I didn't know how to get there, but I knew *exactly* where I wanted to be. I wanted to be close to my husband again. I wanted his support. I wanted to parent as a team.

So, I continued to put one foot in front of the other and head in that direction. It was like walking into a fog. There were hurdles. I jumped over them. There were obstacles. I worked around them. And I also stumbled plenty of times.

But slowly, slowly, things started to become clearer. I was finding a way. Disillusionment, confusion and frustration turned into hope. And then hope turned into a burning desire to make a difference for our next generation of parents and families—including yours.

You learned about relationship stages in **Loving**, and you learned about personal stages in **Growing**. These stages are helpful to break down something big and overwhelming and confusing and chaotic into smaller, more manageable phases. Each developmental phase contains stepping-stones, awareness and skills that lead you through the journey and milestones to mark your progress along the way. You'll get more stuff in your backpack to make the next phase of the journey easier.

And remember I told you that traditionally parenthood is a rite of passage and this involved three stages? Well, times have changed. Our world is so much more complicated these days—you can't just strap your baby to your chest and return to work—and have the support and guidance of your village while you do it. Parenthood still, and always will be, a rite of passage. However, three stages don't begin to describe what happens for parents these days.

I have worked with mothers, fathers and partners for over 20 years as a relationship counselor and educator. I have seen, and helped, and sometimes, sadly, not been able to help, parents and couples as they worked through just about any scenario you could imagine. I have poured over decades of research, hundreds of papers and books that take up a whole wall in my study. I've learned just as much, and earned wisdom, the hard way. And this is what I discovered:

During pregnancy, the first few years of parenthood (and beyond) parents will love, learn and grow through *eight* stages of parenthood. Yes, eight.

People say nothing can prepare parents for parenthood, but that's not true anymore. I want to help you find your bearings, see around corners and choose the better path when there's a fork in the road. I want to help you avoid the swamps where parents before you got stuck, the rockiest parts where they fell and scraped their knees and the dead ends where they just threw up their hands and gave up. Even more than that, I want to support you to trust yourself and to trust each other—even when you're heading into the great unknown—so you actually *know how to* create the family you dreamed about.

**Stage One** will see you through the time of thinking about a baby, conception and pregnancy. **Stage Two** will see you through your family's first few months. **Stages Three** and **Four** will guide you through the first six months or so, and **Stages Five** to **Eight** apply to the next few years and "forever."

Each time you welcome a little person into your family, you get to go through all the stages. If it's not your first time, you get a "do over" of any steps you may have stumbled on previously. This is one of the many gifts of the parenthood adventure.

And don't be surprised if you find yourself going through the later stages again and again as your children grow. Big changes in your family, like moving to another state, starting a new school or the loss of someone close, will cycle your family through most of the stages again.

So here I am about to walk you along a trail map of parenthood. No matter where you are in your journey right now, you're about to embark on a new adventure. If you have children now, you're probably going to wish you'd had this guide before. But I hope you'll also be grateful you found it now, because in some parts I will tell you, "here's where you want to stop and back away, because you're getting close to a ledge."

Along the way, you will find the biggest and most common challenges for parents who have travelled these stages before you. For each challenge, if it doesn't apply to you, your partner, or someone else you care about, you can just jump over it and move on.

If it does apply to you, I'm going to ask you to stop and check your compass. I'm going to tell you what I know can lie ahead in each direction. Sometimes I'm going to ask you to look backwards. Or inwards. Challenge you to think about what you might be seeing. I'm hoping this will help you to discover new angles and multiple viewpoints, different ways to go forward.

Sometimes you'll walk the path ahead hand-in-hand with your partner. Sometimes they'll be helping you over a rough patch and other times you'll be helping them. Sometimes, often even, there will be times when you can't agree on the best way forward, so you'll take different paths around an obstacle or even go off on your own for a while. Sometimes you'll be farther apart than you thought possible—maybe with one of you on a motorcycle and the other pedaling a tandem bicycle alone. Other times you'll realize you're just around the corner from your partner, but you couldn't see them because something was blocking your view. All of this is OK. And no matter the distance between you, I'll guide you through ways to get back to each other again and again.

Then, I'll encourage you to put any types of vehicles aside so you can take your time to explore the landscape of parenthood on foot. I'll suggest some steps for you and your partner that have helped parents travel that same terrain before you. These steps can help you get closer to your desired destination of a happy, healthy and stable family—and closer to each other.

Some of them are baby steps. Some of them are big. Grab those backpacks because your adventure is about to begin.

# Stage One: Preparing for Your Baby

## (Before Your Baby Joins You)

Your journey into becoming a family can begin long before your baby is born. Even before they're dreamed about, the space for a child can be created between a couple. It might be a desire to find a partner who also wants a big family, or only one child. Or maybe it's even a partner who doesn't want to have a child, but you find it happening anyway and you must then create the space for them. Either way, it's a space filled with hope and possibility.

And then pregnancy is a time of expecting—of waiting. But with changes on the horizon, you're much better served to use this time for *preparing*. At first, it's the physical changes you will have noticed: the ripening and blossoming of breasts and belly, the first flutters of movement, the wonder of another life inside, and then the momentous miracle of birth, which transforms your old "us" into a new one overnight.

The more preparation you have done beforehand, the less adjusting there is likely to be afterwards. This gives you more time, energy and focus for the important work of becoming familiar with the newness of each other. And new aspects of yourself.

As bellies grow, baby stuff is purchased, and booties are knitted by excited relatives you may also experience an evolving sense of who you will be as a new parent. As you prepare to farewell your old life and perhaps your old job too, it opens a new space inside you, ready to be filled.

Even with second or more children. Aspects of pregnancy, birth and parenthood can change during a second or more time around. Things that weren't noticed in the newness of the first time can come to the foreground. You may circle back to old issues again, but you'll have more insight and experience to deal with them differently.

As your baby's birth day gets closer, you might find yourself so preoccupied with the practicalities of getting ready, and the prospect of birth is so huge, that it's hard to focus on anything else. But as you both anticipate meeting and bonding with your new baby, be aware that the bond between the two of you is just as important—and this bond supports your baby too.

So as you think about your future, about where you want to go, think also about what you may need to get you there. Sure, you may need some extra equipment, but more important than this you may need some direction and skills for any challenges that lie ahead.

So pack your bags carefully. Think about what you're taking with you. Because your adventure starts now.

## Life Changes

*Some friends have warned us to be prepared for some big changes. Should we be worried?*

You have some *very* caring friends. Should you be worried? No. Should you prepare? Yes. Examine your life to find areas with potential for improvements and address them: work/life balance, nutrition, physical and mental health, communication, stress relief, family relationships etc. You can't prepare for everything, but you can prepare for lots.

**CHECK YOUR COMPASS:**

**Some questions.** Who is responsible for earning money or running the household? Who does the work of maintaining your relationship? Imagine how these things may change when your time and energy is going into your absolutely adorable, but-will-suck-you-dry for a while, baby, and how you might change things around or get your own needs and wants met differently. What can you do now that will simplify life after your baby comes?

**STEPS:**

**Talk to others who have gone before.** Encourage them to be honest about the changes and challenges they've faced. Ask how they worked through these changes—or how they would have liked to. These conversations before and after the baby help you adjust.

**Be prepared.** Encourage willing family members to start cooking and freezing meals now so you have time and energy afterwards for more important things, like resting. Establish a shared daily ritual (e.g., a late hot chocolate or evening walk together) to check in.

**Declutter.** Have you ever heard of the 80/20 rule? You only use 20 percent of your stuff 80 percent of the time (clothes, cooking utensils, etc.). One afternoon of getting rid of the rest could save you years of unnecessary dusting. Less stuff is easier when you have toddlers too.

*Now that my wife is heavily pregnant, I have so much to do. How long do I need to keep this up?*

It's great that you're asking this now. While most people recognize the challenges for a heavily pregnant woman, the same can't be said for her partner. There's also the assumption that a woman in late pregnancy needs help, but not so much awareness that one with a new baby needs even more. It's likely that she will need you even more in all sorts of ways. This can be a challenge for some partners.

**CHECK YOUR COMPASS:**

Quality is just as important, if not more, than quantity. Realize the ways you're most important to her and focus on these. Ask her if you don't know.

**Where is your energy going?** You may be doing things that will take time and energy from your new family. Now's the time to start scaling them down a little.

**You need to take care of yourself.** Make sure you are eating well, getting a good night's sleep and exercising regularly. Often, we're exhausted simply because we aren't looking after ourselves.

**She will need you.** After the baby comes, she will have little time for normal household tasks including cooking, cleaning and shopping. The intense focus and energy required for bonding and breastfeeding, as well as general fatigue, will mean that doing things that require details, or a long attention span, can be challenging. She'll be experiencing physical and emotional changes that she may want to share with someone in order to make sense of them. You're the person she probably prefers to share all this with.

**She will have new needs.** A new mother and baby's vulnerability mean she may look to you for an increased level of both strength and sensitivity.

She may need you to look after her as well as the baby. This may mean shielding them from too many visitors or phone calls, providing her with a snack or drink while she's feeding the baby, or setting limits with intrusive grandparents.

**Steps:**

**Embrace vulnerability.** Your partner and children will need your care now and forever. Parenthood is the perfect time for you to tap into and develop your nurturing side.

**Talk about it.** Partners may hesitate to share their concerns for fear of stressing their mate, yet women tend to bond with their partner when they share their vulnerabilities. Sharing concerns connects you both at a deeper, more trusting level. It may also take her mind off her own worries for a while. The closeness that comes from sharing concerns can lessen worry and make problems disappear.

**Get to know other dads.** Dads need friends to debrief with, call on for help, take timeout with and get advice from—which can be lifesaving. This helps you to cope with the realities of parenthood, laugh or commiserate, take away from it all for a couple of hours and remind you that you (and your partner) are normal.

**Build up a support network.** You were never meant to do it alone. It really does take a village. Start gathering your tribe together now.

## Expectations

*Now that I'm pregnant, I want my partner to treat me differently. I want him to be more considerate of my feelings.*

It's normal and common to feel more vulnerable, sensitive and in need of care at this time, and there are good reasons for you to feel the way you do. How well your partner is able to respond to these new needs will, in part, depend on how you request them.

*We've been waiting for a long time to adopt our baby. I want my partner to realize how this is affecting me.*

*This is our second baby, I don't know about my partner, but I want it to be different this time.*

A common issue for couples after having a new baby is that their expectations of each other have remained unspoken and then they actually turned into assumptions. So, before baby comes (and sleep deprivation sets in) is the time to start talking about your hopes and concerns.

**CHECK YOUR COMPASS:**

**Expectant parenthood is a time of self-discovery.** Take time to look inwards and put words to what you're sensing inside.

**What do you want for your relationship?** This very special and unique time in life has great potential for a more intimate level of sharing between you.

**Expecting, wanting and asking are different things.** It's fine for you to want something from your partner, and anticipate receiving it, but as much as you might like it, your partner isn't likely to be able to read your mind—so share your hopes or expectations with them and develop the confidence to ask openly for what you need.

**STEPS:**

**Ask early**. When you ask, and the way you ask will affect how your partner responds. Too often we wait for our mate to intuit our needs, so by the time we have to ask, we're already resentful.

**Frame your words**. If you frame a request as a criticism, "you never think of me," or a demand, "you should think of me," your partner will only hear the criticism or demand, and the request gets lost.

*I thought when I announced my pregnancy that my mom would be thrilled. I'm shocked and hurt that she wasn't.*

It's normal to assume other people's reactions reveal their feelings towards you, but this isn't usually the case. More often other people's reactions reveal more about their feelings about themselves, or their own situation and so they may not make sense to you at the time.

**CHECK YOUR COMPASS:**

**Becoming a grandparent is a milestone** that can mean different things for different people, and it's commonly a time for grandparents-to-be to revisit aspects of their own past.

**Your parents' experience.** If your mother struggled with her own pregnancy, she may be fearful for yours. If she remembers having troubles in her marriage during that time, she may worry for your relationship. If your father remembers his own parents or in-laws being either intrusive or absent after you arrived, he may worry about what the right level of involvement will be with your baby.

**STEPS:**

**Notice gently**. You could say something like, "I noticed you went very quiet/seemed uncomfortable/changed the subject when I told you our news. I was wondering what was going on for you."

By sensitively bringing your parents' reaction to their attention, you may unearth a back-story of which you were completely unaware. As well as creating opportunities to know your family better, you'll have more family knowledge to pass on to your child one day. And maybe you'll find new understanding and healing too.

**Ask them about their history.** Find out what that time was like, their concerns and fears and see if there are any links or context that helps you understand their reaction.

*I didn't really think much about the baby. My wife was very capable. I was sure she'd take care of everything.*

For at least the first few weeks, but very likely the first few months of motherhood, a mother will be in survival mode. She may struggle to meet her own needs as she finds her way of meeting the needs of the new addition. She'll need your help, and probably even more.

For a start, your baby comes with plenty of decisions to be made that involve and affect you: where are you going to have the baby? What does she need from you for the birth? Where is your baby going to sleep? Is she planning to breastfeed? Are you going to circumcise or vaccinate your child? How much time are you each going to take off work?

**CHECK YOUR COMPASS:**

**Some changes will directly affect you**. It's likely she'll need you more than ever (even if she doesn't tell you). What might this mean for your current lifestyle? You may have to be prepared to suspend or scale things down a bit.

**What are your priorities?** Think about your careers and stabilize it for the time being if you can. Now is not the time for promotions or job changes where you'll have to work longer or harder. Mothers need their partner home earlier, not later. And less stressed, not more.

**Little things can make a big difference**. New mommas spend a lot of time at home, especially early on, so it's nice to have a comfy space to relax in. If you're a fixer-upper, do what you can around your home so she can focus on herself and the baby. Hang a hammock; get some new curtains or cushions; fix a stuck window or do some landscaping so she has fresh air and a nice view while she's stuck at home.

**Your children will like roots.** Children also need a sense of home to grow up in. It's a good idea to stay put while you have a young family. Kids like the security and predictability of familiar streets, knowing the best trees to climb, other kids to play with and which neighborhood dogs you can pet. Familiar neighbors and great local cafes and playgrounds also help alleviate the isolation that's challenging for new moms.

**What makes a home?** More important than bricks and mortar and a familiar block is the atmosphere inside your home. A calm, happy and loving home is the best start in life for your baby. It helps them relax and feel secure.

**STEPS:**

**Make time for your baby.** Start thinking now about the different ways to make your new family a priority and create some space in your life for those things to happen.

**Go to prenatal appointments together.** Sure, you have to work, but even one session to ask questions about things that are important to you can make a big difference to how you cope and adjust after your baby joins you. Consider hiring a doula. Doulas provide practical and emotional support for all aspects of pregnancy, birth and early parenthood.

**Do some research.** Read up and talk with parents you know to get a realistic picture of what life will be like and share what you're learning with your partner. In these ways you can begin to make room in your relationship for your new little-one-to-come.

**Turn the page.** The easiest way to adjust your expectations of the ways you will be needed is to keep reading.

## Mixed Feelings

*Since I found out I was pregnant I have been really up and down. My partner must think I'm crazy!*

*There's so much to get done before the baby comes. I'm excited and terrified too.*

Thanks to hormones, the anticipation of life changes on the horizon and adjusting to the "bigness" of the news, mixed feelings at this time are normal and are a good training ground for the just-as-common emotional turbulence of early parenthood.

If you've had to go through IVF, or a rigorous adoption process (or both), you're likely to find this time is a particularly challenging rollercoaster ride—and need more emotional support.

**CHECK YOUR COMPASS:**

**Welcome to your inner world.** Having a baby and getting to know them is also a time of getting to know a fuller version of yourself.

**You have an inside voice.** Expecting a family is the beginning of changes inside you, and inside your partner. Pay attention to your thoughts, feelings and desires and take time to put words to them: "I think… I feel… I need…"

**You're both going through changes.** You and your partner are both experiencing huge mental and emotional adjustments. It can be hard to find words to describe what might only be inklings or intuitions. When this happens, it's easy for either of you to become preoccupied with what's going on inside you and withdraw into yourself, leaving your partner out.

**STEPS:**

**Talk about your thoughts and feelings** with your partner and with trusted friends. This helps the feelings to pass naturally.

**Write them down.** Parenthood is a journey of the self and of your relationship. Just as you may keep a travel journal to track the highs and lows of a great adventure, you can benefit from bearing witness to this experience.

Motherhood researcher, Wendy le Blanc, recommends that while you're still expecting, write a list of all that you've achieved up until now, and the qualities you have that helped you get there. These same qualities will come in very handy down the track.

**Be mindful of your diet.** Stimulants like caffeine, sugar and alcohol can make mood swings worse. Some foods affect blood sugar levels, causing them to spike and then drop quickly, which can make you irritable. Avoid foods containing artificial sweeteners, like most diet foods and soft drinks. They can lower your mood and may not be good for your baby either.

**Start good self-care now and build it into your routine.** Then, by the time the baby comes, it will already be a good habit. Exercise releases endorphins, creating a natural high. Search for a gym with baby care or find some prenatal exercise videos for home.

**Slow down.** Babies have a very different idea of time. They don't like to be rushed. Start noticing the ways you may be rushing in your life now and take it down a notch or three. That way you'll be more used to a pace that your baby is likely to be more comfortable with.

**Rest throughout the day** to combat fatigue, which always makes things worse. Relax when you can. This is good practice for after the baby comes and it can be harder to do, but even more important. You'll see what I mean when you get there.

**Learn to switch off**. Relaxation doesn't come naturally for some, especially if you've been working full-time and had a crazy social life too. Pregnancy is a time of taking life down a notch or two; it's good preparation for the marathon of early parenthood.

**Experiment.** Different relaxation techniques work for different people and now's the perfect time to experiment—prenatal yoga, meditation apps, spending time in nature, listening to music or luxuriating in a herbal bath—or all of them.

*My girlfriend has been in tears on and off since we found out about the baby. Is this normal? I don't know what to do; everything I say just seems to make it worse.*

Is it normal? Absolutely. There are several things that could be going on for her. Mixed feelings and mood swings are natural with all the hormonal and emotional adjustments of pregnancy, especially if the pregnancy was unplanned, sooner than expected in your timeline or if there're some feelings of ambivalence about having a baby—even when a baby is part of the plan.

**CHECK YOUR COMPASS:**

**What's happening for her?** She may be experiencing emotions that are hard for her to make sense of.

**What's happening for you?** You will have a natural internal (and external) reaction to her being emotional. Check in with yourself and ask what it is. Is it confusion, helplessness, frustration or something else?

**Your reaction will affect her**. Relationships are reciprocal. You influence each other. Knowing this gives you more control over what happens between you. If you know how your reaction helps or hinders her, you can use this new knowledge to guide your responses, so this time is easier and more enjoyable for both of you.

**STEPS:**

**Encourage her to talk**. You're probably both going through a rollercoaster of emotions, which can look chaotic on the outside. Talking about what's going on inside is a great way for people to have a better understanding of themselves. Sometimes just getting it out can be enough. Using the Thriving skills to create a platform for her to link her thoughts, feelings and reactions is empowering for both of you.

**Don't try to give advice**. This is not a problem that needs solving. By just listening and caring, you're providing a safe place for her to explore her emerging mother-self. She will be grateful for it.

**Ask her what she needs—it may be less than you think**. For results-driven or problem-solving individuals, just listening can seem like doing nothing. But nothing is further from the truth. By caring enough to listen you are supporting her emotional process.

**Get support for yourself too**. Just as it's good for your partner to be able to talk things out, it's also good for you. Surround yourself with good friends and good listeners, preferably those who are also becoming a family, so you have lots in common.

> *When I announced our pregnancy to my husband, I thought he would be overjoyed—we've been planning it for a while. Even though he was thrilled at the beginning, he doesn't seem so happy now. He won't say much. I'm devastated.*

It may be difficult for you to make sense of your partner's reactions. But his silence may not mean disappointment. He may be grappling with thoughts about life changes as they get closer or feeling overwhelmed. It's common for men particularly, to stress about the practical and financial aspects of becoming a dad, and any of these reasons, and more, are going to affect how happy he seems.

### CHECK YOUR COMPASS:

**Does he have concerns?** Most dads-to-be have concerns, but they don't always voice them. It may be through fear of stressing their partner, that they talk themselves out of them, or maybe because they lack the confidence to speak their fears. Worries common to most new dads are financial concerns, feeling left out, coping with changes to love life and lifestyle—and how you'll both cope with all that.

**What can you talk about now?** Now's a time to work on creating safety and developing skills, so that no subject needs to be off limits. Where one or both partners refuse to discuss a serious issue, your relationship is likely to suffer in other ways, too.

**A deeper relationship.** Opening up and sharing yourselves on a deeper emotional level is good preparation for the years of parenting you have ahead, and the even longer years you'll have a relationship with your children. Sharing feelings brings you closer to others.

**STEPS:**

**Open the lines of communication.** There will be a gazillion sensitive parenting conversations to be had over the coming weeks, months and years. The sooner you start initiating these talks, the more practice you'll get in before baby joins you.

**Let them know you know.** Ask if anything is bothering your partner. It might be something entirely different to what you thought. While it may be uncomfortable at first, airing concerns helps alleviate them, because it gives them an opportunity to be heard, to explore options of find some relief. You have your Thriving skills for this.

**Deal with stress proactively.** High stress in expecting dads is closely linked with an increased risk for Paternal Postpartum Depression after baby. Now is the time to build regular family-friendly stress relief into both your days.

**Get help if you need it**. If your conversations reveal that either of you have concerns about your partnership, visit a relationship counselor or marriage and family counselor to sort out any issues now. Studies have consistently shown that those with relationship problems find the transition into family much more challenging.

## Bonding

*At our pregnancy classes, they talk about bonding, but I don't really understand what they mean.*

Bonding is the sense of connection you have with your baby. Bonding begins during pregnancy and grows as you get to know your new little person. Bonding is the beginning of your baby's attachment style that you learned about earlier.

While bonding with baby is what they talk about most in classes, there are actually three bonds that are vital for a stable, secure and loving family: the bond between you and your baby; the bond between your partner and your baby; and the bond between you and your partner.

**CHECK YOUR COMPASS:**

**Bonding is important for your whole family**. The connection you have with your baby and with each other is special and makes you feel special. This bond gives you each a sense of security, nurturing, protection, unconditional love and acceptance.

**Look into your baby's future**. A secure bond with parents and caregivers who are close, available and responsive sets your child up to have positive self-esteem, reach their potential and have healthy relationships in their life.

**STEPS:**

**Wonder.** What's going on for your baby as awareness of this strange new world grows? What's this experience like for your partner and how is it affecting them? Being interested and curious are the beginnings of empathy.

**Make the time.** Deep bonding with your baby doesn't necessarily happen straight away, especially if the birth experience has been challenging. Bonding unfolds as mama recovers and you all spend days together becoming more acquainted. You form attachment bonds through holding and cuddling your baby, gazing into their eyes (they'll look away when they need a break), learning to read their signals for attention and care, and through the warmth of your voice. All these things increase your baby's relational brain development and their sense of being supported and loved, particularly if they're receiving this attention from both parents.

**Be prepared to learn.** Parents normally start out misreading their baby's signals 70 percent of the time according to Gottman. You may think they need to be fed when they don't, or you may jiggle them when they just want to be left alone to sleep. You'll figure it out.

**Be prepared to learn about your partner**. Partners send out little signals too. And you can misread those as well. When you express appreciation for each other in small ways regularly throughout the day, then you strengthen your bond.

**Use your words.** "Please" and "thank you" help prevent resentment and thinking you're being taken for granted. Endearments like "sweetheart" or "darling" leave you feeling loved. Massaging tired shoulders shows thoughtfulness. Complementing each other shows attention—especially as your baby is getting most of it.

**Be prepared to get support**. New parenthood is a time of extra pressures and responsibilities, so it's the best time to expand your comfort zone around asking for help so you can have as much attention and energy as possible to care for each other. Your baby benefits from this too.

## Anxiety and Depression During Pregnancy

*My wife seems to be feeling really low a lot. I've heard of postpartum depression, but is it possible to be depressed during pregnancy as well?*

*My partner is stressing over every little thing. She gets frustrated over every speck of dust. I've heard of nesting, but this is ridiculous.*

Every pregnant woman can have bad days. Days when she may feel bloated, tired, stressed or hormonal. If you've noticed that these seem frequent or prolonged, you may be dealing with antenatal depression (AND) or antenatal anxiety or (ANA).

Mild to moderate depression and anxiety during pregnancy is much more common than most people think, with depression affecting around 10 per cent of pregnant mothers and current research suggesting that anxiety is much more common. Don't panic, I'm going to show you how to reduce the risks for this.

And it's good that this is on your radar now, because if left untreated, those with anxiety during pregnancy have a 50 per cent chance of becoming depressed after their baby's birth (PPD). We'll talk more about this in Part III.

If it turns out your partner does have depression or anxiety, getting support now will greatly reduce her chances. A good place to start researching (and find support ahead of time) is Postpartum Support International (PSI).

Antenatal depression or anxiety can be hard to identify because many of the symptoms (fatigue, worries about the baby or becoming a mother or moodiness) are all perfectly normal at this time. Things to watch for, though, are: a persistent sense of dread, feeling hopeless or an inability to enjoy things that usually bring pleasure, significant changes to eating or sleeping habits (not pregnancy-related), a lack of motivation or extreme fatigue that doesn't let up, difficulty concentrating and making decisions, obsessive behaviors including cleaning, intrusive worries that won't go away or uncontrollable crying.

**CHECK YOUR COMPASS:**

**What you're doing right now can make a difference.** Gottman's research found that for expectant parents who had relationship education during pregnancy, only 22.5 percent of the group experienced depression after baby compared with 66.5 percent who had no relationship preparation. A study of over 50,000 women in Norway found the single biggest contributing factor to anxiety during pregnancy was a woman's relationship with her partner. This guidebook can help you both work with feelings of anxiety and depression.

**Steps:**

**Know how much you matter.** You have a profound ability to keep your partner feeling safe and supported and reduce feelings of anxiety. Care and reassurance go a long, long way. Get support for yourself if you need it so you can sustain your efforts.

**Step in if your partner is struggling.** A big contributing factor to depression at any time in parenthood is a lack of partner involvement. Partners can help momma look after herself by pitching in around the home, and later taking on joint responsibilities of caring for baby. As well as making her happy, it is a way of supporting baby too, and increasing the wellness of your whole family.

**Grow closer to reduce stress.** People feel less stressed when they feel like they're not in it alone. Bonding with each other is done the same way as you will both bond with your baby: being close, paying attention and making eye contact, touching, reading each other's signals, and responding in a supportive way. Now's the perfect time to practice on each other.

**Encourage her to talk.** Another big contributing factor to depression is holding stuff inside. It helps mom to be aware of her self-talk and get comfortable talking things out. Ongoing, mutual conversations daily are good preparation now for negotiating all the adjustments that will come after your baby joins you.

**Research your expectations**. The gap between your expectations of life after baby and the reality of it can determine how you both cope and adjust. The easiest way to research? Keep reading.

**Help mom get her feelings out**. As well as talking things out verbally, mom benefits from letting her feelings out physically, too. Having a good cry every now and then is very therapeutic. Expressing anger and frustration in an appropriate way can also be helpful. The more her partner can get comfortable with her expressing her emotions and with revealing their own, the more you'll find emotional wellbeing for both of you—and this is good practice for parenting.

**Go together to see a professional if she's comfortable.** Some mothers prefer to discuss things privately; others appreciate the presence of a partner. It might also be helpful for the midwife or other professional to hear things from both perspectives.

If mom feels anxious about visiting a professional out of fear of being put on medication, chances are this won't be an issue. Mild to moderate depression or anxiety responds well to natural therapies. You may need to talk to different providers to explore your options. If she does decide to take medication, you can explore options that are safe for your baby.

**Enlist family and friends**. Especially in late pregnancy, a mom is less likely to want to cook or do heavy housework. It can be difficult to move with a baby in her tummy. Partners, and others can step in and be a big help by doing chores. It's good practice for after the baby comes too.

**Remind her to care for herself**—to eat small, regular meals to keep blood sugar levels balanced. If a pregnant momma is feeling well, support her in getting some regular exercise, like yoga, walking or swimming, which all stimulate feel-good endorphins. Resting and doing something she enjoys regularly also supports her mental and emotional wellbeing.

*My husband seems to be a lot touchier and withdrawn lately. He's also been going out more and wanting to spend time with his friends. When I ask him what's wrong, he says he doesn't want to talk about it.*

Some anxiety or feeling a little low may be a normal part of his adjusting to the changes. They may pass naturally, especially if you can talk about them. If he becomes more withdrawn or touchy, it could be he has some deeper feelings—triggered by his own early experience of family, or a reaction to his attachment style. Either way, it's important to address it now. There is a correlation between dad's stress levels during pregnancy and risk for Paternal Postpartum Depression (PPPD) afterwards.

**STEPS:**

**Help your partner to open up**. To open the lines of communication, you first need to have their trust. It's only when they feel generally accepted and appreciated by you that they will feel safe to reveal more. Gently notice your partner's behavior, engage in talking about what's going on inside and offer your support.

**Help them become aware of their self-talk.** Self-talk is like dreaming—we all do it, even if we're not aware of it. Negative self-talk ("I'm an idiot," "I can't handle this," "I'm such a failure") can contribute to feelings of anxiety or depression. Being aware when you're talking yourself up or down can stop the negative thoughts that fuel negative feelings. Mindfulness is good for this and there are some great apps, so check them out. Challenge your negative thoughts and replace them with more positive and productive ones like "I can handle this" or "It's OK to ask for help."

**Share your own concerns.** You're both human and you're both in this together. Pretending you don't have any concerns of your own may make him feel worse and more alone. Share your worries and ask if your partner has the same, or different ones. If they react defensively—it might be because of the way you've asked, so be prepared to try again.

## Preparing for Birth

*My best friend had a difficult labor and delivery. As it gets closer, my partner and I are both a bit anxious.*

*I'd really like a home birth. My husband says "no way."*

The best way to prepare for whatever the experience will be that brings your baby into this world is to educate yourself about different birth options and birth interventions. You'll know as much as possible what to expect. Then you can have more say about the process and your bases are covered in case of any complications.

**CHECK YOUR COMPASS:**

**Birth is a joint venture.** You got here together, so research together, ask questions together and draw strength from the knowledge that no matter how this experience unfolds, you're in it together.

**Preparation is important for *both* of you.** Some birth professionals, like midwives, OB/GYN's or doulas will be more comfortable working with both of you than others. Choose your birth team carefully.

**STEPS:**

**Find a professional who will include both of you.** Get the best preparation for your experiences of the birth. Find someone who will acknowledge the normal and common emotions and needs for both of you (including fears and anxieties) and prepare the birth partner for the different roles they can take during labor.

**Employing a birth doula might be a wise investment.** You and your partner are less likely to be freaked out by the birth if you feel prepared and supported by a professional who cares about you both as well as your baby. A good doula will facilitate the bond between you all during the labor, even better, because this reduces your risk of experiencing the birth as traumatic too.

Let's take a quick pause here while we're walking. Our son's birth could have been traumatic because he was born with the umbilical cord wrapped around his neck. He had to be rushed off to the special care nursery. This wasn't great, but I never felt that he was in danger and became traumatized because of the expertise of our midwife. OK, more steps for you….

**Talk to friends and family who have gone before**. Ask questions and encourage honest answers. This will give you a range of birth experiences—and remember, yours will still be different.

**Research birth and parenthood preparation classes.** Hospital classes often cover only birth basics, so investigate other options in your area that have a wider focus and cater to both partner's needs. Research shows that feeling prepared for what comes beyond the birth actually leads to better birth outcomes. You may even find there's a Becoming Us trained professional near you. If there isn't, you might like to recommend your favorite birth professional do the training, so they know how to support both of you and set your family up for your very best beginning.

**Prepare physically**. Relaxation and deep breathing exercises (partner can coach) help the cervix soften and open. Acupressure helps cope with pain (partner can learn to do this, too). Although it's counter-intuitive, relaxing into and "going with" the waves of contractions like you're surfing them and then fully relaxing during the periods of respite in between can make for a calmer and gentler birth. It may sound weird, but a natural birth is a bit like sitting back, letting your brain have a break, trusting your body and letting it take over.

**Know when to let go**. Becoming a parent is embracing a life you cannot control. You develop a new relationship with uncertainty and grow to accept its presence in your life. As for birth, if an intervention or situation develops that is not part of your birth plan, it can feel frightening. This is not a failure on your part. You will have professionals to guide you and your partner to hold your hand. We all find our own way. And if you end up feeling lost or abandoned for any reason, there are other professionals to support and guide you for the next part of your journey.

**Research the signs and treatments for birth trauma** so you're not afraid of the unknown. Talk to your physician, obstetrician, midwife, nurse or doula and ask them to refer you for debriefing if you're distressed after the birth. Some will try to minimize this, but don't let them fob you off; birth trauma is real and needs treatment. I'll circle back to this with you in Part III."

## Sex

*Is it OK for my wife and me to have sex throughout pregnancy?*

Physically, sex is fine right through, unless your pregnancy care provider has told you otherwise. Many couples find the second trimester is a particularly sexy time. As the end of pregnancy gets closer you may have to be creative about positions (try side-by-side, hugging her from behind or her on top). Be prepared that sex in the final week or so can help to bring labor on. Oh, and you don't have to worry about the baby when having sex—the uterus changes position during pregnancy to keep the baby private and safe.

While it can be awkward physically at some stages of her pregnancy, it can also feel uncomfortable emotionally. With the normal mood swings of pregnancy, her libido will also be up and down, so be sensitive, patient, and take your cues from her.

*My husband is as keen as ever, but I just can't right now.*

While you understandably feel awkward about having sex during pregnancy, it's something that requires sensitive negotiation. When a woman says no to sex, some men can take it very personally.

**CHECK YOUR COMPASS:**

**New understanding.** Some people believe sex is more important to men than to women. And while this may sound obvious, the reasons why may not be. Some men feel the most bonded with their partner, the most well-loved through sex, in which case, the loss of sexual intimacy could be devastating. It's good to talk about this.

**STEPS:**

**Make it clear it's not a rejection of your partner**—that you still find them desirable, and work with them on creating other ways of connecting intimately. We'll get there in Stage Eight.

*Now I'm pregnant, I've never felt so horny. It's driving me crazy but my husband keeps making excuses not to have sex and it's starting to hurt my feelings. Who's normal here?*

Short answer: you both are. Changes to both partner's libido during pregnancy are common, so don't be alarmed. Pregnancy can be the beginning of a mismatch in sex drives, something you're likely to need to work through at some stage in your relationship—whether it's due to a period of stress, ill health or aging.

**CHECK YOUR COMPASS:**

**Is it about you?** Probably not. Partners can be stressed about upcoming life changes, even if they aren't talking about it, and stress tends to kill libido. Other things can affect desire, too. If you had to work hard at getting pregnant, they might want a break to let feelings for fun-sex return. Maybe they're preoccupied with the upcoming role or more aware of your vulnerability. None of this means their feelings for you have changed.

**Comfort levels.** Talking openly might be enough to relieve any fears, or you might be able to find ways or positions that make you both feel more comfortable.

**STEPS:**

**Talk about it.** Men can feel awkward, both physically and emotionally, having sex during late pregnancy. Some can feel embarrassed—like the baby is watching, or even that the baby can get hurt during sex. Talk about your sexual desires and needs now, because it will make the postnatal period much easier to navigate through. Oh, and he doesn't have to worry about the baby when having sex with you—the uterus changes position during pregnancy to keep the baby private and safe.

**Take responsibility for your sexuality.** None of us like to feel pressured to meet our partner's sexual needs. If you haven't already, become comfortable with pleasuring yourself. This reduces disappointment or resentment towards your partner and takes stress off you both. Embracing sexuality post-baby can be a challenge for some moms, so being appreciative of your body now is great.

*With her full breasts and rounded belly, my partner has never looked so sexy, but she says she's just not interested.*

Lots of partners find the ripeness of pregnancy a turn-on. You may like what you see on the outside, but chances are she's more preoccupied with what's going on inside.

**CHECK YOUR COMPASS:**

**Is it about you?** Probably not. There are good reasons she feels the way she does, and none of them have much to do with you. Fatigue, feeling unwell or self-conscious about her changing body will all affect her libido. She may also have concerns about the upcoming changes to her life and even some confusing feelings about sexuality and motherhood. All these might mean your sexual needs just aren't on her radar right now.

**Some perspective.** Most couples find their sex life changes temporarily leading up to and after birth—but if this isn't handled sensitively, this issue can become more permanent than passing. Making sure the lines of communication remain open will mean a higher chance of resuming mutually satisfying sex sooner.

**STEPS:**

**Find other ways to connect.** Where one partner may feel connected through sex, another may feel equally, or even more, connected through intimacy. More on this in Stage Eight.

**Ramp up the romance**. Romance lubricates a relationship; it keeps the engine running. If yours wasn't particularly romantic before, it's the perfect time to introduce this helpful ingredient. The loving bond you create through romance will make up over time for the lack of sex. Romance doesn't have to be costly or fancy. Read her a touching paragraph from a book. Pick a flower when you go for a walk. Give her a regular foot massage (she will appreciate this particularly in late pregnancy).

**Help her talk through her feelings**, accept and validate them, and share your feelings with her. The emotional closeness that comes from these intimate conversations paves the way for physical intimacy when you're both ready for it again.

## Grandparents-to-Be

*My husband comes from a different cultural background to me. His mother is trying to be very helpful but her advice is a bit out there. It's causing tension for all of us.*

Trouble with in-laws rates a hefty 29 on the Life Events stress scale, so it's a real and pressing issue for some couples. It's also a tricky one and needs to be handled delicately. There's potential for this to get worse after your baby is born, when you may find you actually need your in-laws more but have less time and energy to sort things out with them. The last thing you want is for your mate to be the meat in the sandwich—feeling torn between you and their mother.

### CHECK YOUR COMPASS:

**Your relationship has a foundation.** Parenthood is a time when the dynamic, the underlying structure and functioning of your primary relationship, is changing. And it can be knocked off balance by other strong family relationship dynamics (such as between you or your partner's relationship with parents). This issue really needs to be worked through. If you try to avoid it, it's likely to become a wedge *way, waaay* into the future.

**You have boundaries.** When you and your partner become parents, it's the beginning of a new family unit, one that may well operate very differently from the previous generation. How do you want to be as a family? How do you want to be different? What values do you want to pass on? You'll need to jointly decide what's right for the family you're building together.

**Whose problem is it?** Is it your problem, but you're expecting your partner to deal with it? Is it theirs, but they're expecting you to? Or is it both of yours? Working out who owns the problem means you can work out who takes primary responsibility for it. Responsibility (think about these words: response-*ability)* means taking control. Issues can become more complicated when you assign the control of them to others, when the problem really is yours. Can you see how this keeps you stuck?

**What you'll need.** Respectful assertiveness is a skill you'll both need as you go into parenthood. It's the best way to deal with issues after baby—you won't have the time or energy for anything else.

**Silence implies consent**. If you don't speak up about this (or any other issue), both your mother-in-law and your partner are likely to assume you're OK with it. The longer it goes on and you remain silent, the harder it will be to backtrack.

**STEPS:**

Educate yourselves. Advice on the best ways to care for a baby and raise a child has changed considerably over the past few generations. This is a great time for you both to do some homework before baby comes (and you have less time)—to have discussions so you're both on the same parenting path.

**Talk about options.** Regardless who is going to speak with the in-laws, agree on how it's going to be done. Best-case scenario, you provide a united front (even if not in person, one of you could say something like "we have spoken about this" or "we have decided."

**Separate the problem from the person.** Your mother-in-law is giving you advice because she cares about you and her future grandchild—her intentions are good. It's the advice that may be outdated or inappropriate. So the problem is not her, it's the actual information. This focus of your conversation will likely bring better results.

**Communicate sensitively.** If you speak in a negative way, you increase the chances of your partner feeling the need to defend or side with their mother.

Use the feedback sandwich—positive, negative, positive. For example: "We really like that you want to be involved, but we're not so sure about ____. What we'd really appreciate is ____ instead." This way you protect the relationship but can stand firm on the issue.

*I've always had a tricky relationship with my parents. I'm worried how becoming a parent myself will affect me and my relationship with them.*

It's good that you're aware of these concerns, because becoming a parent is a time of revisiting the past, often unconsciously for most people. So if you moved several times during your childhood, you may have a stronger need to stay in one place for your child. If your father abandoned your family when you were six, you might find yourself being extra anxious when your child is about the same age. Whatever prevented you from having a close relationship with a parent before now can return and cause concern. These fears are normal in the context of new parenthood, and to be expected.

**CHECK YOUR COMPASS:**

**You're not alone.** Most parents want to do better than their own parents did. This is largely because we now have more awareness about what babies and children need. There're a multitude of books, courses and other resources available that weren't there for your parents. The times your parents may have failed you wasn't usually out of maliciousness, but more from a lack of awareness, or due to their own circumstances at the time.

**See your parents differently.** Becoming a family is a time of seeing your parents as vulnerable human beings with the same stresses and concerns (or even more of them) than you. For some it can bring a parent down a notch or two from the pedestal you may have put them on. For others, your own experiences of parenthood can shed new light on the perceived failings of your parents. Either way, new insight and compassion can bring relief, healing and connection.

**You can experience your parents differently.** You might be pleasantly surprised that instead of being a source of tension, your new experiences create a bond of shared understanding and renewed appreciation. One study found the mother-daughter relationship was tolerant of more upsets than any other family tie.

**STEPS:**

**Use this time before the baby comes to address this**. Seek the support of a counselor or therapist if you need help. Talking through painful issues through with an empathetic listener gives you the opportunity to re-experience old events in a new, safe way, gaining insight, perspective and healing. This can releases you from old attitudes and patterns from the past that can color what's happening in your present—and potentially influence your child's future. Making peace with your parents—in whatever ways possible—is an important step in parenthood.

**Go inwards**. Spend some time reflecting on the circumstances of your birth and your childhood and try to get in touch with the child inside you.

What did you need and want at that time? You are becoming a parent yourself. See if you can find ways to give yourself what you didn't get as a child from your parents.

**Go backwards.** Consciously reflecting on your past and making choices to change attitudes and family patterns means you can use the wisdom of your experience to shape our child's future, rather than just passing your past on to them. Use your experience of your parent's relationship styles as inspiration to find your own, and make your own way.

**Don't try too hard.** Some parents can try to make up for the past so much that they overdo it. Don't try to be perfect—a relaxed, happy and healed parent is the best thing for your baby.

## Dadding Concerns

*My dad wasn't around much when I was a kid. And when he was, he didn't have much time for us. With no role model, I worry I'm not going to be a good dad.*

Down the track, we'll talk more about how becoming a father can affect dads, but for now, let's start with this. When you start a family, you're caught between two generations—how you were raised and how you want to raise your children. This is a particularly common concern for "fatherless" fathers.

Even if they were around physically, some dads in previous generations could be distant emotionally. It's only recently, with more flexible work patterns and a better understanding of emotional intelligence, that attitudes are changing, and fathers can be more available for their children, both in person and in spirit.

The fact that you *are* concerned means you have the right attitude to be a *great* dad. Some of the best dads are the ones who either learned by example what *not* to do or those who didn't have a role model to follow and so had to consciously and intentionally make it up as they went along. Dads who missed out in some way can be more motivated to be there for their own children.

**CHECK YOUR COMPASS:**

**You are needed.** Two parents interacting with their baby increases development of her brain. You mold your child's personal and social development from birth. There are ways that only you are likely to expand your child's experience of the world.

**You expand your baby's capacity for connection.** Here's some food for thought: fathers or partners are usually the first person to pass on to their children the ability to love more than one person at a time—the basis for the rest of their relationships through life.

**STEPS:**

**Ask yourself.** What did you want from your dad? What did you need? To feel important enough to have his time and attention? His guidance? To teach you how to do stuff? What might this have looked like on a day-to-day basis? How can you give this to your own kids? Or will they want something different from you? Being the dad you and your kids want you to be helps heal losses from your own childhood. For more on loss, see Part III.

**Turn it around.** Think of your role models and follow their lead. Even if it's someone you admire in movies or on TV, whatever works.

**Find resources.** There are some great books, DVDs, websites and online communities to prepare you for active and involved fathering, so do some research if you need more reassurance.

## Finances

*My wife earns more than me. I'm worried how we're going to cope after the baby comes. Should I take on an extra job?*

Shouldering the family's financial burden is a common and pressing concern for dads or partners. What you might find, though, is that finances are only part of a bigger conversation you'll both benefit from having about how you want family life to be.

**CHECK YOUR COMPASS:**

**A different perspective.** What will it cost if you don't work two jobs compared to what might it cost if you do? Being absent from a child's life can affect children of all ages—bonding in infancy; language skills as toddlers; poorer social competence—and more behavioral problems at school. Fathers are important in a child's life.

Can you both work part-time and share your child's care? What are momma's plans/desires for returning to work? Have you jointly considered the pros and cons of you being a stay-at-home dad?

**Re-evaluation of priorities and commitments.** Your wife needs you to be a partner in every sense of the word. Your children need you to be there for them. While financial pressure can erode the security of a family, your continued absence could do even more damage.

Similarly, she may want to assess her desire to work and retain employability. Sometimes this is only possible after the baby is born. Explore ways to approach work and baby care so it will be less of a sacrifice for your family.

**STEPS:**

**Make a family plan.** Most people are pretty clear about their career plans, or at least the importance of having one. Intentional conversations about family plans are important too. How many children do you want? How far apart? How will this affect work? Holidays: where, how often, how expensive? Schooling: public or private? Home: stay, move or renovate? Cars: do you need two, downsize or upgrade? Can any investments wait a few more years? What childcare is available? Little ones need predictable, responsive, loving care to support secure bonding.

**Find ways to save money or reduce spending**. What do you really need? What can you do without? Forget expensive baby stuff—it's a waste of money. Budget, cut back on expenses, re-finance the mortgage. Use some of your time at home to do jobs around the house you would normally have to pay for.

**Get advice**. Explore options and discuss which ones might be best. Making decisions now that benefit your family in the long-term will take a lot of pressure off your relationship.

## Taking Time Off Work

*Our baby is due soon. I'm not sure how much leave I should take from work.*

Your willingness and ability to support your new family is crucial, so check what your leave entitlements are and discuss your range of options with your partner and employer.

The amount of outside help available will impact whether you take all your leave at once or over several months. It may be more useful when the excitement of the new arrival has worn off and help is slowing down. Flexibility is key and may come in different forms, such as starting or leaving early or taking one day off a week for a while.

**CHECK YOUR COMPASS:**

**Your parenting matters, right from the beginning.** In their first few weeks your baby knows and responds to your voice and your touch. This is the beginning of the bond between you. The more time you spend with your baby, the more opportunities for bonding, and the stronger the bond.

**Your partner needs you too.** New parenthood is a vulnerable time for her and for your relationship. She needs a partner in every sense of the word.

**What's most important?** There're times when you're forced to let go of whatever it is you're caught up in to focus on what's most important in life—a health crisis, when you lose someone close to you, a major life change. *Now* is one of those times.

**Anticipate the ways you can be involved.** Partners can do everything except breastfeed, so there's a whole repertoire of tasks up for the taking: bathing, changing, soothing and settling. And if you're planning on being up for the nightshift, you won't be able to work much during the day anyway.

**STEPS:**

**Plan ahead.** What areas of life can you simplify so you can focus on your new family? Now is not the time for new career strategies (unless it means spending more time at home) or planning major home renovations. Sometimes, however, it's unavoidable. This is where support networks, backup plans and being realistic about what you can cope with are important.

**Be aware.** Most new parents aren't prepared for the impact of sleep deprivation. For at least the first couple of months, momma will be up most of the night feeding and settling and will need someone around to look after the baby so she can sleep or rest during the day. Even when the baby starts feeding quicker and less frequently, nighttime feeds are tiring. You might =consider co-sleeping to help with this.

**Talk about expectations.** Get clear what they look like in real terms. Now is *not t*he time for misunderstandings—they are a major contributing factor to unnecessary arguments.

**Be involved.** You might find that all the uncertainties and stresses of new parenthood can make you want to avoid going home and instead put in overtime at work. But the benefits of being at home are immeasurable—especially in the long term. Research tells us that children grow up having a better relationship with their dads and a lower risk of getting caught up with drugs, alcohol, crime and unhealthy personal relationships. That's massive.

Ok, so here you are at the end of the first stage of your journey into parenthood. I hope you have more than enough to prepare for your launch into the next, most exciting, one.

If I were to give you one piece of advice as you're about to step over the threshold into parenthood, it's this: life does change, people do change, and relationships do change when you have a baby. Don't fight the changes, or you may end up fighting each other. Embrace the changes and embrace your partner. Lash those life rafts together and get ready for the ride of your lives.

I'll see you on the other side soon.

# Stage Two: Building a Nest

## (Your Family's First Few Weeks)

You're here. You've landed—congratulations! I hope it was a relatively soft one for you, but it's possible you may have hit some turbulence along the way. Or maybe you even had an emergency landing?

Or is it that you're not there yet and taking this whole being-prepared thing seriously and reading ahead while you're still pregnant, which is awesome.

So now, here you are, about to embark on stage two of your parenthood journey. Important changes are happening to each of you in your family's first month or two. Your baby is adjusting to life outside the perfect environment that they've been growing in, getting used to lights, sounds and other sensations.

And at the same time, you and your partner are adjusting to your new roles as parents and partners in parenting. Caring for a baby is not just about tasks. There will be new decisions to be made, advice to weigh and unexpected challenges to face. How you start to manage these early issues will affect the tone in your home—the nest, you're bringing your baby into.

So, take the pressure off as much as you can and hunker down. Shut everything else out; buy as much time as you can to focus on what's happening at home. You know how you get jetlag when you're travelling to a new time zone? Well, you're likely to feel a lot like that in the next few months, as you're travelling to a new life zone. Time has a whole new meaning when you're becoming your new "us."

## Breastfeeding

*I've started breastfeeding and I'd like to continue, but a couple of friends had a hard time with it, so I'm not sure if it will be right for me. My husband says he supports me either way.*

You may have been led to believe that it's easy, convenient and will come naturally. The bad news is most women struggle with breastfeeding at first. It needs to be learned by both you and your baby and initially can be time consuming, painful and difficult, both physically and emotionally. Some women experience tender breasts and inverted or cracked nipples and mastitis. You may worry about your baby not getting enough milk, but this is rarely the case.

The great news is breastfeeding does get easier, quicker, less frequent and not painful and the long-term advantages can far outweigh early struggles. It's cheap, convenient and nutritionally perfect for your baby. For many women it's also a very pleasurable, bonding and empowering experience. Whichever way feeding your baby is right for you, you'll both benefit from the support of your partner.

### CHECK YOUR COMPASS:

**Learning something new is frustrating**, especially if you expect it to come easily or you pressure yourself to do it better. Then you may feel like a failure. Help and support at this time is vital. Don't be afraid to ask for it; let go of expectations and go gently on yourself.

**Your partner's attitude.** If your partner is supportive, you are more likely to attempt and persevere with breastfeeding. Let your partner know this is important to you and how they can help.

**Breastfeeding saps energy**, so you'll need to rest regularly, especially in the first few weeks when your supply is becoming established, and in the afternoons, when your energy is likely to dip.

### STEPS:

**Research.** Talk to other new mothers, but remember your experiences may differ; read, and talk to midwives and lactation consultants. Check out breastfeeding websites (such as Breastfeeding USA and La Leche League). The more information you have, the more you'll have contingency plans for different feeding situations.

**Talk together.** About your hopes, preferred options and backup plans. For example, you might decide to try to express milk a couple of times a week so your partner can bottle-feed, and you have a much-needed break. Or you can have a night out together using a babysitter.

Be prepared for things to change. Sometimes things don't go as planned and you need help to increase your supply or deal with mastitis or changing to formula. These can be difficult times and hard decisions. Having your partner's support makes it easier and ensures you don't feel alone on this part of the journey.

## Exhaustion

*I was entirely unprepared for how much time and effort it takes to just keep a baby alive, let alone be a great mom.*

It used to take a village, it still takes a village and it will *always* take some sort of village to care for a baby. John Travis, MD, one of the founding fathers of the wellness movement both for adults and infants, estimates it takes 3.87 pairs of arms per infant to meet everyone's needs—now you know why.

It's a shock for most of us to find that simply feeding and changing can take up most of a normal new-baby day—and night. Breastfeeding is tiring and broken sleep is exhausting for everyone in the family. While you can't avoid this, there are things you can do to stop drowning in exhaustion and getting swallowed up in the washing pile.

**CHECK YOUR COMPASS:**

**What's your aim?** Early parenthood isn't about "getting back to normal," it's about working together to create the "new normal" that's right for your family. Instead of aiming for less important chores to be done, aim for healthy, happy and rested instead.

**You have a rhythm**. Early parenthood is as a much about managing energy as it is about managing time. Your energy naturally peaks and dips throughout the day, which can be frustrating if you're dipping at the same time your baby is peaking.

**Your baby has a rhythm**. As for managing time, your baby is used to going around three times slower than you. When you go at their pace they can bond more easily. Slow down.

**What are you trying to prove**? Putting too much pressure on yourself to do everything perfectly, or even better-than-just-OK is needless self-sacrifice that doesn't help anybody. As far as your baby is concerned, you don't need to prove anything to anybody to be a good mom.

**STEPS:**

**Lower your expectations.** Resist the urge to "achieve." Just doing what's needed is achievement enough at this stage—and it is a stage, it will pass.

**Reassess your goals.** Especially if you're the sort of person who normally writes thank you notes, irons dish towels and mops the floor every day, you may have to accept that life as you knew it, will just be a little different from now on. The time and effort you'd normally put into the home, or elsewhere, will be better used on looking after yourself and your baby.

**Work with your rhythm.** If you're at your best in the morning, do something that takes the pressure off you later in the day. Chop up fruit or a salad so you have a snack ready for afternoon or dinnertime. Chuck some meat and veggies into a big slow cooker and freeze extra meals. Go for a walk early so you can rest or nap later.

**Prioritize yourself.** You come first (you can't look after baby if you're hospitalized for exhaustion). Make your nutrition, rest and exercise a daily priority. Enlist your partner, family and friends to do the same.

**Exercise.** It may feel counterintuitive, but regular exercise increases energy levels, promotes sounder sleep, reduces stress fatigue and boosts self-esteem. It can even allay depression and anxiety. All good stuff and all needed now.

If you were exercising regularly beforehand, check with your birth professional when it's safe to pick it up again. Try gentler variations while you work your way back up. If you're exercise-averse, start with walking. Keep it up for a couple of weeks and, trust me, you'll see for yourself the difference it can make.

**Reduce stimulants.** Fatigue increases cravings for things that give you a boost, but stimulants like caffeine and sugar create a spike that's soon followed by a plunge. Recent research has even linked sugar with inflammation that can contribute to depression. Research low glycemic index (G.I.) foods that even out blood sugar and provide sustained energy for longer.

## Isolation

*We've moved away from family and friends and I worry about how I'm going to cope without their support.*

*My husband just started a new job and is working long hours. I hate being at home on my own all day—I need more help.*

*I live close to my family, but I'm not close to them—if you know what I mean.*

Isolation is a very real challenge for many new moms and is a big contributing factor to postpartum depression. It may not be just physical isolation either. The emotional disconnection of not feeling understood by your partner, not sharing a common experience with close friends or having the support of a sympathetic community can leave you feeling alone too.

Stay-at-home dads and same-sex parents have their own challenges in this area. There are fewer social resources like playgroups or father-friendly baby facilities. Old-fashioned attitudes to contend with can increase isolation.

**CHECK YOUR COMPASS:**

**Find replacements.** Whenever you're separated (either geographically or emotionally) from a support system, it's important to find replacements. A sense of belonging is good for your emotional wellbeing. Knowing there are people other than your family who can provide support and meet your needs just as well (or even better) is liberating and empowering. Support organizations (search online) are also a great resource.

**Focus on the relationship you do have—the one with your partner.** This is an opportunity for your partner to step up and step into your world and provide some of the support you may have relied on others for. Let them know you're grateful for it.

**STEPS:**

**Let your partner know you need them.** Discuss what help you need and how your partner can best support you. If they aren't getting involved, it's not likely that they don't care; it's more likely that they don't know how.

**Find ways to stay connected.** The benefit of having far-flung family that you get on with is spending holidays with them. Keep up regular connection in the meantime through phone calls and online. They may want to be included just as much as you want them to be.

**Find your tribe**. Being part of a group provides emotional and practical support, widens what can feel like a very small world and provides ongoing opportunities for finding new friendships. Online support groups can also be a great resource for both moms and dads. Now that you're in this stage, you'll be discovering why only other new parents can understand.

Many communities have mothers' or parents' groups. Are there any playgroups, local libraries with story time or special services for new families in your area? All can be valuable sources of support. Shop around until you find people you really like. They may be friends for life—for both you and your child.

**Become part of your community.** Make friends with people you come into regular contact with—shopkeepers, other parents at your local park, neighbors or the lady who walks her dog in the evening. These are the people your child will come into regular contact with too.

**Invest in more support**. A postpartum doula can help you get settled in. The reliable teenager down the road can babysit. You can hire help to clean the house, deliver meals or tidy the yard.

If you can afford it, instead of thinking that these expenses are a waste of money, see them as an investment in the wellbeing of your family. Outsourcing things that can be done by others reduces stress and frees you up to nurture yourself and each other—the best antidote for exhaustion.

> *My mom is around, but we've never gotten on particularly well. I find her to be very negative. Even though she's here every other day, I still feel lonely.*

For some, becoming a parent can bring them closer to their own parents. Seeing grandparents excited with the news of a baby, making plans to be involved and delighting in their new grandchild can mend old hurts.

For others, it can mean opening old wounds. If this is the case, you might find yourself struggling with reactions or emotions you haven't experienced before (or for a long time) and at a time when you have the least energy to deal with them.

**CHECK YOUR COMPASS:**

**Is now the time?** Recovering from birth may not be the best time for deep and meaningful conversations with parents, especially if they could potentially go awry. If you've not had a good relationship for years, there's no reason sensitive conversations can't wait for a few months more until you feel more like yourself again. Don't let them slide, though, they will be important, so keep them for later.

**Gaps can be filled.** Sometimes the easiest way to manage your sadness about not being close to someone is to get closer to someone else. This can heal some of the hurt while you're waiting to talk to your mom. Do you have a favorite aunt, older friend or mom of a girlfriend that you get on with? Reach out to them.

**STEPS:**

**Look into her.** Often people react to you in ways that may be painful because of something that's happening inside them, but they're unaware of how they are coming across. When the time is right, gently question your mother about her life's experiences. You may gain enough information that makes more sense about her. When you can understand other people, it's easier to forgive and feel more connected to them.

**Go gently**. You'll have to use all your Thriving skills.

**Ask for what you need**, so she gets what she needs. Underneath negativity there is often a need that isn't being expressed in a way that you can respond to positively. Help her turn criticisms and complaints into requests so you can hear her message more clearly—and respond more supportively. You can do the same with your own needs.

## First Conflicts

*For some reason, there seems to be a lot of misunderstandings between us now.*

Gah! Parenthood can bring down even master communicators. You're both likely to be stressed and time-poor and won't have the energy to talk and work things out as you used to. When there are new experiences and changes happening in your world, and you're not able to communicate them regularly, this period is a prime time for miscommunication, misunderstanding and assumption making. So, KISS: Keep it Simple Sweetheart.

In fact, most problems in relationships occur, not because there's anything wrong with either partner, but with how they relate to each other. For these reasons it's vital that, if you aren't already good at communicating, you learn to do it well—for your baby's sake as well as your own.

**CHECK YOUR COMPASS:**

**Misunderstandings are opportunities.** Clearing them up as you go is the best way to keep conflict from escalating.

**Learning deepens intimacy.** Misunderstandings often occur when you aren't aware of what's going on in your partner's deeper layers. At the same time, it's your partner's responsibility to reveal themselves if they want you to know them well. Misunderstandings are the perfect opportunity to communicate more intimately.

#### STEPS:

**Reassure her.** New mothers need to feel understood, so make the extra effort to listen well and get a feel for what she's going through. Research shows that feeling misunderstood can be particularly distressing for new mothers and contributes to PPD.

**Don't panic.** Hiccups in a relationship are a normal and natural part of *becoming us.* Remain calm, breathe and have the grace to work things through. This will leave you both in a stronger place than beforehand.

**Deal with problems without getting heated.** It's not differences and disagreements that negatively affect babies—it's when these aren't managed.

**Think ahead.** When new issues come up (and trust me, they will) aim to manage the issues rather than "resolve" them. In his research, Gottman found that 69 percent of couple's issues can't be resolved—they're just differences. Managing this kind of conflict without animosity, however, makes it less of a problem. More on this in Stage Seven.

**Be curious.** You may think you know your partner inside and out, but parenthood changes aspects of a person, and if you're not up with the changes, you may be missing something. Couples who have been together happily for decades experience their relationship as a journey of discovery. As lives reshape around events, they rediscover each other.

> *I'm exhausted by the time my husband gets home from work and desperate for a break. He gets home tired and cranky and doesn't seem to want to help.*

It's important you find ways to work through this. How to divide up the overwhelming workload that comes with a baby (it really is too much for two people) is the biggest issue that causes conflict between couples in their baby's first two years.

#### CHECK YOUR COMPASS:

**How do you think?** One of the big things having a family does is to challenge you to start thinking in an "and/both" way instead of "either/or." So instead of competing over who had the worst day, consider that you both had a bad day, so you both need some down time. Even just being empathetic with each other can be enough.

**Work/home transitions can be stressful.** It's easy to carry time pressures, traffic worries and to-do lists in your head. And have you ever noticed that you're more sensitive at times of saying goodbye or hello (especially after a particularly hard day)? Pleasantries when reuniting that are rushed or overlooked can leave us feeling flat.

**The first five minutes.** After a day apart, pleasant greetings set the tone for the rest of your evening. A poor reception can take longer then an evening to recover from!

**Commitment protects your relationship** from the stresses that threaten it—work, parenting, whatever. You're beginning to build a partnership wide and deep enough to cope with the various challenges your family will need to deal with over the coming weeks, months and years.

**STEPS:**

**Separate work from home**. Home is the sanctuary where you retreat to from work and the world, but this is of no use if someone continues to carry work around in their head. If your partner can't do it on the way home, they may benefit from 15 minutes transition time to shift roles, so they're not preoccupied for the rest of the evening.

Those who work from home need to find their own ways to do this. Allowing your partner time to do this can mean they are more present and engaged and can provide the sanctuary you need after a day with the baby.

**Greet each other warmly.** Especially in these early months after very different days of separation, it's important to reconnect. Let your partner know how glad you are to see them and share a cuddle. Take 15 minutes (after transition time) to just relax and enjoy each other's company before you get to chores and more.

**Debrief your days.** When you're both ready to talk, talk about what may have stressed you during the day. This is not a time to talk about relationship stress. This is a time to unite against the stresses outside your home.

**Make a list.** The working-out-in-the-world parent probably isn't aware of the time and effort it takes to look after a baby, so a list of things that need to be done may be eye opening. Make a list of everything you think you need to do and cross off anything that's not super important or can be left for another day. Prioritize what's left. Each chooses the chores they prefer. Divvy up the leftovers fairly. You'll only have to do this a few times until it becomes a new routine.

## Postpartum Depression

*At our prenatal classes, we were told about postpartum depression. Now that we've had the baby what should my wife and I be prepared for?*

Your first point of contact after the birth, your family doctor, obstetrician, midwife or pediatrician, may also be responsible for evaluating how your partner is coping and may need use the Edinburgh Postnatal Depression Scale (EPDS) or other test to screen for depression. Testing for fathers is coming too.

But since you're the closest person to her, you're the person most likely to notice any changes in her mood or behavior and get help.

### CHECK YOUR COMPASS:

**Be a partner in every sense of the word**. Your partner doesn't want to feel like she's in this on her own. Sharing day-to-day tasks, responsibility for making decisions, as well as your own struggles—and being open to hearing hers—keeps you bonded and provides her with a strong sense of support. Mothers are much less likely to become depressed if they feel part of a team.

**There's a link between isolation and depression**. Not only does she need you there physically, but emotionally and mentally too. Being around but being distracted or emotionally unavailable could make her feel even more isolated—and depressed.

**Your attitude matters.** Your appreciation and encouragement directly affect her level of satisfaction, feelings of achievement, level of confidence and enjoyment of her new role. More than that, in the absence of other things that might have contributed to her feeling good about herself, *you* might be her only support for self-esteem for a while.

**Culture check.** In some cultures, becoming a mother elevates a woman's status in society. Unfortunately, this is not true of ours. Your esteem of her will build her self-esteem.

### STEPS:

**Rescue her when she needs it (sometimes from herself).** Now's your time to step up and be there for her like never before. Help her work out ways to get things done. Let her know it's OK to let go of stuff; you can live with a messy living room and takeout for dinner. Get the baby ready and whisk them out for a coffee (or breastfeeding-friendly chai latte). Some days will be harder than others. Some days she will need you more.

**Pay her attention.** With everyone's attention on your adorable baby, give her your attention so she isn't being neglected or feeling invisible. Many moms do feel this way.

**Tell her:** That she's beautiful. That she's doing a great job. That you're there for her. How much you love her. Thoughtful actions—a note, a text message, a flower on her pillow, some cut-up fruit in the fridge—little things can make a big difference.

## Resuming Sex

*Our doctor has given the go-ahead, but I'm not so sure.*

For some couples, the first attempts at sex after baby are spontaneous, for others, it's after months of a delicate dance of "does she or doesn't she?"

**CHECK YOUR COMPASS:**

**You may both be anxious**. Sex after baby is usually unadvisable for six to eight weeks, or longer, depending on the impact of the birth. New moms can be understandably nervous. The rigors of childbirth, any resulting tissue injuries and a decrease in vaginal lubrication are all considerations. Fathers and partners, too, can be anxious about this.

**It may take time.** Getting back to a "normal" sex life can take *a lot* longer than most couples expect. Months and months…and months…even. Knowing this can take some pressure off.

**Review your sex life**. Share what you like about your sex life together and what you, or your partner, might like to modify.

**Sex is good for you.** It's a great stress-buster and lowers blood pressure. It's also good exercise and improves your immune system. Oxytocin is released during orgasm, making you feel more bonded and giving you a lovely floaty sense of wellbeing. If you've ever had issues with your sex life before, now's a good time to get professional help—like many other new parents.

**STEPS:**

**Share your concerns.** Talking is important because unspoken feelings can lead to frustration and resentment—and resentment is the most effective contraceptive I know of. A woman likes to feel that she's still attractive to her partner—even if she is having mixed feelings about sex. Men like to know they are valued and loved, even if her desire has disappeared for a bit.

**Stay connected on other levels**. Relating easily with each other leads to intimacy, which leads to a desire for sex. (We'll cover this fully in Stage Eight).

## Not Coping

*I just don't feel normal. I can't focus or remember things and I'm also very emotional. I'm worried it means I'm not coping.*

"Baby brain" is a normal part of new motherhood and actually a good thing. It's because the neurons in your brain that you usually use for a whole bunch of other random tasks band together for the sole purpose of bonding with your infant and learning your new baby-care skills.

As your learning becomes easier, neurons go back to their own business and you'll feel more normal again. Scans show the brain of a new mother actually grows *a*fter birth—in the part that that promotes sensitivity to your baby. So tell that to anyone who might be complaining.

There're lots of reasons for being more emotional too—often mainly due to hormonal changes and fatigue. There're lots you can do to find supported and support yourself to cope. In fact, that's a whole stage, Stage Five—not too far ahead.

**CHECK YOUR COMPASS:**

**Perspective**. If the birth, or the period afterward, was stressful, your brain and body will adapt so you can get through the immediate stresses. At the same time, you may use up considerably more mental and emotional energy than you realize.

Stress fatigue accumulates, sometimes days or weeks after the stress has passed, so it's likely you're actually still recovering from the birth and maybe have the "Baby Blues," which is normal.

Stress fatigue shows up like this: thinking can become foggy, trouble with decision making or even stringing together a sentence. Moms can be more emotional, teary or irritable, but not sure why. If the birth was traumatic, these things are a normal reaction to an abnormal amount of stress, and usually pass as things settle down. We'll talk more about birth trauma if you need to in Part III.

**What does "not coping" mean**? Most parents feel like they're not coping at some stage. Parenting has massively steep learning curves; feeling out of your depth is normal. That doesn't mean you shouldn't reach out for help—it means you *should*. If you don't have support on hand for any reason, Postpartum Support International is a great organization to connect with.

You might also want to readjust your notion of what "not coping" is.

I'm going to pull you aside on the path here for a bit so we can have a private chat. I used to think if I cried, it meant I wasn't coping. I have since embraced crying (and screaming into a pillow and cursing—gosh I love doing that sometimes). Allow yourself to let go and let it out—it's much, much better for you to fall apart sometimes and get support than pretend you're coping and keeping it all in. I tried that for a while and it didn't work.

My best friend and I were fortunate to have our babies at the same time and started having regular, honest conversations about how we were going. This helped us both to cope better.

Are you ready to go on?

**A little bit of not coping can be a good thing.** Sometimes it's better than only just coping. You're more likely to ask for, accept and get offers of support when you let people know you need it. Just coping can mean wearing a mask and limping along, sometimes for years. This will take a toll on both you and your family. I want better for you all.

**Signs for needing professional support**. Physical changes like not being able to relax, sleep or weight changes are some. There are also mental and emotional signs for needing professional support (see Part III).

**STEPS:**

**Let your mate into your head.** Describe what it's like for you, how hard it is and ask for support. Your partner may be taking your reactions personally. Also, any unreasonable expectations from your partner or others, that you should be functioning normally at this time, will only stress you further.

**Know your limits.** Parenthood is a great opportunity to develop new limits. "Not coping" can look different for different people. You know yourself better than anybody else, so monitor yourself, your thoughts, feelings and reactions. When you notice something that doesn't feel like you, make a note of it. A diary or journal is one way.

**Get backup.** Let your partner and a trusted friend know what's going on and get them to check in with you regularly. Ask them to (gently) let you know if they have concerns.

**Schedule regular pampering**. Create your own 15-minute coping strategies: flick through a magazine; have a nice cup of tea (I even bought a nice tea set for this); listen to your favorite music; putter in the garden; phone a friend; binge on your favorite Netflix series; take a warm scented bath, have dark chocolate—maybe all at the same time on really bad days. What other ways can you think of that would work for you?

**Accept all offers of help**. Welcome others into your family. Find something for them to do (most will at least be happy to cuddle the baby while you shower), appreciate them and send out massive hints for casseroles and babysitting.

## Messy House

*We both hate how the house is always messy,*
*but I just don't have the energy for it.*

**CHECK YOUR COMPASS:**

**New priorities.** Your newborn family period only lasts for a short time. Relish it. Let go of things that make it more stressful than it needs to be.

**Old expectations.** *I*f either you, your partner (or anyone else) expects you to keep a perfect home now, somebody is up for disappointment. You and your baby need what time and energy you have. Your partner needs any that's left over. Your home doesn't.

**What's your body telling you?** If you don't have the energy, it's because you're using it up on more important things. Your body is telling you to rest. Listen to it.

**STEPS:**

**Decide how important it is**. If tidying the home helps keep you sane or stops you from wilting with boredom, then do it. But don't overdo it, this can lead to burnout. If it's more important to your partner than to you, then it's their problem and their responsibility. This may change their attitude.

**Have designated areas**. Choose the room where you spend the most time and focus your efforts there. The rest will recover eventually. Even Marie Kondo said her house was messy when she had young kids.

## Dad's Involvement

*We've just brought our daughter home from the hospital. I want to be involved but sometimes I feel like I'm useless and other times like I'm intruding. Yesterday I suggested we should get our baby into a routine and she nearly bit my head off.*

Fathers and partners often aren't aware of or prepared for the crucial role they play in the early stages of their new family. The following might help.

**CHECK YOUR COMPASS:**

**Birth takes a toll.** No matter how smoothly the birth went, your partner has been through a physical, psychological and emotional trial that will take her some time to fully recover from. She will be exhausted and overwhelmed. Your baby has to adjust to new noises and sensations that are very different from the environment she has known. This makes them both sensitive and it's up to you to keep them safe as they adjust.

**Hospitals do not welcome** new mothers to stay for as long as is ideal or provide the optimum environment for those crucial early days, but you can create the nest to bring your baby home to (or have your baby in if you're having a home birth).

For example, you might decide to limit visitors in the first few days or weeks to give you all time to recover from the birth, some privacy to find your feet without feeling self-conscious and to bond as a family. You can assist bonding by minimizing disruptions (outside stresses, trivialities, things that can wait until later).

In the early weeks, your partner's sensitivity is actually a survival mechanism for your baby—it supports her in intuiting your baby's needs. She needs you to manage other things initially, so she has the energy and focus this level of receptiveness requires.

As well as supporting your partner's bond with your baby, you can also create your own by sharing in all aspects of your baby's care.

**Are you rushing?** Sometimes we can be so keen to help we can come across too strongly. These early weeks are a time to relax into your new roles, rather than trying to get into a routine (this can come later). You all need time and space to experience what's going on and enjoy the newness of each other. Resist the urge to rush things.

**Are you in step?** Some high-achieving new dads can feel resentment at having to "help" their partner, as if they're taking a supporting role. Protecting and caring for your partner, as well as developing a relationship with your baby at the same time, means stepping in, not stepping back.

**STEPS:**

**Be the gatekeeper**—from overbearing people or from visitors who stay too long. Protect her from herself if she's trying to do too much, too soon. Protect her from the concerns of the outside world. Join her in focusing on the baby. All else can wait.

**Do it all**—feeding, changing, bathing, settling and sleeping. Some for your partner too. Be prepared to be flexible as your needs and circumstances change. Some partners like to get up during the night to do the change after the feed; others prefer to sleep through so they can take better care of their family during the day. You'll find the routine that works best for all of you.

*I work very long hours and I'm exhausted by the time I get home. I want to spend time with our baby, but I just can't, and my wife isn't happy. Does it matter?*

While quality is generally more important than quantity in terms of time, both are important in these sensitive first few months.

**CHECK YOUR COMPASS:**

**A wakeup call.** If you think you have no time—you're locked into and constrained by your commitments and obligations—you feel like you have no breathing space and no control over the situation, this is your wake-up call. These are sure signs of stress—which have bigger implications for you and your new family. If you're working too hard now, you're probably working too hard, period.

**A reality check.** Parenthood is the best time you'll have in life to step off the treadmill, reassess your values and re-design your life.

**People can lose themselves in their jobs.** Your wife and baby need you now. In the scheme of things, it's only for a very short time.

**STEPS:**

**Make a list of priorities.** Does the amount of focus, energy and commitment in each of those areas reflect their importance? Are your choices and behaviors consistent with your priorities? If not, what's stopping them?

**Be honest with yourself.** Do you feel anxious about spending time with your baby? Lots of dads or partners do. So do lots of new moms. This is understandable, but you might have to ask yourself if you're working longer hours to avoid it.

Some dads compensate for the jabs of inadequacy that can come with new parenthood by increasing their prowess at work. The rewards of work are tangible and measurable. The rewards of parenting—well-balanced children and great family relationships—won't show up for years but are much more rewarding.

*I thought my main job would be changing diapers but my wife gets impatient with me, saying I'm "not doing it right."*

*My wife won't leave me alone with the baby; she thinks I'm going to drop him or something.*

*I must admit, I'm feeling a bit excluded.*

Expecting and newborn mothers are usually so engrossed with experiencing pregnancy and preoccupied with caring for their baby afterwards, that there's room for little else. When only women family members or friends come to visit mom and baby it can leave new dads feeling left out.

Perinatal services focus mainly on mothers (have you noticed?) excluding or even alienating dads or partners. All this can add to feeling left out, unimportant—or even rejected or jealous.

Remember, in a new family there are three bonds that need nurturing: mom and baby; dad (or partner) and baby; and mom and partner. It's important that mom supports you in bonding with your baby and that you support her to do the same. It's also important to your relationship with your baby that you have a good relationship with your wife Gottman's research found babies will emotionally withdraw from dads who are not happy with their relationship to their partner. They pick up the vibes—we are all intertwined.

**CHECK YOUR COMPASS:**

**You both affect your baby.** In one study, researchers Belsky and Kelly found that when a mother entered the room, a father's interaction with their baby changed—for worse in unhappy relationships and for better in happy ones.

**Below the surface.** What usually drive a partner's behavior are the thoughts and feelings they're having at the time. You will interpret their behavior in a way that's meaningful to you, but unless you know what they're thinking and feeling, your judgments may not be accurate.

For example, some mothers can take their new role so seriously, and have it become such a big part of their identity, that their sense of self can actually feel threatened if they feel someone is "intruding." You might interpret this as her thinking you aren't up to the task.

Remember, your partner is also finding her feet and, when she does things well, is probably starting to feel confident and competent, just as she did in her pre-baby life. It may not be about you at all.

**Are you contributing**? If she's upset or snappy, it's likely because she's exhausted and really needs a break. Don't make the mistake of suppressing your feelings by withdrawing from your partner or your baby or spending more time at work; this brings on more problems.

**STEPS:**

**Gently tease out the issues.** Let her know you've noticed: "It seems to me when I try to change the diapers, you get impatient." Question what's going on for her and listen well so she can get it out. Chances are that she's so exhausted she's been on autopilot and not even aware that you have a point of view.

**Gently assert your right to be involved**. Being engaged with your children makes for a happier father or partner, mother, baby and family. You have the right to find your own way with your baby, and to be treated respectfully by your partner. You can do everything except breastfeed—and science may soon find a way even for that. Notice what tasks she's struggling with, those she enjoys the least, those she has to do at the same time as something else, or those you enjoy the most or have the most time for.

**Share your thoughts and feelings.** Let her know you want to be involved and together find ways that work for both of you. As she begins to trust herself and let go of the reins more, she will have more trust in your ability to take them too.

**Reconnect.** When you're both focusing on the baby so much, it can be easy to lose sight of each other. Take moments throughout the day to make eye contact, smile, just notice and "be" with each other. Connection reduces anxiety for you both, and connected parents make the best parenting team.

*I've been asking my husband to spend more time at home but, when he tries to help with the baby, he's not very good at a couple of things, I get so impatient that I might as well do it myself.*

It's important to realize your attitude towards your partner affects their parenting ability, their relationship with the baby and also their relationship with you.

### CHECK YOUR COMPASS:

**Awareness of what you're asking.** When you ask your partner to spend more time with the family, you may be asking him to step away from his work, which might be an important source of self-esteem for him at a time when he may be feeling unsure of himself. I am not saying that you shouldn't ask, just be mindful of other factors when you do.

**Your tone is important.** Belsky and Kelly's research showed when a mother and father interact, the tone of communication also affects their baby—so make sure it's positive.

### STEPS:

**Step back.** Some mothers can get a bit territorial, acting as if they "own" the baby. Don't think of looking after the baby as your sole responsibility, and of your partner as "helping" you. They are developing their own relationship with your little one.

**Share the responsibility—and the joy.** You went into this together, so stay in it together. Parenthood is a more rewarding and fulfilling journey—both in the short and long term—for your whole family when you share it with your partner.

**Affirm your partner.** There are aspects of being a parent that are likely to scare the heck out of both of you. Build confidence for each other by noticing and appreciating what you like about each other's parenting.

The view is great from this ridge. Oh, look over there. There're some water buffalo down by the river. Before we climb down from here and get among them, I want to share one of my favorite memories with you. The first time my husband changed our son's diaper, he asked me how I thought he should do it. I realized I had a choice here, I could try to be the expert or I could admit to still feeling a lack of confidence myself, so I laughed and said: "I don't know, you're his dad, you'll work it out." He told me many years later how good for him to hear this. It was a throw-away comment for me, but it set the tone for our parenting partnership—one that I still appreciate to this day.

And how are you doing? Time for a break? Maybe a cup of tea and a few minutes in the sun? I'll be here when you get back.

# Stage Three: Managing Your Expectations

## (Your Family's First Few Months)

You've taken the leap of faith. You've gotten through the otherworld of birth. You've experienced some of those incredible first joys and gritty parts of parenthood and now you're climbing down out of the nest you created so carefully—and coming back down to earth.

Over these first few months you'll be finding your feet as parents—and you may not necessarily find yourself where you thought you'd be. Just like looking at a map can only give you an idea of the territory you'll be travelling through—this stage is where you compare what you thought parenthood would look like with the reality of it. A map is flat, but some of the learning curves of parenthood come around suddenly and are very, very *steep*.

Before you got here, you probably had a picture of what life with a baby would be like—that picture is what you've been working towards until now.

But kind of like those glossy travel brochures we can drool over, during the next few months you're going to be discovering that the images of parenthood you've seen on TV, in movies and on Instagram aren't giving you the whole picture of parenthood. And yet, those images are likely to have informed your expectations—probably more than you realize.

Most parents expect that some aspects of *becoming us* will be unfamiliar or challenging and are willing to find ways to manage this. But what can be more challenging is that becoming a family can be tricky, not only *in ways that you don't expect,* but in ways that you have never, as a couple, experienced.

Expectations are powerful. They shape what you think the future will be like and determine how you will adjust when you get there. Expectations can be both helpful and unhelpful. If you expect mutual respect in your partnership, you will give and receive accordingly. But expectations that are unrealistic create unnecessary pressure.

Expecting a baby often comes with high expectations. It's called *expecting,* after all. Whenever you go into a situation with high hopes that aren't met, you'll naturally be disappointed. The higher and less realistic your expectations are, the more disillusioned you will be. Here's the thing; most people don't think their expectations are unrealistic.

On the other hand, you *can* expect not to know everything and that it will take some time to find your feet. Each stage of your children's growth will also require some adjusting. You can give yourself and your partner time and space to figure out what's normal for now—it's not so much about getting back on track as about creating a new one.

Navigating expectations with your partner reduces blame and resentment. It brings you closer and prepares you for the time when your expectations will be directed towards your children. And that will come sooner than you think.

In this stage of your journey, we'll examine some of the more common "expectation maps" of parents who have travelled before you. If their expectations start to look and feel uncomfortably familiar to you or your partner, now's the time to put your loving, learning and growing skills into practice so you can start to work towards the reality you want to create for your family.

## Expectations of Your Relationship

*Now with a baby, I thought we'd be more in love than ever.*

*I have two children already from my ex-husband. I'm in a same sex relationship now and I expected things to be different. They're not.*

*We spent a lot of money, time and heartache to finally become parents. We both love our adopted son, but I'm not sure we can say the same about each other right now.*

Nothing beats the warm, fuzzy first feelings of family, but let's face it, those first few months can be really rough too. There's going to have some sort of fallout for you, your partner and your relationship. But remember, this time is only temporary. Things will settle down.

**CHECK YOUR COMPASS:**

**You're normal.** Around two thirds of couples report a drop in relationship satisfaction in early parenthood according to Gottman. This can be a huge shock if you expect to feel more in love. But if you think of the effects of fatigue, sleep deprivation, financial and time pressures on a couple, it's not surprising. The reality for most parents is that *in some ways* you may feel more in love or more complete than ever and *in other ways* you may feel like complete strangers!

**It's temporary.** Fatigue and sleep deprivation pass eventually. Finances and time pressures can be renegotiated. Assumptions can be examined, laughed about and forgiven. The more you're prepared for, and deal with, the challenges, the quicker you'll get through them and the less scrapes you'll both get along the way.

**Why it's happening**. Even with couples that consider themselves similar, new differences in priorities, needs, values, family backgrounds, perspectives, feelings and personality are likely to arise. New differences raise the potential for relationship dissatisfaction. Navigating new differences is a big thing for parents; it's a whole stage you'll pass through (Stage Seven).

**It's common.** Shock or disappointment over unmet expectations is one of the biggest issues that relationship counselors deal with in new-parent partnerships. That two thirds of couples said their relationship took a hit after baby tells us that with this is *common.*

**What the other one third were doing differently:** they were friends—before and afterwards. They had a deep knowledge of each other and each other's lives, and were able to retain intimacy and goodwill throughout the transition. They grew *together*. You know how to do that now.

**Where did your expectations come from?** Instead of trying to fit your life with your partner into your expectations, it's easier to examine if your expectations ever actually fit for your partner in the first place. What were your expectations based on? Movies, TV, social media? What your family and friends have shared? These can all be misleading, as they tend to show only the romantic and fun images of parenthood. Sure, they're part of it. But—they're only part of it.

**Did you grow up with a baby?** Unless you actually lived with a baby in your house, most of us have very limited experience of what life with a new baby is like, so there's little opportunity for realistic expectations. Books and courses like *Becoming Us* can take you about as far as you can get, but there's still a long way for you to walk on your own. It's much better when it's hand-in-hand.

**STEPS:**

**Give yourself time**—to both adjust to your new roles and to truly feel like a family. For some, this may not be until your last child joins you.

Reflect on your expectations and assumptions and where they came from, especially when you're shocked or disappointed. This is your opportunity to take off the rose-colored glasses, look at your partner through clear eyes and embrace the reality of your family. It's only then when new, and even better, possibilities can emerge.

**Don't blame your partner**. Did the words "yeah, but…." just pop into your head as you read this? Read it again.

**Let go**. Unrealistic expectations are premeditated resentment. They're harmful to you and damaging to your family. Let go of them.

**Open up**. It's common for couples to have "no go" zones. But talking about your hopes reduces unnecessary disappointment and resentment and brings you closer. Share what you've learned about your expectations with your partner in a non-blaming way. Reassure your partner that you don't blame them for your (maybe unrealistic) expectations. Hug.

**Invite your partner to open up**. Do you ever wonder about your partner's expectations of you, themselves or your family after baby? Are they the same or different? In what ways? Be curious about your partner's experiences. Use the steps in Thriving.

## Expectations of Others

*Why the heck didn't someone tell us it would be like this?*

You know what? This is a *really* good question. It's one I asked many years ago, and one that's been asked of me many times since.

Whether you've dreamed about becoming parents for years, or pregnancy was an unexpected surprise (or even a *shock),* either way, you only have eight or nine months (or until the adoption is finalized) to prepare. Which is not a lot of time for the biggest life change you're ever likely to experience. If you were moving overseas, you'd likely give it 12 months—at least.

So, you may have read magazines and books, talked to friends and family, attended prenatal classes and had appointments with physicians or midwives. Your expectations of parenthood would largely have formed around the information you got from these sources and resources.

But here's the thing. Nobody talks much about this stuff (unless you're lucky to have found a *Becoming Us* trained professional in which case I hope they were extra helpful).

As you now know, normally there's a *lot* that's left unsaid. Looking back, it might seem like you were lulled into a false sense of security, or even thought it was "a conspiracy of silence," as one parent put it—you were padded with a nice thick layer of bubble wrap. For a number of reasons, the media, health care professionals and even friends and family may have kept you in the dark.

### CHECK YOUR COMPASS:

**Understanding others.** When you're expecting, others may be unwilling to share their own frustrations or disappointments of parenthood to protect you. Friends and family will have experienced their own challenges as they were adjusting and may not know how to prepare you for the shock. Because people don't generally share their troubles honestly, this can leave us thinking we're the only ones having problems—not realizing the issues are shared by most of us.

**There can be social pressure**. New parents can be wary of admitting being overwhelmed, stressed or depressed for fear of being judged and are afraid it means they aren't coping. Others are ashamed to admit parenthood isn't coming as naturally as they'd expected. The reality is most of us feel a bit dazed and confused for a while. Pressures can frequently challenge coping strategies, and parenthood *has* very steep learning curves.

### STEPS:

**Share your experience with a good listener.** Unmet expectations come with a fair dose of shock. Talking about them helps the shock to wear off and any other feelings like anger or disappointment to wash through you. This speeds your ability to adjust and is particularly important when you may feel some sense of shame about something. Shame breeds in the darkness. When you open up and shine a light on it, it loses power. Saying "I feel ashamed" is an act of courage.

**Talk to other mothers**. Finding others who are also struggling helps reduce the resentment you may feel towards your partner—if you're convinced that you're struggling because of them.

**Don't blame your partner.** Chances are they were just as uninformed, or even more, than you. Don't let them blame you either. Even if you read all the books, there's much more between the lines.

Blame is something people do when they don't feel strong enough to handle something. As parents, you both benefit from resisting the temptation to blame, because there will be times when you will both feel out of your depth. Blame doesn't work—support does.

**Break the code of silence.** Share your experiences in honest, sensitive ways to help other parents. Recommend any great resources that you've found along the way to help them adjust their expectations.

## Expectations of Yourself

*I don't know how my mother did it. I feel like I'm failing all round.*

*My brother has six kids. Six! I can't even handle one.*

One of the largest sources of expectations of you as parents is likely to be from your own family. It's easy to fall into the trap of negatively comparing yourself to them. Don't set yourself, or your partner, up for failure.

**CHECK YOUR COMPASS:**

**You are unique.** As you learned in Part I, one of the tasks of growing into an adult is embracing your sense of yourself as a distinct individual. Parenthood is the perfect time to do this. You were a unique human being before you had your child. Having them has added a whole new layer to your personality. Now's a good time to support yourself by distancing from expectations that can stunt your growth.

**Memories are unreliable.** Your first memories are likely to have formed when you were between two and five years old. By this time your parents had adjusted and acquired a couple of years' experience. You're unlikely to have a conscious memory of how they coped when you were an infant or very young child.

**Don't compare.** We live in a very different society from previous generations. Parenthood is unchartered territory for most of us. Some of the stresses you face now may not have been faced by your parents. They faced different stresses, sure, but also may have had more support from extended family or community.

**Understand context.** Remember: fathers were primarily breadwinners and mothers were homemakers. Mother was the nurturer and father the disciplinarian. There was no confusion about responsibilities—roles were clearly defined.

Many parents haven't seen their mother weighed down with the stress and guilt of juggling demands from children, partner and boss. Most of us never saw our fathers doing the same. Ours is a pioneering parenting generation, with new frontiers and so we're having to figure it out as we go.

**Build confidence**. Your level of confidence is inversely affected by your expectations. The higher the expectation, the harder it is likely to be for you to meet. Do yourself a favor—lower your expectations of yourself (and your partner) a notch or two and give your confidence room to grow.

**STEPS:**

**Talk honestly with your parents about your early childhood**. Explore how they really coped. You might find they were just as human then as you are now. Sharing this discovery with your parents can be very bonding. It can heal past hurts and leave the door open for more help and support from them.

**Practice mindful self-care**. Comparing yourself with any parent, past or present, is not good self-care. Nobody in the world has the exact same combination of life circumstances, history, influences, experiences or temperament as you. You are unique. Any comparison is unfair. Learning not to compare is good preparation for parenthood. Children don't like to be compared either, and if you have more than one, this can especially cause problems between siblings.

**Be your own best friend**. Unfavorable comparisons damage self-esteem. You probably don't like it when other people judge you—so why on earth would you judge yourself? Are you feeling pressured by family, friends or society? Let go of other's ideals. You're better off conserving your desperately needed energy for more constructive and meaningful things.

Check in with your partner. They can be hard on themselves too, so see if this is an issue for your mate. Sharing personal disappointments in other areas of our lives, finding empathy and encouragement is very bonding.

*After years of infertility and finally adopting, I thought I'd have everything under control. I didn't realize being a mom would be so hard.*

*I was determined to be a "supermom." Have the baby, go back to work, be the perfect wife. Ha! That's a joke.*

*I'm a midwife for goodness sake! I shouldn't be struggling like this. I feel like such a failure.*

Starting a family can feel like a natural progression for many couples. You may expect becoming a mother will just feel right—that you will bond immediately with your baby and that mother-craft skills will magically arrive just in time—especially if looking after babies or young children has been in your professional role.

In reality, most new mothers feel clumsy and disorganized, dazed and confused for a while.

**CHECK YOUR COMPASS:**

**Some words have great power.** The word "mother" can have powerful associations (Mother Earth, mother love, Madonna) attached to a whole set of expectations. You may expect to be suffused with loving feelings, to feel complete as a woman, fulfilled, whole, capable and content, that things will come naturally, that it will be easy or even a spiritual experience. What were *your* imaginings?

**There's always a flip side**—frustration for not getting things right; resentment towards your partner for being able to "escape"; worry about your abilities; deflated by the monotony of day-to-day tasks. It's all part of the real picture. Learning to manage strong emotions is a whole other stage of parenthood that we'll get to soon.

Here I'm going to pause and point out some dangerous territory that I'd like you to be aware of.

**The media are a trap.** Onscreen mothers are frequently portrayed as highly organized, completely unselfish, well dressed, hair styled and possessing enough energy to do ten things at once. Families have tidy homes, ironed clothes and rarely have realistic arguments. There's usually a neat little happy ending at the finish. Don't buy into it: it's better to be the real you than a recycled version of a fantasy. Thankfully, with more relatable shows out now, this is changing.

**There are unrealistic pressures.** You can stress yourself out trying to be perfect, cope with more than you can and give an endless supply of love and nurturing—to the point of burnout. Where you find your expectations aren't met, you may wonder if there's something wrong with you, feel guilty, think you're a bad mother or that you're not cut out for this. These not-true thoughts can lead to depression.

**STEPS:**

**Know you're normal**. Researcher Wendy Le Blanc found 88% of mothers experienced what she called Postpartum Stress. Dads and partners suffer from this as well.

**Embrace the fullness of yourself**. You are who you are, there's no getting away from it. The sooner you accept this, the quicker you'll learn to work with, rather than against, yourself—and the easier you'll adjust. The same is true for your partner.

**Embrace flexibility.** You may expect that motherhood will just fit in with the future you'd planned for yourself. The reality is that mothers often find maternity leave is not long enough, childcare is expensive or hard to find and good part-time jobs even harder. Motherhood is more exhausting than most of us expect—we don't have the energy to work outside the home because we're too tired from the night shift.

Some good news to come from this is that one of the fastest growing business sectors is entrepreneurial moms and dads who've beat the system by working from home.

**Share it.** Talk with other mothers. The more you share your experiences, the more you'll realize you're not alone and the more support you can muster.

**Invite your partner in**. Share your thoughts, feelings and hopes. And wonder how they're going. Are they experiencing anything similar?

## Expectations of Your Partner

*I thought my husband would be more involved with the baby. He seems to be more interested in his own life.*

*As a gay couple, I expected my husband would get what it's like for me.*

Parenthood comes with hopes, dreams and desires. Those that have remained unspoken, even if they're reasonable, are the ones your partner may be most unprepared for. The way you handle this will directly impact your outcome.

**CHECK YOUR COMPASS:**

**Be mindful of mind reading.** Have you spoken to them? Until you've actually verbalized your hopes or expectations to your partner, they remain assumptions. Assumptions breed misunderstanding and frustration, so resist expecting your partner to read your mind.

**Your needs.** With all the nurturing you give to your baby, you will find you have an increased need to be nurtured yourself. Naturally, you'll want this from your partner. You might expect they'll be able to rise to the challenge, but this can be very difficult if your partner is the one used to being "looked after."

**Your partner's intentions.** When partners become parents, they may turn their attention to areas in which they think they can make the most contribution to their new family—like working harder. And to cope with the pressure of working harder, they might have an increased need for stress relief, which can mean they're spending less time with you rather than the increased time you hoped for.

**Expectations influence relationships.** Expectations shape beliefs and influence communication. This can be a good thing. If you expect your relationship to be a mutually respectful one, you will speak to your partner accordingly and improve your chances of getting a respectful response. The opposite can also be true. If you think your partner is angry with you and you expect an angry response from them, your tone is more likely to sound angry, and that's exactly what you're likely to get back from them.

**STEPS:**

**Don't set your partner up for failure.** Gently check out your expectations before they become a problem.

**Invite your partner in.** It's human nature to withdraw from unfamiliar situations to protect yourself from feelings of vulnerability. Your partner might need to know you need and want them to be involved.

**Know that both parents need time to find their feet.** If your partner is feeling out of their depth, they'll appreciate reassurance and appreciation, just as you do.

**Realize unspoken expectations are uncomfortable for you both.** You won't know their feelings and where your partner is coming from unless it's safe for them to say. The way you frame the conversation will directly affect its outcome. (See Thriving for guidelines).

**Be clear.** If you feel awkward about broaching a subject, do you try to talk around it instead of stating it clearly? This can be confusing and frustrating, especially for a goal-oriented mate.

## Expectations of Your Little One

*I expected my baby would sleep all night and that I could play with them in the daytime. I didn't expect to feel like a robot.*

You're not alone in this. None of us ever feel adequately prepared for the reality of life with a little one—and this is a very real problem. Research shows mothers most at risk of burnout are those who underestimate the amount of work involved and who put too much pressure on themselves to live up to unrealistic expectations.

**CHECK YOUR COMPASS:**

**"Normal" after baby is different to "normal" before.** You may have been led to believe that when you settle your baby into a routine, life will get back to "normal." You may expect to be sleep deprived for the first few weeks, but that it can go on for 12 months or longer is a shock to most parents. Whatever "normal" was for you as a couple—sporty, musical, love-the-beach/snow/camping, cultural or creative—may not be a passion shared by your baby or toddler, so you'll have to find work-arounds.

**Other expectations will remain unfulfilled.** Visions of the perfect baby—one that meets or exceeds initial milestones of weight gain, first smile, first tooth, first word and first step. Particularly with a firstborn, any failure to meet an expected target may cause anxiety or disappointment.

You may have hoped your baby would be a boy or a girl; fair haired or dark; have your nose or your partner's eyes because you love that part of them the most. Any unmet expectations will require some adjustment.

Here's where I stop and draw your attention to a pool beside us. I'm going to ask you to look below the surface and notice what you see that you otherwise might easily miss.

Be honest with yourself about these feelings, even if you don't share them with anyone else. Because here's the thing—anything you don't allow yourself to acknowledge can show up in other ways in your relationship. If you don't admit to yourself that you wanted X instead of Y, you're more likely to snap at your partner if they express the exact same thing. The more adjusting you do as you go along, the better you will get through the challenges and get on with the great stuff of building your happy and healthy family. If you want help with any of this below-the-surface stuff," you might consider working with a counselor. They're pretty great at this.

**Beware the "If my child is perfect, it means I'm a good parent" trap.** We can put a lot of pressure on children to be a certain way if we think they're a reflection of us, rather than little people in their own right. Yeah, sure, you can guide them, they'll need this from you, but children thrive most when you support them to become who they are rather than who you think they should be. Cherish their uniqueness.

**Do you expect to be in control?** Most parents expect to have more control over their children than they will. Many are dismayed when not having control leads to feelings of being out of control. When you experience your toddler's first tantrum, you'll know what I mean.

**There's a lifetime of expectations to come.** That your child will have great soccer skills, want to ride horses (because you love to), get good grades, choose the right college, follow in your career footsteps—the sooner you learn to manage your expectations the better.

**STEPS:**

**Learn to "go with."** Do you feel like things are going "against" you? It would serve you better to learn to go with them. Once you let go of the need to control, you may find a whole new side of yourself. For many, it feels like a new sense of freedom. Some people like to send what they can't control on to a higher power before they let go. Others develop the ability to self-soothe. "Happy and relaxed" (not perfect) can be your new mantra.

**Know that this, too, shall pass**. Like all challenging aspects of life, when you adjust, it gets better. Parenthood is the same. As your baby settles, becomes more predictable and eventually gets into a routine, you'll find it easier to manage things. And then you'll find their routine will change again. Toddlers eventually learn to channel their frustration, children to finish their homework and teenagers to do the dishes occasionally.

**Face feelings of failure.** If you find it hard to deal with failure (or disappointment or rejection or anxiety or…) you might find that you try to control people and things around you so that you will never have to feel bad. If this sounds like you, or your partner, it may be tapping into some issues from your own childhood. This is something you or your partner may like to work through with a counselor.

*We're very active and we always thought our children would just fit in with our lifestyle. It's dawning on us that this might never happen.*

*We were planning a trip to Europe with our baby at the end of the year, but now we realize it's just going to be too hard. We're so disappointed.*

Ahhh, remember when you used to think "we'll just take the baby with us." How long did that last? Three months? Two? One week? Finding something to wear that fits and doesn't have milk stains on it, packing a diaper bag and negotiating a stroller just to get out of the house can be just too much trouble on some days. Being unable to socialize or travel can be another big disappointment. Gone are the lazy Sunday sleep-ins, tidy homes, romantic weekends or fancy dinners—for a while at least.

**CHECK YOUR COMPASS:**

**You're in *very* good company.** In the book, *Babyshock!,* Elizabeth Martyn found only a tiny *4 percent* of couples said raising children lived up to their expectations. I don't think this means there is something wrong with 96 percent of children. Almost 50 percent of new parents say they would have delayed starting a family if they'd known what the reality was going to be. That's a lot of parents.

**Re-evaluate**. Know what's important to keep and what to let go of, or at least scale down for a while. For example: it's important to exercise, but it may not be fair to the family to do it for two hours every night. It's also important to have regular holidays, but it might be a cabin at the beach, rather than a suite at the casino.

**All the payoffs**. Little ones teach us what's important in life; the blessings of good relationships and what unconditional love feels like. Develop new aspects of your partnership while other parts are on hold for a while, like how to listen well or respond empathetically—these are the things that will see you through until then, and beyond.

**STEPS:**

**Talk together**. What have been the major lifestyle adjustments for each of you? Empathize with each other. Talk about what you're happy to let go of and share what you're finding hardest.

Let go. There may be some sense of loss in this. We'll get to that in Stage 5.

**Start to appreciate the small things**. Many parents delight in the unexpected pleasure of the smaller, simpler things in life after baby. It may not be a three-course meal, but you have a new appreciation of sweet potatoes when your baby's thumping enthusiastically on the highchair tray.

**Be creative.** Brainstorm all the crazy and silly things you can do. You might just surprise yourselves—and each other.

## Partner's Expectations

*I didn't expect things to change much; my wife is very capable. I guess I expected to follow her lead.*

*I enjoy the baby, but I didn't think I would have to do so much at home. I feel quite resentful towards my partner.*

*I thought my wife would go back to work sooner.*

Many modern partners go into parenthood with a true intention of equality. They expect to take part in basic baby care and household chores, share responsibility for decision making, and anticipate that their partner will likely return to work either full- or part-time at some stage, again sharing the financial responsibilities.

Some partners don't have any expectations at all. And ignorance is bliss—until it wears off. Some see thinking and worrying about the ins and outs of infant care as the stay-at-home parent's responsibility—but unless this arrangement suits *both* of you, it can lead to problems down the track.

**CHECK YOUR COMPASS:**

**There is more to fathering than meets the eye.** Notions of fatherhood tend to center on the practicalities of looking after children—providing for them and giving them the best possible life. This may be the "model" of fatherhood you grew up with.

Today's fathers, however, tend to be more actively involved in all the responsibilities (and the joys and challenges) that come with parenting. The "bigness" of this can take some adjustment. Parenthood can take you to places inside yourself and in your relationship that weren't on your radar.

**You're not just committing to your baby**. Remember, you're re-committing to your partner—to work together, be friends, be a team, be lovers, repair damage when you cause it and to forgive.

**STEPS:**

**Deal with reality.** I hate to be the one to break this to you, but I said I was going to be straight. As long as you hang on to unspoken expectations, you're in denial. Denial causes you to avoid dealing with problems and increases their chance of escalating.

**Work as a team**. When the going gets tougher than expected, you might find yourself drifting almost unconsciously back into traditional gender roles. While baby and household-related tasks may be shared in the beginning, most mothers end up doing the majority of the work. Fathers often find they take on more of the discipline issues and, thanks to the gender pay gaps and glass ceilings that still exist, carry the heavier financial burden. Talk about your roles and your hopes.

**Be honest with yourself.** Work on issues that stand in the way of your relationship with your children, either on your own or with a counselor.

**Share with your partner**. Your expectations say something about you, but until you discuss them openly, your partner is likely to take them personally. Own what's going on inside you and share it. Use the tips in Thriving so your conversations are helpful for you both.

## Parenting Versus Housework

*We agreed I would continue to work while my wife stayed home with the baby. I thought she'd take care of the housework as well.*

*My husband thinks I should be able to have dinner on the table every night. He just doesn't get how much effort that is sometimes.*

*Now our baby is in daycare, and I have returned to work part-time, my partner expects me to be in charge of the house too. That was fair in theory, but I'm no less exhausted now than when I was at home full-time.*

One of the biggest problems for couples is when expectations clash over the double-barreled issues of parenting and housework. If you're the stay-at-home parent, you'll expect to take on most of the parenting responsibility, but you may not necessarily see housework as part of this.

You may instead expect that, as you're busy most of the day with baby care, which can be exhausting, that your partner will pitch in and take on chores. Your partner however, may see housework as part and parcel of the parenting role, anticipating it will be your responsibility.

Oh, and by the way, in case you were wondering, research tells us gay and lesbian families have an advantage here—roles tend to be more fairly negotiated and shared.

**CHECK YOUR COMPASS:**

**Fairness and equality**. Whether it's inside or outside the home, the fact is that both of you are working. In terms of the success of your family, unpaid chores at home are no less valid or important than paid work in the labor force. You are *both* contributing to the wellbeing of your family and you *both* deserve support, appreciation and timeout from your responsibilities.

**Caring for a baby is 24/7** in the beginning and housework is *on top of that.* No one person can realistically achieve it all without burning out very, very quickly. Plus, if you're still in the first few months of parenthood, you're probably still dealing with transition stress, which is tiring in itself. Putting pressure on the stay-at-home parent to do more than they're capable of isn't good for them, you or your family.

I'm going to pull you aside again here because we're passing another one of those pools that looks shallow from the surface, but it's deceptively deep.

Housework is one of those tricky issues that can look like it's just about the laundry or the dishes, but it can hide a concern underneath—that you don't respect me, don't value me, that sort of thing.

**STEPS:**

**Negotiate.** Housework is something you're likely to argue about for the next 20 years, so it makes sense to start either getting to the bottom of it now (if there is a bottom—it may actually just be about the dishes this time), so use all your Thriving skills here.

Be prepared that your (paid) work lives may change or increase as your children grow, so other roles and responsibilities will need to be re-negotiated too.

**Listen to your inner voice and then pause.** It will probably be saying some pretty strong things. Catch your thoughts and feelings and modify them into words that your partner will be able to take in before they leave your lips.

Outsource chores to family, friends and neighbors for a few months or enlist paid help. It's much cheaper than divorce!

## Expectations of Society and the Workplace

*When I was pregnant, strangers made a fuss and went out of their way to help. Now our baby is in a stroller, I feel like I'm either invisible, or an inconvenience, especially when I'm breastfeeding.*

*I felt very respected and valued in my job. Now, as a mother, I'm doing "the hardest and most important job in the world," but I don't feel like I'm getting any respect at all.*

*I didn't realize how my own feelings of being undervalued as a mother affected me—and led to me allowing my partner to treat me less than well—until I went back to work and regained my self-esteem.*

We'll talk more about self-esteem and your sense of identity in Stage Six, because that's a big thing with parenthood, but right now, what's important is to acknowledge the differences between expectations and reality.

The changes that happen for you when you become a family don't just show up inside you and in your home, but also how you perceive your wider world too—and sometimes how you're treated by it. Have you noticed that yet?

Like when you were pregnant, you may have received extra knowing smiles, been approached by motherly types who wanted to chat. Hopefully people had the good grace to offer their bus seats. You may have felt special. Due to the privilege of living in a developed country, you are likely to have had plenty of support and so you may well have expected that this would just continue, or even get better after you had your baby.

In terms of your work-world, you probably educated yourself, trained and worked hard at your job before you became a mother, likely expecting to return to the same, or another fulfilling role when you were ready.

Afterwards, however, you may have discovered that not everyone wanted to give way to a stroller, was supportive of breastfeeding or tolerant of a grumpy baby.

You may have found that your local park didn't have enough shade, comfortable seating or clean toilets. I didn't realize how bad (or non-existent) some footpaths were on my block until I was pushing a stroller. It's frustrating that late-night, drive-through facilities exist for fast food, but not for baby food, pain relief, diapers or sanitary pads. Queuing for anything is a nightmare with a toddler, unless there's a basket of toys for them to play with.

**CHECK YOUR COMPASS:**

**A different perspective**. Remember, traditionally, parenthood was considered a rite of passage, a special time supported by the whole community—a time of reverence, ritual and celebration. Parents were elevated in their value to society. In our world, sadly, these values have been lost. Parenthood should be valued still.

**Do you value yourself and other parents** for the incredible responsibility we all carry out? When you're proud of yourself, you have more resolve to expect respect and request support from others. Also, you can support other parents to expect the same. If we all work together with a shared voice, we can, community-by-community, change things for the better.

**STEPS:**

**Believe in yourself.** As new parents, you're encountering a whole new set of experiences in a short space of time. Under these unique circumstances, you may naturally lack confidence and think the problem is within you, when in fact, it is more likely that you are having to do without—without the support, recognition and rise in social status that parenthood would have afforded you had you been born into another culture or another time.

This realization can give you the boost to work towards changing situations that aren't acceptable. More than likely, most other new parents are feeling the same way.

**Start noticing things**—like a lack of clean and functional public baby change rooms (especially ones that can be used by fathers); too few play areas or parks (especially ones that are fenced); ones that don't have toilets or shade; a lack of designated parents' parking spots (or people that thoughtlessly take up stroller parking spots); lengthy retailer queues (especially when the store can afford to employ more staff); and retailers that deliberately leave candy bars within toddler-tempting distance and then expect you to pay for the damage. Don't.

**Start noticing things** if you've gone back to work. Common work frustrations include: being expected to work too-long days; a lack of flexibility in starting or ending times (including managers that make meetings for times or days you aren't in the office or who nominate which days of the week you must work); stalling on return-to-work arrangements making it difficult to obtain or confirm childcare; lacking amenities for breastfeeding or expressing (would you eat your lunch in the toilet?); assuming that working from home is an easy option, that you must be seen at work to be taken seriously; or that part-time workers aren't committed.

**Make suggestions** that can benefit all parents and build your own confidence. Some people find it easier to speak on behalf of someone else.

**Speak up!** Phone or email your local council. I have seen parks revamped and dangerous equipment removed due to diligent parents.

**Let store managers know.** There's nothing more frustrating than dirty parents' rooms with broken facilities or the absence of at least one change room that's big enough to fit yourself, a stroller and the clothes you're trying on without pulling a muscle. Elevators or escalators out of order in train stations or shopping malls need to be reported—you'll be doing anyone with a disability a favor too. Too hard at the time? Phone or email later.

**Suggest that retail stores provide toys** so toddlers get their needs met and shoppers can browse in peace. One day you'll appreciate this.

*I expected to go back to work after our baby comes, but my boss made my job redundant. I'm keen to get back to my career and my mom will mind the baby. But there's virtually nothing available. It's so unfair—I trained for years to do this profession.*

After returning from maternity leave, it can be shocking and disheartening to find your job have been downgraded (particularly if you're returning part-time), has disappeared entirely or that the work culture now makes it impossible to sustain.

**CHECK YOUR COMPASS:**

**And it doesn't end here**. Women are still having to fight for equality in the workplace, especially at the higher end of the ladder. In executive management, on boards and in government, women make up at best, a small minority. Despite what we're lead to believe, it seems that today's woman can't, in fact, have it all—especially if she has children.

**See this as a family issue, not just a women's issue.** Negotiate conditions that make it possible to do your job and have a family life too. Ask your partner to do the same. If partners, actively push for the changes in their own workplace, we're more likely to turn this around. Imagine what it would be like for all of us if childcare were integrated with employment.

**STEPS:**

**Get political.** Government relies on advocates to alert them to important issues. Use your voice, find avenues, and ask questions. Contact your local government and attend meetings, talk to representatives and voice your frustrations or concerns. Join with other advocates and combine your power to influence policy.

**Go global.** The web joins you to the wider world. Join organizations and sign online petitions to protest injustices around the globe.

**Research.** Some clever moms and dads working from home have set up websites to help other parents return to work. Find recruitment agencies that specialize in listing family-friendly employers. Contact your industry's association to see if there're courses to refresh your skills if you're ready to take them on.

Stay in touch with what's going on in your profession. Reconnect with former colleagues and browse the newspaper and industry publications. That way, when it's time to return to the workforce, you'll be ready.

Let social media contacts know you're thinking about returning to work—managers may be happy to avoid the advertising and interviewing merry-go-round when they have a personal recommendation instead.

**Make yourself known** to a particular company or industry if you think you can add value. If they agree, and they really want you (not just someone who can do that role), it can be on your terms.

**Join a temp agency.** One mom I know got free training in all the latest computer software, worked a few days a week for some local employers and ended up with three job offers to choose from.

Keep sight of the valuable skills of parenting: multitasking, negotiating, time managing, thinking on your feet, having grace under fire, infinite patience—the list goes on. What other skills have you gained?

This may have been a tough stage of the journey for you—it is for most parents as they have to adjust to the difference between what they thought life would look like and the reality of it. Share what you've learned with your partner, a friend or someone else who's a good listener or write in your journal. And remember this—parenthood is not about the destination. It's not about getting to where you thought you would be. It's about the very real journey you are taking along the way. And it's a journey for life.

And the good news? You're about to get a bit of a break.

# Stage Four: Setting Up Base Camp

## (Whenever You Can)

Here's the stage in your parenting journey when you can stop and rest a bit. You've done such a great job of nurturing your baby for a few months now, (you kept them alive, yay for you!) that they're thriving and life is also finally starting to settle down a bit—so now's the time to now turn your attention to yourself and your partner. Chances are, with all that time, energy and focus going into that gorgeous baby of yours, you both may be needing some extra TLC.

So, we're going to look at some basic relationship survival supports. Some foundational stuff. You're going to set up Base Camp. This is going to prepare you for all the stages to come.

Your journey also starts to change here. Until now, the stages of parenthood—of *becoming us*—have applied mainly to new babies and first-time parents. You'll find however, that if you have a second or more children, or even older children, that you'll circle back to this stage, and the following stages time and time again. You never stop becoming, so the guidance in this stage applies whenever your family is under stress for any reason: an illness, a death, a job loss or a move to a new place—with any big changes, you can come back to Base Camp.

And once you know how to set yourselves up, you'll be able to set up base camp whenever life throws you and your family another challenge. It's where you can retreat to, regroup and build your resources to move forward as a family again.

I would prefer some other way…? Time for another personal share before we start pitching those tents. My husband and I have three kidults now. The last time we went back to base camp was only a few months ago.

## More Support—Still

*My partner has gone back to work and when he comes home, he's exhausted but I'm tired from being with the baby all day and I still need his help like in the beginning. It feels like we're in a competition of who needs who more.*

*Our baby is still not sleeping through the night. I can't do it all. I'm tired and cranky all the time.*

For most parents, time becomes a luxury, energy becomes a precious commodity and you start to fantasize about sleep, not sex.

When you're constantly sleep-deprived, rushed, and physically exhausted, it's easy to be irritable, forgetful, impatient and/or distracted. You may have expected to be tired and busy for a while, but it may be starting to feel that "while" means forever.

It feels like you're in competition with each other because in many ways you *are*. Recognizing this is the first step to dealing with it.

**CHECK YOUR COMPASS:**

**The depth of change you're dealing with.** When you become a family the dynamics—the underlying structure and functionality of your relationship—changes. In mechanical terms, it's like re-building an engine to make it more powerful. In journey terms, it's like going from an organized bus tour of Europe to solo trekking in the Himalayas—with a new baby.

Before, your partnership involved the negotiation of the needs of two equal people, so the *status quo,* the balance and harmony, between you, is likely to have been fairly stable. You both may have been working, sharing the housework, making decisions, purchasing stuff or renovating or decorating your home as a team. You each would have had your own stress relief and support systems. Similar focus, goals and priorities are likely to have made it easier to support each other in meeting your joint needs.

After baby, you're now looking at the negotiation of the needs of two people and one *very* dependent infant. This means major changes, especially for the stay-at-home parent. Any change for one partner will inevitably affect the other. Change is tiring. Transition stress is a thing. Big transitions over many months take a toll.

**What happened to your needs?** When things have settled down a bit, you may look back and realize you have been sacrificing your own needs for self-care. You may not be connected into your old support systems and stress relief activities as much. To continue coping and giving out, you need to be nurtured yourself. The person you're likely to want to fulfill these new intimate needs for physical and emotional support, is the person closest to you—your partner.

**What about them?** At about the same time, though, your partner may see life returning to "normal," and expect the *status quo* that existed before baby will be returned to—and that their needs will again be important to you. At this stage, you may find yourselves in competition with each other. Who most needs rest, time away from their responsibilities or time to get stuff done?

**Your needs may be incompatible.** In a traditional relationship for example, a mother's need to rest, reclaim her body, have recognition for all her (less visible) hard work and get no-strings-attached affection may be in conflict with a partner's desire to come home to a clean and tidy home, to relax and have dinner already prepared, and to be validated for all their hard work—and a return to a normal sex life.

**You have extra needs when you're under stress.** As well as basic needs for good nutrition, sleep, rest and a comfortable environment, people also have needs for company, variety and a sense of purpose to be happy. When you're under stress, you'll have additional needs for outlets and emotional support. The same is true for your partner. Not just with a new family, but for any stage in the future when there're big life changes.

**You will have new limits.** When you have a baby or young children, or your family is under stress for any reason, it can be a struggle to meet your own basic needs, let alone have time or energy to do all the things that make you happy and feel fulfilled.

**Do you expect to do it all?** It's just not realistic and not possible, at least most of the time.

**Some perspective.** These days, parents frantically rush to get ready, drive from place to place, drop big kids off at school, take little ones to play gym, rush home for lunch and naptime, pick up big ones, get them changed, squeeze in snacks, take them to sports or music practice, supervise homework, prepare dinner on a daily basis as well as regularly work, pay bills, sign notes, help at school, do fundraising, carpool, shop and run errands. Even if this isn't you yet, it probably is the neighbor who, a generation ago, may have been able to help you out.

**Technology pressures your body clock.** The relentlessness of ringing and pinging phones, emails, social media messages and movies to catch up on. There's a lot to cram in these days, all of which can put even more pressure on time-strapped parents. Our body clocks have been replaced by digital clocks, which means we can very easily disconnect *from ourselves.* We need to slow down to cope.

**Needs are interdependent.** If your needs are being met, you're better able to meet your partner's needs. And *vice versa.* An extra challenge for those who give too much is to feel comfortable receiving, and for those used to getting, it's to give. Now's the time to practice this. And if both your needs are being met, the better you are *both* able to meet the needs of your little one.

**STEPS:**

**Don't fight your needs, accept them.** Your needs are what make you human. Getting them met is what determines how you cope, the quality of your life and your satisfaction in your relationship.

**Don't fight your partner's needs, accept them.** It's easy to lose sight of your partner's needs when you're not getting your own met. Ask your partner to take responsibility for their needs and share them with you in a way that will motivate you to support them. Use your Thriving skills to work through this so both your needs get met.

**Remember, think "both/and" not "either/or."** A baby is the ultimate joint venture. Thinking in terms of "both/and" builds equality and mutuality into your relationship. You need assistance and he needs time to relax. You both need support. You and your partner need time out. Put your energy into making these things happen rather than arguing about them, which just takes more energy that you won't have.

**Don't blame your partner.** Re-read this sentence. Again.

Value yourself. Your partner may be unaware that you need extra support, especially if you're embarrassed to ask for it. This can be exacerbated by a society that expects women to be "supermoms."

**Value your partner.** Your partner will want to feel included and appreciated so they don't just feel like a helping hand.

**Remember "this too, shall pass."** Navigating new needs is a normal (and relatively temporary) stage. The better you negotiate it, the quicker it will pass.

**Organize your needs.** Write a list of your current needs and work out which ones you can meet yourself, which ones you rely on your partner to meet, those family or friends can help with them, and the ones you can outsource to professional help.

**Get back to basics.** What stresses you? What relieves it? What do you need for comfort? Particularly when you're under stress, eating well, resting and exercise are vital. Initially your fitness routine might have to be gentle and sporadic, but work up to it being a regular, predictable time out you that you can look forward to.

**Expand the circle of people you can depend on.** Enlist support and encourage your partner to do the same—they need support too. Despite concerns about this, most who are able to help a new family are delighted to—especially if they get to cuddle the baby.

If you have older children, make friends with your child's friends, and their parents. One thing that still brings us great joy in our family are the close relationships we have with the parents of our children's friends. Play dates or sporting activities become a chance to catch up with our friends as well. Holidays with other families are great fun for all. You can trade babysitting favors too.

**Eat simply and well.** Keep an airtight container in the fridge with washed and prepared salad vegetables. You'll have what you need for a healthy sandwich and a salad for dinnertime too.

**Relieve stress**—and do it regularly.

## To Feel Secure

*I've been feeling really anxious since I became a mother.*

It's normal for new and unexpected vulnerabilities to arise for mothers, especially around relationship security—that you'll be there for me, care for me, desire me. And also for partners—that you're still interested in me, that I can look after us all and that the baby hasn't replaced me in your life.

The security of knowing that your partner is strong enough to have your back, but gentle enough to be a soft place to fall, comes through trust and commitment. Security is essential to start building at this stage of becoming a family. Because it's the foundation for everything to come.

*When we discuss things, it gets out of hand pretty quickly.*
*It's better not to try.*

More issues, more potential for conflict, less sleep, less time and energy—all a recipe for disaster. The very first thing you need to cope with all this is a joint commitment to create safety in your partnership. Going forward, you'll need to be able to talk openly and honestly without fear of the types of arguments that can potentially damage your bond.

Strong emotions escalate conflict and can make you feel unsafe, so you need to find ways to manage them. That's ahead in Stage Five and Stage Seven. If lack of physical or emotional safety is an issue in your relationship, you might want to skip ahead to Part III.

*Ok, I admit I've been going out drinking a bit more lately, but since our baby came, it feels like my wife wants to change me, she keeps nagging....*

She may want to change you, but maybe not in the way you think.

Having a baby ups the ante on her dependency on you to provide the security and stability that she and your baby need.

Some previously ignored aspects of your relationship may now take center stage. She may want to "fix" something that makes her feel less secure, knowing instinctively that a sound relationship is best for your whole family. Most partners, naturally, don't like being "fixed."

**CHECK YOUR COMPASS:**

**Your relationship is like a garden.** You can tidy it up every once in a while, and it will look OK. If you neglect it, it will wilt, wither and die. Make it a priority, tend it with skill and care enough to create something you're proud of and it will reward you *every single day.*

**Security is the bedrock.** Trust is the layer of soil on top of it. Without safety and security, trust cannot be built. Without trust you cannot go inwards or deeper into yourself or into your partner to fully give your love. Your relationship stays shallow. You can build trust—in lots of ways. This is the garden your children will play in one day. Two gardeners working together can achieve more than one alone.

**There are different types of security**. The best way you may know how to provide security for your family is to work hard to pay the bills to keep a roof over their heads. But the stay-at-home parent is likely to see you working harder at this time as a lack of support, which can be confusing if you think you're doing more.

**Does stuff make you feel secure?** Another thing that can be confusing or frustrating is when mothers seek a sense of security through (often expensive or unnecessary) baby *stuff*—like the "right" stroller or bassinette.

Advertisers can take advantage of this. Wanting expensive stuff also sends a message to you that you'll need to work harder.

**Become transparent**. Transparency builds trust. Where partners aren't open and honest about their feelings and needs, relationships become stunted. Whenever you think, "Wow, that really hurt," but your outside voice says, "you don't know what you're talking about, you idiot!" you know there's room for growth.

**STEPS:**

**Respect the vulnerability of your family**. Don't make selfish decisions (like starting or continuing risky activities). Don't stress financial resources by spending unnecessary amounts. Don't make major plans or big decisions without talking them through with your partner and seeing things from their perspective. You want to be putting into your family in this stage, not taking away from it. And this stage is temporary; there will be more time for you in the future.

**Notice how you communicate.** It's easy to get into patterns of relating (like nagging, being critical or defensive) that make the trusting and intimate talks you need to feel bonded, loving and loved almost impossible. Turn your communication around and you turn your relationship around.

**Have agreements.** Agree not to say or do things that threaten the security of your family (like threatening to leave). If you say something you regret, repair it. It's easier to repair a broken agreement than a broken home.

**Self-soothe.** You need to be able rely on yourself to calm down, not on your partner—there will be times they won't be able to be there for you. Being able to self-soothe means you're less likely to lose control and throw out words in anger that you'll forget, but which can cut your partner deeply. Your partner needs to learn this too.

**Talk to yourself.** Think about the ways you feel secure—in your home, your relationship, your community, your financial situation. Think about the ways you feel less secure. Ask yourself what you really need. Is a superficial need covering a deeper one? Do you really need to hop on that motorcycle to escape, or do you just need your partner to ease up a bit? Is it that expensive change table really needed, or reassurance that you'll all be OK?

**Crosscheck your perceptions**. Use the skills in Thriving for this. A need for security is often a hidden concern (we'll get to that down the track a bit in Stage 7). Talking about concerns openly for half an hour could save you a decade of arguments. After first discussing your hopes and concerns, you can then move into brainstorming and problem solving.

## To Be Seen

*I know what the baby needs, I know what my husband needs—he makes that very clear. But what about me? I feel like I'm drowning in everybody else's demands.*

*My needs and wants are so often put aside or delayed for the sake of the children or the family. It's usually by choice, which is OK, but sometimes it adds up and I just want it to be my turn.*

**CHECK YOUR COMPASS:**

**Do you need to be needed?** I have walked this part of the path ahead and I don't recommend it. I'm going to show you an alternate route. You might believe the more you give, the more you'll get in return. Putting your own needs first can feel selfish, I get it. But putting your own needs last leads to burnout and even health risks. Here's something that will shock you if you need more convincing: women during the childbearing years are 75 percent more likely to suffer from autoimmune diseases than men.

Women have been trained for generations to be caretakers. But it's much better to be wanted and loved than to be needed. There is a big difference.

**You are a whole person, not "just" a mother.** You are unique. Becoming a mother has added new aspects that make you even more unique than you were before. These aspects are there to discover, not conceal. We'll talk more about this in Stage Six.

**STEPS:**

**Insist that your partner, and others, see you as a person too.** Resist the expectations that come with the role of mother if they aren't right for you. Resist the "supermom" myth. You still have the same personality and ambitions you had before. Expect support from those close to you so your hopes can come to fruition when the time is right.

**Hold on to yourself.** Stay connected with meaningful aspects of your pre-baby self: friends, interests, and activities. Expect your partner's support in this too. These things will tide you over while you find other resources in your mother-self.

**Give your needs a voice.** As you become more aware of your needs, your expectation that your partner will meet them may increase. The problem is of course that your partner won't be aware of our needs unless you voice them. Sometimes you may do this in a blaming way, such as "You never think of me!" All your partner will hear is the blame. Your needs will go on voiceless and unmet.

**Meet your partner's needs at the same time.** It's likely that your partner's self-esteem is important to them. If you communicate in a way that makes them feel bad about themselves, they will shut you out—and you won't get your needs met either. You both lose.

**Don't give up**. If you think that you're asking, but your need is being rejected, you're likely to give up. This can lead to resentment. You can give up in other ways too. You may start denying or minimizing your needs. But when you'll start to shut down, you risk becoming depressed.

If your partner is unable to find a voice for their needs, they can do the same. You each need to take the risk, find your voice and tell your truth. The more sensitively you do this, the less risky it will be.

In *The New Rules of Marriage,* author Terrence Real says instead of asking women to "back down" from their relationship demands, we should support men to "step up and meet them." The double-dilemma for a woman is if she doesn't challenge her partner to increase his awareness and ability to meet her needs, they'll go unmet. On the other hand, if she challenges too much, he will be unwilling to meet her needs—and they still go unmet. You can learn how to tread this fine line.

## To Feel Understood

*When I get home, the first thing my wife says is that she needs a break. She's home all day, what does she need a break from?*

*My husband is stressed about his work, that's nothing compared to my stress about the baby.*

*Our baby is seven months old. I just lost my job, so my wife went back to work. She doesn't understand how much of a challenge being at home with the baby has been for me—I don't have the experience she's gotten.*

When relationships are challenged, it's not usually because there's anything wrong with either partner, but because partners are simply unaware of each other's needs, especially their emotional ones. We're usually so preoccupied with our own issues that we miss what's going on for our partner. This can be especially true in the early stages of parenthood when our lives can become so different.

**CHECK YOUR COMPASS:**

**What can you see?** Parents need to stretch themselves to have multiple viewpoints. To see things from where your partner stands, to get a sense of what their perspective means to them and to value their views as equal to our own.

**Your partner is more like you than you think.** Both of you will want the best for your family; both of you have your own obstacles that get in the way. Both of you are learning and trying and occasionally messing up. Both of you will want acknowledgement and understanding and to share struggles so you get support, comfort and relief. Your baby wants all of this for both of you too.

**STEPS:**

**Be real.** Risk being vulnerable. Share your struggles, problems, concerns and frustrations. We all tend to have a rosy view of parenthood until we get there; and this may be the image one parent continues to see until the partner who's closest to the action shows them how it really is.

At-the-job-all-day partners can be particularly unaware of the stresses and strains for the stay-at-home parent, who can sometimes make the mistake of trying to cover them up to prove they're coping. Be careful, there's a pothole there.

**Pull back and re-focus**. The more immersed you are in your own experience, the harder it is to see someone else's.

Admit what you can't see. Admit you may not recognize or understand what some of your partner's concerns are. Let them know you still care, even if you don't fully understand.

**Ask questions—clarify.** What's it like for you? What does that mean? How long have you felt this way? When you have the answers, things will make more sense to you and you'll have more empathy.

**Work towards understanding.** It's the first step in navigating your needs and can bring about momentous, lasting change that creates wonderful things for your family.

## To Feel Accepted and Respected

*I never realized until now how different my partner is to me.*
*I worry what this means for us.*

It can be a shock when unexpected sides of your partner, or differences in your relationship, arise at this stage. But remember, parenthood is a time of increased individuality (because both parents roles and days can be so different) as well as increased differences (thanks to new issues to work through).

**CHECK YOUR COMPASS:**

**Do you accept yourself?** You cannot fully expect from others what you don't first give to yourself. The ways you treat yourself models for others how to treat you. Your self-acceptance and self-respect threshold forms your expectations and sends a clear message to others. Expect respect.

**Do you accept your partner?** Your partner is now and forever your child's other parent. Your child has them in their heart as much as you are. If you criticize, mistreat or leave your partner out, it hurts the child that loves them too.

**Respect your differences.** The word respect comes from the Latin *respicere,* which means, "to look back, to consider or regard." Differences are something to explore and reflect on. We'll cover this territory more in Stage Seven.

**What do you need?** One of you may need more order or structure to manage uncertainty anxiety. The other may have a need for variety or flexibility to manage feelings of boredom. Each of these needs are valid but can conflict with each other.

**There are different ways of getting the same need met.** You may need to relieve stress by dancing around the living room with the music full blast. Your partner may need to relieve stress through meditation at the same time.

**Some differences aren't so different.** Surface differences are often based on common underlying needs. We all have the need for acceptance, trust and respect, but may have different ways of trying to gain these.

**STEPS:**

**Commit to both your needs being equal.** Eliminate competition.

Be the expert on you. For example, you know exercise is good for you, but you may not be so excited about the learning to surf/play tennis/rock-climb that your partner may be insisting on. Your partner is better off conserving their energy for the surfing/tennis/rock-climbing and supporting you to find what works for you. Having said that, rock climbing might be more fun than you think.

**Talk regularly.** Needs shift and change with life's ups and downs and children's stages of development. Re-negotiate things regularly to ensure you continue working as a team.

## To Be a True Partnership

*I feel like I'm the only one that's putting in any effort—except in the bedroom!*

Relationships tend to topple when they're one-sided. A true partnership builds and deepens through intimacy. There are two conditions for intimacy to thrive. The first is that because intimacy involves risk and vulnerability, it grows between two people who consider themselves equals. The second is that it must be reciprocal. Reciprocity is the ability to give as well as receive. Where intimacy is one-sided, the giver will give up eventually. Intimacy is so important for parents that we'll be walking towards it in Stage Eight.

*My wife's driving me crazy, ordering me around and telling me to "grow up and act like a father."*

*I asked my husband for help with the kids the other day. He said "I've just worked a 12-hour shift—you do it!"*

Give and take is part of a normal healthy relationship. But with a new baby and older children, stress and needs pile up so rapidly that give and take can look more like push and pull.

I'm going to point out something else you'll want to avoid here: see the beach over there, there's a powerful current there and if you get caught in it, it could be dangerous so I'm going to describe what I have seen happen for parents who get caught in it. Then you can see it ahead of time.

If push and pull becomes an ingrained power struggle, it can become treacherous for a family, especially if it's about looking after the baby—because your baby can become caught in the middle of it.

**CHECK YOUR COMPASS:**

**There's a link between competition and power.** When mothers bear and raise a baby, in some ways they relinquish control of their body and life for a time, which can leave some women feeling powerless. This can mean they're more sensitive to the power balance in their relationship, and this can fuel competition.

**Beware of over-parenting.** When you feel like your sense of power is reduced, it can cause anxiety. Some parents can make up for the sense of power reduction in other areas by claiming more power over the baby. Sometimes they even do this by putting their partner's efforts down.

This can also happen when a parent becomes less bonded with a partner and over-compensates by becoming overly bonded with a child (co-dependency). This can lead to anxious, helicopter-style over-parenting. As well as creating relationship problems, this style of parenting will have a negative impact on a child.

**There's a slippery slope here.** Let's say you start off happy to do more of the baby care. After a few months, however you may begin to feel overburdened and overwhelmed. If you feel guilty on top of this, you may redouble your efforts—further widening the gap between what you and your partner are doing. We'll talk about guilt in the next Stage.

Some mothers try to address this imbalance by trying to change their partner, which increases the partner's resistance, and may cause them to withdraw—under-parenting even more.

While both partners may initially be happy for the less-parenting partner to have other responsibilities (like breadwinning), a few months later, that partner can feel excluded, nagged and under-appreciated. Rather than acknowledging their part in leaving the stay-at-home parent with more responsibility, they may do even less, or do it in a resentful way.

That current is going to carry anything in it towards the rocks. Can you see where they are? No? I'm going to lend you my binoculars so you can see them more clearly.

**This dynamic can escalate**. The more one partner does, the less the other will do, and *vice versa.* Each position reinforces the other. This can end up in 10 years' time with one parent who is martyr and another who isn't around much. And children who aren't so happy. I want you to avoid this.

**Inequality destabilizes your relationship**. The most satisfying and stable long-term relationships are ones in which power (influence, decision-making and getting needs met) are shared—where couples can accept each other's point of view (even if they don't fully understand it) and have the willingness to find and build on common ground. Common ground is the best foundation for family.

**STEPS:**

**Don't blame.** If this is you, accept your own responsibility in this and recognize how it affects your partner.

Commit to sharing responsibility—practically and emotionally. Even when the breadwinner can't be at home, they can be emotionally engaged in the stay-at-home parent's day or in the decision-making process. Even though the caregiver may not be earning the money, they can be aware of the family's financial stresses and help problem solve this and other issues.

**Make joint decisions.** This can be challenging if you grew up to be very independent, or had dominating parents and you're still trying to assert your own individuality. These reactions are understandable in their historical context, but can undermine the foundations of the family you're trying to build. Joint decisions become joint goals and are easier to work towards as a team—and reap all the rewards of as a family.

**Share the baby.** Commit to sharing care, taking responsibility and making decisions about your little ones. Equality for you may not always be 50:50, or the same as the couple's next door, but more what's considered "fair" by each of you. The spirit of sharing is more important—it's like fertilizer for your relationship garden.

## To Regain a Sense of Balance

*I don't understand my partner, we've been wanting a baby for years and now that we finally have one, all of a sudden, all she wants is to go out with her girlfriends.*

It's confusing when your partner seemingly suddenly starts to act differently. But all of us are a mix of contradictory needs. We can want control in some areas but want to be given direction in others—to have stability, but also to break out at times. When you become parents, this delicate balancing act gets knocked out of whack. You need a new level of awareness and ability to work out what's going on both inside and between you.

Your partner might be seeking an outlet to express or rebalance a need that's been put on hold while she was waiting for your baby. If you had to go through IVF, or an adoption process, and didn't have regular stress relief along the way, she'll have an added need to get it out—as might you.

*I felt as though I completely lost my spontaneity—I couldn't even go to the supermarket without it being a big deal.*

**We need both security and freedom.** When you're responsible for a little one all day and night, day in and day out, it's easy to feel restricted, deprived—trapped even. Well into your children's future, you can feel the stress and responsibility of raising them. To balance these frustrations, both parents can crave—and should have—regular time out.

**Lack of freedom causes resentment** towards the partner you may perceive is able to "escape" (and who may be confused by the resentment).

**Another common need is to feel in control.** Parents can feel almost assaulted by the chaos that accompanies early childhood. Babies are loud and messy, toddlers even more so. They can act in ways that are unpredictable and confusing, and defy all your efforts to calm or control them. Adolescents, too. Your child's need to express themselves is likely to undermine your need to feel accomplished or masterful. As a result, we can *all* feel frustrated with each other.

*My wife used to be very independent, but since we became parents, she's become very clingy. To be honest, it's making me a bit uncomfortable.*

*I'm getting very mixed messages from my partner. One minute he needs my help and support and the next he wants me to leave him alone.*

From the time you're born, one of the things you need to learn is how to regulate your conflicting needs for connection and independence. This is the attachment-style stuff we talked about earlier. It's a lifelong journey. Parenthood ups the ante on this particular dynamic. On the one hand, it increases your dependence on one another, and on the other, becoming a parent inspires you to grow in new ways.

**CHECK YOUR COMPASS:**

**Needs play out in different ways.** Throughout the day, you're likely to have periods where you want to be together and, when you've had enough of each other, to move apart. You're likely to be sensitive to any times your partner moves too quickly for you, or forcefully in a different direction.

**Your partner has these needs too, but maybe in different areas.** You may want to spend more time together (desire for closeness) but also want to spend more time with your friends (need for independence). Your partner may express these dual needs through behavior that seems erratic to you, asking for support with the baby and then dismissing you. You may get your sense of closeness through sex (and feel deprived if you don't get it). Your partner may get hers through talking (and feel deprived if you won't). The more one partner pushes, the more the other tends to pull away.

**This push-pull dynamic escalates in times of stress.** If this is starting to sound eerily familiar to you, it's because these relationship dances tap into your original attachment styles (secure, preoccupied, dismissive or disorganized). This push-pull dance can take on a life of its own and cripple both of you if you get caught up in it. If you can't extract yourself, find a counselor who can.

**STEPS:**

**Have intentional conversations around closeness versus distance.** In what ways do you feel close? In what ways you feel distant? How would you like to feel closer? In what ways would you appreciate more space? Let me tell you here, one 20-minute conversation at this level can prevent 20 years of arguments.

**Think in steps.** When your partner says or does something, think "When you do/say that, I feel X steps closer (or X steps farther away from) you." Share this with them and swap. You may both be surprised.

**Find a rhythm.** If you know you need to cuddle when you wake up, but not at night, tell your partner. If you know you need some time alone in the evening to decompress from the day, say so. Owning your needs for closeness and distance, making your partner aware of them (and you of theirs) and working together, means you can choreograph your dance, rather than blaming your partner for not knowing the moves.

## Friendship and Fun

*I miss my wife!*

Friendship is the core of a long-term relationship. When you become parents, taking time to talk, relax and share a laugh, often gets crowded out by all the responsibilities. But it's liking each other and wanting to be together that provides motivation to work through problems, overcome obstacles and restore harmony in your home.

**CHECK YOUR COMPASS:**

Laughing is like a pressure-relief valve. You'll need it. Fun relieves anxiety and can make even the scratchiest times more bearable.

**Your partner may need a promotion.** If you can apply the loving, learning and growing skills in this stage, you'll find that you bring out the best in your partner, like them more and love them more, and they may even end up being your best friend, if they're not already.

**STEPS:**

**Use the "best friend" rule.** Ask yourself: "Would I speak to my best friend this way?" "Would I get upset if it was my best friend who did that?" "What would I do if this were my best friend?" You want your partner to be a best friend too.

**Share**. One of the first things we teach our kids is to share with friends. How much do you keep to yourself and from your partner?

**Clean up after yourself.** We all make a mess of things at times. So, as not to cause ongoing bitterness, make up and make amends so you can be friends again.

**Make a list of the things you both enjoy doing** and find ways to build them into your life. As your children get older, they can be included too, and on the other side of your journey, when they leave home, you'll have lots in common that you can still share as a couple. I'm going to give you some special look-into-the-future goggles here: The biggest trend in separation now is with older couples after their children leave home. It's called the "empty nest divorce." It's so sad, and in many cases, preventable.

**Have play dates—with your partner.** Regularly. Time away from your baby or children to shore up your bond as a couple also strengthens your family's foundations. Plan small, bigger, and biggest things on a weekly, monthly and annual basis. Have a child-free weekend or holiday every so often as a reward for all the hard work you've put in. You deserve it!

How have you been doing so far? I have given you a lot to think about. There's some shade here, this might be a good time to stop and have a cold drink.

You may not have noticed, so I'll point it out here, that how well you navigate each stage of early parenthood will affect how the next stage unfolds. The more prepared you are for taking your leap of faith in the first stage, the better you're likely to land in the Nest Building stage. The more time and space you create for your new normal in Nest Building, the more wiggle room you give yourself and your partner for your expectations to settle down into reality. With this stage, the more self-care and couple-care you can cram in, the easier the following stages will be.

In fact, now is a good time to pause and put down the book, practice this and just enjoy your family for a while. Because it's not the reading of this guide that can make the most difference, it's putting the advice and skills into action. And you'll be glad you did this now—because the next stage of your journey is going to be a little different. There's a large tidal ocean pool just around the bend…

We're going to take a dive. You're going to look inwards and see how the way you work at a deeper level can challenge you, your partner and your relationship. You'll also see how the way you work at a deeper level has rewards for you, your partner and your relationship—like you may have never seen before.

We're going snorkeling. When you're ready, let's wade in.

# Stage Five: Embracing Your Emotions

## (Your Family's First Year and Beyond)

One of the things that surprises—actually let's get really real here and say shocks or even appalls—most new parents, is the strength of emotions that can wash over you like a Grade Three tsunami. You'll discover yourself capable of elated highs and depressing lows—and everything in between. You're likely to feel extremes—love until it hurts, protectiveness so intense you could kill if you had to, and that some parts of some days are so boring you could scream. A level of patience you never knew you had, or joy so acute it feels like flying. Some days you might feel like a balloon with too much air. Ready to pop.

You might also be plagued with new worries and insecurities. The awesome responsibility of caring for a little one can easily overwhelm you; unending daily chores can leave you feeling depleted or depressed. Physical exhaustion, sleep deprivation and the steep learning curves in every stage of parenting, and especially in the beginning, can introduce you to the rawness of yourself. And your partner too. And that's OK.

But the problem is—most of us weren't taught how to manage strong emotions, either in ourselves or in others. And yet, your emotions are what make you human and as you're likely to be finding how, there's no more human time than the early years of family. With the expanded and deepened experiences that come with the territory, you and your partner's emotions will be expanded and deepened too.

Your emotions are also what bond you to your partner. They bring richness and depth to your relationship. Embracing your vulnerability and supporting your partner to embrace theirs too (and *vice versa)*, takes your relationship to a whole new level.

Emotional awareness is something you'll want to teach your children for their own mental, emotional and relationship wellbeing. Because they're not likely to learn this from anyone else—unless they end up in therapy as adults. Let's make it easier for them.

Goggles and flippers on? Got your snorkel? Are you ready to dive in? I'm going to show you what's happening underneath the surface for most parents. I want you to know if any of what you see while we're down here looks familiar to you, you're normal and you're not alone. The more you keep practicing self-care and couple-care, the more often you'll be able to come up for air when you need to, the more you'll enjoy swimming below the surface with your partner and the more you'll both begin to appreciate the hidden wonders in the deep.

## Feeling Shocked

*I can't believe being a parent is such constant, unrelenting activity and responsibility. When does it get easier? I feel.... I don't even know the word for it!*

Feeling like things will never be quite the same again, on the outside, on the inside and maybe between you and your partner, it's no wonder you're feeling overwhelmed. Writer Meredith Jelbart describes the disorientation, powerlessness and panic of early parenthood as "free-falling." Does this fit for you?

**CHECK YOUR COMPASS:**

**You're normal.** Most parents feel dazed and confused for a while and it's easy to be unsettled with all the new issues and responsibilities that come with parenthood. Shock has a purpose—it acts as a buffer, numbing and protecting your brain from being too overwhelmed initially. Shock gradually wears off, allowing you to eventually adjust to the reality of your situation. Water is cold when you first get in, but start to swim, and you'll warm up.

**"Babyshock" might not affect you straight away**. When you're in the middle of a stressful situation, all your focus and energy tend to go into coping with the immediate concerns. You might find you get a delayed reaction and the after-effects creep up some time later. Some couples can pull together in the middle of a crisis, draw on each other for support, only to find that they start unraveling after it's passed and they finally come up for air, and then they're left wondering "why now?" This is a normal reaction to an unexpected stress.

**Knowledge is power**. Research tells us some couples will be more shocked at the changes than others. If you considered yourselves alike and equal before your baby, you're more likely to be taken aback at the drift into traditional gender roles we spoke about before, where there's a greater divide between your worlds. The more equal beforehand, the bigger the shock may be afterwards. Professional couples, especially highly educated ones who delayed starting a family, will tend to be more impacted because life before and life after can be so different. Not fun at the time—but normal.

**STEPS:**

**Give yourself permission to be a learner**. You don't have to be an expert—learning is so much more fun! Take a step back; give yourself (and your partner) room to grow and time to find your feet. Don't put pressure on yourselves to know or do more than you're capable of.

**Don't keep it inside.** Get it out. Talking about what's shocking to you helps it to wear off and allows you to integrate new experiences into your growing mother- or father-selves. It also gives other parents permission to share in return. This could be the beginning of some great friendships.

**Break things down**. Re-examine expectations. Scale down goals. Prioritize them. Do one at a time. For more on coping with extreme shock, such as from a distressing birth experience, see Part III.

## Feeling Out of Control

*I was led to believe that once I got the baby to sleep through the night in a few months, I would have it all under control. That's what my partner expected too. What a joke! Our son is 11 months now and some nights he's still in our bed.*

*I got so frustrated I had to lock myself in the bedroom for a while.*

*I nearly spanked our toddler the other day, but then I realized it might have made me feel better, but it wasn't actually going to help her.*

Parents are often dismayed by how out of control they feel. "Getting the baby into a routine" sounds so much simpler in theory, doesn't it? So does "managing a tantrum" or "being consistent with discipline." Yeah, right.

We can cope with feeling out of control for a little while, but it's hard to prepare for what this means with a baby or child. At the point where you realize you're unable to establish control, you may feel as if you're is "losing" to the baby.

But "OK, you win," can be a slippery slope from powerlessness to despondency to despair. When you hope for things to be a certain way, but feel stuck in what you don't want, and feel unable to do anything about them, it can lead to depression.

Partners can give up too—sometimes by leaving it up to moms.

**CHECK YOUR COMPASS:**

**This too, shall pass.** As you and your baby or growing child become more familiar with each other's moods and rhythms, some sense of getting on top of things will return. It tends to happen in increments—when the baby settles into a routine, when they *finally* start sleeping through the night or when they begin daycare or preschool. By reclaiming little chunks of your life, you'll start to feel like yourself again. There's more to come on this in the next stage.

**The Serenity Prayer**: "God grant me the serenity to accept the things I cannot change; courage to change the things I can; and wisdom to know the difference." Repeat as needed. And again.

**Frustration can fuel motivation** for working on the things you *can* change. One of the things you have the most control over is the quality of your relationship with your little ones. Have a great connection with them and as they grow and learn self-mastery, they will naturally want to please you. This reduces the potential for negative behavior—and the need for discipline.

**STEPS:**

**Share your struggles.** Let your partner know what you're going through. They may, or may not, understand but expect them to respect your experience and be supportive. If they struggle with this, you might have to urge them to become more empathetic.

**Be slow to blame.** When you feel out of control, it's easier to blame others. This is a protective reaction that says, "I can't deal with this, so you'll just have to." But remember, when you blame someone, you assign responsibility and control to them and leave yourself even more powerless. When you take responsibility (response-ability) for a situation, you can start to manage it.

**Acknowledge your feelings.** Admit to feeling out of control and share these feelings. Owning feelings helps them to wash through you, rather than being stored up and risk becoming fuel for out-of-control behavior.

**Connect with other parents.** The more you share with others, the more normal you'll feel. Unless they give you funny looks. In which case, they're the wrong type of parent to be around. Find some others.

**Yield, don't surrender.** Surrendering means completely letting go of your power. It won't feel like a choice and may leave you resentful. Yielding means choosing not to use your power at that time. You can concede in that particular situation just to get through it, then recover and gather your resources to be prepared for the next one.

## Feeling Overwhelmed

*I'm exhausted just from the intensity of it all—the responsibility, the demands, the worry, the guilt.*

*I'm stretched to the limit with one and we're just about to have our second.*

Early parenthood *is* overwhelming. So is having more than one little person in the house, especially if the second (or third, or more…) pregnancy is a surprise, or closer than expected with the others.

Parents of children of all ages can still feel overwhelmed at times. I often hear parents say they don't feel ready or prepared for the stage their children are at, even parents of teens.

**CHECK YOUR COMPASS:**

**Expectations—again.** Separate what you can do, from what you can't. Some of what overwhelms you may be due to unrealistic expectations from yourself or others. Let go of them. Let them float away. This becomes easier the more children you have.

**What are you feeling?** When people feel overwhelmed, it's often because they're experiencing a number of mixed emotions simultaneously that they're unable to make sense of. Separating and identifying the different (and often conflicting) emotions is the beginning of a deeper relationship with yourself.

**A good habit.** As you look after your little people and meet their needs, get into the habit of asking yourself throughout the day, "What do *I* need now?"

**You are not in this alone.** Your partner is not only your partner in life but also in parenthood. They're there to share all of it—the worries, the responsibilities, the adjustments—and the joys.

**STEPS:**

**Be prepared.** There will be other times in your life when you feel overwhelmed. Accept this is normal and then you can put your energy into find ways to navigate it.

**Let others in.** Establish your own village—you'll always need it. And it's never too late.

**Say no—to people asking for your time or energy**. As a parent with a young child or family, both of these are limited now. Anyone who really cares about you will understand. Tough luck if they don't.

**Talk about it**. When we're overwhelmed, we often have a need to get stuff out to clear our minds and unburden our hearts and shoulders. Talk to your partner, other parents, friends and family. Notice if they listen well and how they respond to you. Find better listeners if you need to.

**Teach others how to treat you.** If their relationship is important and the person doesn't know how to respond supportively, teach them: "What I really need from you right now is…." Ask them to let you know what they need when their time comes.

Break things down into tasks (what has to be done, not what you want to get done) or periods of time (morning, afternoon, evening) and set small, manageable goals. Ask, "What's most important right now?" It may be to rest and let your head clear.

## Feeling Disenchanted

*This is going to sound silly, but I really thought, as we held our beautiful baby for the first time, that from now on I would always feel this much in love with my husband.*

*My husband always said I was his princess. Since we had the twins, I feel more like Cinderella.*

Thanks to Hollywood, many of us expect that getting married and becoming parents is the "Happily Ever After." You may have heard some parenting horror stories from friends, but it's so easy to believe that anything like that won't happen to you.

Depending on your birth experience, for a time, it can feel blissful. Your baby is so beautiful, and precious, and snuggly, and you're so proud of yourselves, and each other and what you've made together, that it couldn't be any other way.

But slowly (or quickly), thanks to hormones and the reality of life with a tiny baby, delight can all too quickly turn into dismay.

Eventually you come back down to earth. The romance has passed and there might be a feeling of anticlimax, restlessness, dissatisfaction or even confusion or frustration. You can't blame the baby, of course, because the baby is just absolutely and completely gorgeous, so you may look to each other as the source of your disappointment. At this point, you're entering a postpartum period of adjustment that I call "disenchantment."

There's a deep part of the pool just over here where the water is darker. An octopus lives there, can you see it? You may need to look deeper.

**CHECK YOUR COMPASS:**

**Understand why.** Disenchantment is often due to unrealistic expectations. The higher the expectations, the farther the fall.

**Disenchantment is an "in-between" state.** It happens as a result of timing. If you committed to each other, or got married when you were still in the Coming Together stage, then you're already naturally moving towards the Growing Apart stage at about the same time you're starting a family. Disenchantment naturally occurs as romance wears off.

If you're already in the Growing Apart stage when you're becoming parents, having a child is a great distraction; it's easy to get swept up in the excitement and anticipation, taking attention away from potential conflicts. However, the unresolved issues will inevitably come up again—along with feelings of disenchantment.

**Disenchantment is normal.** After the first year or so of being together, issues normally start to creep in, and you may start to feel disillusioned. You may even have thought it's because something is missing and the solution is to have a baby, rather than realizing disenchantment is a natural stage of relationship development.

**STEPS:**

**Include your partner.** Research shows the most disenchanted are mothers who thought their partner would be more involved with the baby before the birth but then had their expectations disappointed. Not surprisingly, they show more dissatisfaction with their relationship.

**Own your part.** If disenchantment is a result of your previously unacknowledged and unspoken expectations, take responsibility for them now that you have the guidelines to share them. Don't blame your partner. Blame is likely to only lead to conflict and leave you both feeling powerless to change things. Put your energy into talking and moving forward together instead.

**Own your hopes and expectations**—they are, of themselves, not a bad thing. You might find your partner had similar expectations and is feeling a disenchanted too. Don't take it personally. It means you're in it together; find empathy for each other.

**Connect with other parents.** Common experiences bring some kind of "normal" back. Find other parents to swim with. Beware though, blowing off steam with someone who enjoys trashing your partner will not be helpful.

## Not Sure What You're Feeling

*I hear so many mothers saying how much they just love being a mom. I'm afraid to say that, right now, I don't. In fact, I don't really know how I feel.*

*I just feel numb.*

It's not unusual for either parent to feel a bit "meh"—some ambivalence—about their role at times, especially when you're new at it, or it's a new stage of your child's development—toddlerhood especially.

It may be because you've started a family because of expectations of your partner, friends or family. If you have unresolved issues with your own parents, or mixed feelings about your childhood, you're more likely to feel ambivalent—so too, if you don't "feel ready," or up for the responsibility of being a parent.

Unmet expectations can also lead to feelings of ambivalence. If you thought you'd feel complete, contented and settled, you may find yourself insecure, anxious or restless instead. This can also affect your confidence and self-esteem.

Mothers can feel ambivalent, especially if your jump from paid work to housework seems more like a downward plunge. Both parents can feel ambivalent when work, social life or personal ambitions have been majorly disrupted.

If your experience of birth was traumatic, you're much more likely to feel ambivalent. We'll explore that closer to the end of our journey in Part III.

**CHECK YOUR COMPASS:**

**Ambivalence can be a mix of emotions**—worry around the "bigness" of parenthood, fear or uncertainty of outcomes, resentment about upended lifestyles, indignation about suddenly becoming a supporting actor in our own life.

**Ambivalence can also be a sign** of unresolved issues from the past. A situation now may remind you of different feelings about a similar situation from long ago.

For example, while we're floating here together for a bit, let me share that I absolutely love Christmas with my husband and our children. But for a long time when our kids were young, I felt a bit ambivalent about the whole day, but I didn't know why. Then I realized that day also reminded me of the sad Christmases of my childhood because my parents were divorced. Somebody was always missing. When I eventually became aware of this, I realized I had mixed feelings. Being aware of the sadness was the beginning of working through it so I could just enjoy this special day with my family.

**In the middle.** Ambivalence is also the space between contradictory feelings. You have always had the capacity to hold contradictory emotions almost simultaneously, but with the massive stretch of parenthood, you'll find the tension between extreme love and extreme frustration is greater.

**Welcome to you.** The better you get to know yourself—what you're feeling, thinking and wanting—the less you will experience ambivalence and the quicker and more easily you will work with your feelings and find yourself happier or more at peace. Don't fight your feelings—let them be. That's part of becoming your new you.

**STEPS:**

**Sit with your feelings.** If you resist or avoid your feelings, they have a curious ability to shape-shift into other emotions. For example, unexpressed sadness or disappointment can often become anger. When you can identify and name your feelings, you can start to deal with them. You'll move more quickly through ambivalence then.

**Share your feelings.** Your partner is the only other person in the world who knows the contradiction of just how joyful and how challenging parenting your child can be. Use this common experience as a joint source of comfort (and maybe have a good laugh) while you work through mixed feelings.

**Use other parents as an anchor.** Share with others who are willing to be honest too, so you know you're normal and not alone.

## Feeling Frustrated and Angry

*Since I became a mother, I've never known myself to be so angry. It just seems to take me over at the drop of spilled milk. Sometimes I take it out on my partner or my sister when she comes to help. I hate myself, but I can't seem to help it.*

*My husband yelled at our toddler for the first time yesterday. It shocked me.*

I take my job as a Parenthood Tour Guide very seriously, so I'm going to share with you that frustration and anger are part and parcel of the parenthood experience. Often these feelings are simple and justified. Anger about the poor condition of play areas, frustration about not being able to go out for a quick coffee without taking a ton of stuff or annoyance that your partner left the fridge door open or the toilet seat up—again.

Simple. But feelings of frustration and anger can also accumulate over days, weeks, months and years—simmering below the surface and threatening to blow up. These festering feelings then get triggered by minor things like spilled milk.

### CHECK YOUR COMPASS:

**What's your soundtrack?** Have you ever noticed that when you're frustrated or angry, you can mull over all the reasons why you should feel this way? Have you ever noticed this just keeps you angry or frustrated longer?

**Below the surface.** Frustration and anger are often the leftovers from a mix of deeper, more vulnerable emotions—powerlessness over a situation you thought you could control—disappointment or guilt over unmet expectations; insecurity or loneliness. They can pressure-cook until they're triggered by a partner or child.

**Into the future**. There's a good chance that frustration and anger, like resentment, can trouble you well into the future in terms of your health, your friendships, your wider family relationships and the environment you create for your own, because they can be stored indefinitely.

**Beware flooding.** Sometimes situations may trigger intense emotions that stress you so much you become physically overwhelmed. You're more likely to lash out and hurt others under these circumstances because your fight/ flight/ freeze reaction has been activated.

**Know how to achieve emotional wellbeing**. You can create this in yourself and support your partner and your child as they grow. Separate the feeling from the behavior. The rule of thumb is this: emotions are always OK (they make us human), but how we *express* our emotions may not be. So, it's OK to be angry, but it's not OK to lash out at someone. Learn to channel your emotions so you don't lose control. And you *do* have to find appropriate ways to express your feelings, because when you don't get stuff out, you're likely to carry it around inside of you and it can affect your mood, which is no fun for you or your family. You may want to find a counselor to guide you farther along this part of the path.

**STEPS:**

**Remember how your brain works.** Automatic, uncontrolled anger is activated in the "bottom" part of your brain. Take a few deep, calming breaths and go "up to the top" by saying to yourself, "I feel____ because _____." This is the beginning of short-circuiting the fight/flight/freeze reaction and gaining self-control. It will get easier with time.

**Contain flooding.** Take time out. Shut yourself in your bedroom or go for a run. Frustration and anger have strong body reactions that often need a physical channel, so punch a pillow or have a good cry and let them wash through you. Come back when you've released them.

**Examine your expectations—again.** Are you getting angry and frustrated with yourself, your partner or your child because one of you hasn't lived up to some half-realized expectation? Go easy.

**Talk things out—regularly.** Frustration and anger are often a result of unspoken experiences that get jumbled up inside you. Talking prevents them from building on top of each other.

**Use energy as motivation.** If you're frustrated or angry because you feel you're being mistreated in some way, use the energy that builds up inside positively. Anger and frustration are source of great energy to harness and assertively address a situation.

**Support your partner to support your child.** If your partner is struggling, reflecting to them what you can see happening (e.g., "I can see you're getting frustrated because he's not cooperating. Do you want me to step in?"), you not only help your partner to calm down, you also prevent a situation from escalating.

## Feeling Resentful

*My husband is doing everything he can to continue living his "before children" mindset. He has it so easy, just going to work each day and then coming home and doing whatever. I think he has no right to go do anything without us, because I never get to do anything without them.*

Resentment is a form of anger, and a normal, natural response towards someone who has broken your trust, acted unfairly or otherwise behaved in ways that infringe on you, but with whom you're also unwilling or unable to confront. Resentment *seems* to "protect" you from people who you feel vulnerable with and who you're afraid to risk being hurt again—but if not recognized, and stored instead, it's harmful for both you and for them.

Because where shame is the cancer of the soul, resentment is the cancer of relationships. Resentment builds when issues go unmanaged and then cause more issues. Resentment clouds your perspective and eats away at happiness. It can linger long after the situation that initially caused it. Resentment can build up over time and ruin a family—even affecting a next generation who can grow up just accepting that parts of their extended family "don't talk." Have you ever noticed this?

**CHECK YOUR COMPASS:**

**Expectations—again.** Resentment is often a result of unrealistic, unspoken or unmet expectations. The first two aren't fair to your partner. Even though you may be resentful, you probably don't really expect your partner to change jobs, give up their friends or become a completely different person.

**Understanding—again**. You may be resentful because you don't have all the facts. Resentment breeds in the muddy waters of misunderstanding, lack of information and assumptions you make about your partner or about how they feel towards you.

I'm going to take you on an even deeper dive here.

It's even possible that the roots of resentment are not in your current relationship but left over from a previous one. Maybe, at some level something your partner did, or the way they said something, reminds you of a parent, older sibling or previous partner.

**STEPS:**

**Shift the focus.** Take the focus off your partner and tune in to what you need and what you can do. In a non-blaming way, share what you've learned about yourself and ask for support.

**Talk together.** Often—not just about the what's, but the why's and the how's. Usually, you'll find it's your partner's behavior that's distressing, but if you understand where they're coming from, it's lessened—the more understanding, the less distress. Your partner needs to understand your what's, why's and how's as well.

**Acknowledge each other.** Often. It's easy to feel overlooked and unappreciated with that gorgeous little one taking center stage. Let your partner know you still see them and are grateful for what they do for your family. The more they feel appreciated, the more involved they'll be—and your lives won't be quite so different anymore.

*Since I became a dad, I can't help but feel resentful towards my old man—that he wasn't a better father to me.*

*My mom let me down in so many ways. I get really angry when I think about her.*

Parenthood is a time of looking back, as well as looking forwards, and you can't help but compare the parent you are, with the one they were. Often, they'll fall short. But blame is not always placed fairly. There may be reasons why your parents parented as they did. A major one is that they had little information about the effects of different parenting styles on a child's development.

**CHECK YOUR COMPASS:**

**Times have changed, thankfully!** Parents in previous generations believed it was their prime responsibility to shape us as model citizens. The old way of thinking was this: if they controlled your behavior, it made you "good" children—and meant they were good parents. Some parents tried too hard. You might feel anger or loss around not having a childhood that met all your needs, and there may be grieving to do. If this is the case, we will work our way to that. Part III has more support for this.

**Parents raise children to fit** into the families or environment they're born into. If a parent experiences the world as a rough, violent place, they'll try to bring up their children with the skills to cope with this—toughen them up, build strong muscles. Sadly, this just creates a world where more of us have to be this way. And if your parents were abusive, you'll likely have a longer journey of unlearning, new learning and healing ahead.

**STEPS:**

**Invite your parents to open up.** If you want, if they're around and your parents are willing, now is a natural time to talk with them about your childhood. In a non-blaming way. Compare your life with your children to theirs when you were the same age and invite them to fill in the gaps. You may gain information that helps alleviate anger, resentment or sadness that you may have carried around for a very, very long time.

**Get rid of the baggage**. It's amazing how much energy you'll find and how much lighter you'll feel if you can off-load the baggage we can all carry around with us. It's such a relief.

**This may involve forgiveness.** If it does, forgive for your own sake—not theirs. Forgiveness doesn't mean forgetting what they've done or letting your guard down. It means letting go of the destructive feelings you have inside you, feelings that cause you distress, but the other person is probably not even aware of. Forgiveness means looking after yourself by putting that energy to better use—for healing. The more resentment you let go, the more space you make for healing. Forgiveness is both a decision and a process.

## Feeling Anxious

*I don't know if this is normal or not, but since we've had a child, I find there is so much more to worry about! I can't make my partner understand.*

*I keep the house spotless—not a thing out of place. I'm always worried my husband or the kids will mess it up.*

Anxiety feels a bit like fear, but with fear, you usually know what you're afraid of. Anxiety, on the other hand, is a response to uncertainty—a fear of the *unknown*—and not knowing its cause, can make you more anxious.

Becoming a family comes with a whole bunch of unknowns, so it's normal to feel some anxiety. Whether it's "normal" or not, depends on the degree and how it's affecting you and your partner.

Anxiety can be mild, with vague, unsettling feelings that come and go (e.g., parental performance anxiety—is she latching on properly? Am I doing this right?). Or it can be from worries about children of all ages (e.g., what if she gets a cold? Are his grades good enough? Will she ever get a boyfriend? Will he ever leave home?) all the way to extreme fears about yourself or your child. Anxiety can be managed, and we'll talk more about how in Part III.

**CHECK YOUR COMPASS:**

**Stress brings out your vulnerabilities**, making you feel more anxious and less secure.

**Anxiety has a ripple effect**, starting inside, but radiating outwards towards your partner and others close to you. This can trigger anxiety in them—even babies and young children can absorb it. At the bottom of it all, you are more likely to get anxious when you feel disconnected—from yourself, from your partner or from a support system. Connection reduces anxiety.

**Where's your focus?** Notice what's going on inside. Anxiety feels uncomfortable, unpleasant or distressing, and you will naturally want to diminish it. You may look to your partner for some relief. You may become more preoccupied with what you're not getting from them and what they should do to make up for this. Maybe it's to behave differently or to admit their mistake. You may over-focus on a particular issue, rather than what's going on inside you.

**Are you sharing?** If you don't share your anxiety openly with your partner, it's more likely to come out "sideways," and affect them more anyway.

**STEPS:**

**Listen to your self-talk**. You can actually escalate anxiety by winding yourself up: "this is terrible," "I can't cope," "this shouldn't be happening," "I don't know what to do." Self-talk like this can leave you feeling powerless and stuck in the anxiety whirlpool. Replace negative self-talk with positive: "I'll be OK," "I can get help if I need it," "I'm just learning, that takes time." Tell yourself what you need to hear, not what you don't.

**Don't blame your partner for your anxiety**. This won't get to the bottom of the problem and is likely to stir up unnecessary conflict that can make you more anxious. You can, however, expect your partner's support.

**Own your feelings.** Anxiety is a normal response to the unknown. Accepting and naming your feelings is the first step to minimizing and managing them. It's when we ignore feelings that they can get stronger.

**Share them.** Share your anxiety in a non-blaming way with your partner. Ask them to support you in finding ways to manage it. Do they ever feel anxious? How can you support them?

*The other day, I felt dizzy and couldn't breathe. I went to the doctor and he said I'd had an anxiety attack. My partner and I are both worried about this.*

Anxiety (or panic) attacks are not at all fun, but they're actually fairly common (35% of people experience them), especially during times of transition like graduation, getting married or starting a family. But they are distressing, especially if it's your first, and particularly if you have little ones with you at the time. Knowing what they are, why they occur and what you can do about them will help.

**CHECK YOUR COMPASS:**

**Your body talks to you.** Panic attacks are a result of an accumulation of anxiety in your body, which you may not even have been aware of at the time. They often occur after a period of intense or prolonged stress or after a period of uncertainty *has passed,* but the effects have accumulated in your body and mind. A panic attack is your body's way of signaling, "hey, you need to pay attention to me!"

**Anxiety is usually triggered by stress.** You're more likely to be stressed if you're not looking after yourself physically, mentally or emotionally.

**STEPS:**

**Know how to help yourself.** Panic attacks aren't pleasant, but they are not physically harmful. If you feel a panic attack coming on, try to distract yourself. Don't start to avoid places you think will trigger you—this can fuel more anxious feelings. If you're in the throes of an attack, reassure yourself that it will pass shortly. Managing symptoms, rather than denying them, builds your confidence to cope if there's a next time.

**Enlist your partner's help.** Have conversations about what's stressing you and ways to manage or minimize them. Sharing stress reduces it.

**Exercise regularly.** The best way to move stress energy is to exercise it out. Daily exercise is a natural anti-anxiety and antidepressant. Put the baby in a sling or a stroller and go.

**Consult a professional.** If anxiety doesn't pass with the above strategies, a psychologist or counselor can help you understand the origins of your anxiety and explore further treatment options if necessary.

## Feeling Disappointed

*I was expecting my husband to help more.*

*I took three weeks off work, but most of the time she left me feeling like a spare tire.*

Some mothers have an idea that their partner will be more involved in parenting—both practically and emotionally—than their partner is willing and are naturally sorely disappointed when their expectations are dashed. Other mothers don't want their partner too involved, seeing childcare as their personal domain, only to risk leaving their partner feeling excluded and rejected.

**CHECK YOUR COMPASS:**

**Awareness**. Your partner may be unaware that you need extra support, especially if you have been embarrassed to ask for it. This is exacerbated by a society that expects mothers to be supermoms.

**What about your partner?** It's likely that your partner needs to feel included and valued so they don't feel like they're just an extra pair of hands or a paycheck at the end of the week.

**STEPS:**

**Be specific about what you want.** Keep communication unclogged to avoid disappointment or resentment building up that can fuel conflict.

**Renegotiate.** Children's needs change over a short amount of time, so stay one step ahead of them and on the same page with each other, by renegotiating your involvement regularly. A partner who isn't very involved in their infant's care due to work commitments can be as equally involved as you by the time your little one is old enough to be read to at night or play ball on the weekends. Some couples completely swap parenting roles when their kids start school.

**Unite and conquer.** Find ways to creatively work together, rather than against each other. For example, discipline is a thorny issue between couples. One of you could take the time to read up on ways to avoid the need for discipline, the other could follow the advice. You both support each other.

## Feeling Sad

*I remember it dawning on me after the birth of my son, this new love I'd never felt before, and how my feelings for my partner suddenly paled in comparison. I felt shocked, guilty and sad that things between us would never be the same again. Our romance had died.*

*It's a huge challenge adjusting to the loss of personal space, time with my wife and enjoying her company the way we used to before kids. I've noticed if we don't "fight" to have quality time with each other, things go downhill.*

*Every time Christmas comes around, even though it's great for my kids, I can't help remembering how lousy it used to be for me.*

*I miss my old life.*

With children there are many, many gains. But in any period of transition there are inevitably some losses too—it might be the loss of expectations, parts of yourself, time spent with your partner, or your sense of freedom. The intensity of your feelings will depend on how significant the loss is to you—some will be minor, others sorely felt.

Some losses may be subtle, unexpected and difficult to explain (like unconsciously missing aspects of your pre-baby self or your pre-baby relationship). It's possible to even grieve the loss of a hope, a future you thought you would have, or a past you never wanted for yourself.

It can be a time of fare-welling a great career, even if you're willing to give it up, regret about not travelling more before you had babies (that's one of mine, but I'm making up for it now), or sadness that you didn't grow up in a loving family of your own.

It's normal for parents to be faced with situations they didn't expect to feel sad about. You may have grieved the end of your pregnancy, the feeling of the baby in the belly. You may have wanted a natural birth, feel that you didn't get to go through "real" labor, and ended up with a cesarean scar instead.

There can be a sense of loss if you needed assisted conception or IVF, and you didn't get to experience a "natural" pregnancy. Or if you weren't able to conceive and found your baby through adoption.

Mothers can feel a sense of loss at being unable to breastfeed or give it up sooner than expected. These situations can leave you feeling that you have somehow "failed" and grieving your first hopes for your mother-self.

Fathers experience their own losses too. They can miss being the most important person in their partner's life—that they have somehow been replaced. Changes in lifestyle, loss of independence (especially if they're the ones at home with the baby) and an absence of a satisfying sex life are other big adjustments for most dads.

There are other things to miss as well: time, spontaneity, freedom and privacy. I remember grieving the end of my relationship with my husband as we knew it, the easy, lingering, uninterrupted times of fun, sharing and relaxation.

If the degree of loss is significant enough, it's likely to send you through a process similar to the one of grief. We'll talk about that in a moment.

**CHECK YOUR COMPASS:**

**You're normal.** Most parents anticipate the gains and good times, but not the losses or farewells, and then think there must be something wrong with them. They will have conflicting emotions about the various pluses and minuses of parenthood. It's normal and OK. It doesn't mean you don't love your child, or love being parents, or love each other. It just means you're human.

**Parenthood is bittersweet.** Each milestone—first word, first step, first ride on a bike—can bring mixed feelings "he's not a baby anymore" and "they just grow up so fast." Parents of twins (who only wanted two children) can feel sad that they won't get to do the whole "baby thing" again, as some have described it.

**It will continue**—the first day of: preschool, middle, high school, college. Each new stage means saying goodbye to the old one. You have a lifetime of this ahead of you, so the earlier you accept and learn to ride the waves of loss, and comfort each other through them, the easier it will become.

**Parenthood is a time for new aspects of old grief**. If one or both of your own parents are ailing or have died, parenthood is a time when you're likely to feel this keenly, even if it was some time ago. And it's not just during the birth and newborn period that you may be aware of your sadness. Birthdays and celebrations are likely to be times when your parents are missed all over again.

**What's your relationship with your parents like?** As your relationship with your growing child unfolds, if you didn't have a good relationship with your own parents, you might start to feel the loss from missing out. Special occasions can trigger old memories and the feelings that go with them. Old grief may resurface and need to be dealt with again. If handled sensitively, however, this can lead to healing and reconnecting with your own parents. Even if they have died.

Feelings of loss are common—even if nobody's talking about them.

**STEPS:**

**Get good at grieving**. Knowing how to grieve well is a life skill. Experiencing and expressing pangs of sadness or regret helps them to pass more quickly. Grieving and healing go hand-in-hand. When you allow feelings to wash through you, it creates space for healing.

**Share your feelings with a trusted listener**. If you don't, your emotions can build up over time. Sharing feelings gives others the opportunity to comfort you and allows you to heal.

*I've been feeling all over the place since my baby was born 14 weeks ago. Is this normal or is it postpartum depression?*

A period of emotional adjustment, even though most don't expect it, is completely normal for new parents, and I actually think the stages of grief apply here. Let me explain.

Because most of us go into parenthood so unaware, so unprepared and maybe with such unrealistic expectations, the realities of parenthood can be a huge shock for us—and this can set the stages (in bold) in motion.

For example, with our first baby, I remember being shocked at how constant and relentless it was looking after a new baby. I was almost manic trying to prove to myself, my husband and everybody else how well I was coping (denial). I was constantly irritated with myself and my husband (anger). I came up with all these schemes to get better organized (bargaining), but they only lasted a day or so because I was too tired and scattered to keep them up. I didn't realize I was depressed—I just thought I was totally exhausted. Talking with close mother-friends helped (expression). I did finally come to accept my situation, and things started to improve after that. Looking back, I have to wonder if I was, in fact, grieving.

**CHECK YOUR COMPASS:**

**Are you grieving?** It's normal for new parents, mothers especially, to grieve (perhaps without realizing it) over some parts of their old lives or their old selves, including aspects of the relationship with their partner. But there is little or no recognition of this, which can leave you feeling confused, guilty or ashamed.

Worse than that, not acknowledging, allowing and supporting the "loss" aspect of parenthood can mean that you can get stuck in the process, especially in depression. I actually think the lack of preparation for loss and the lack of opportunity for a facilitated process of adjustment is a contributing factor to the growing number of parents who are experiencing postpartum anxiety (PPA) and depression (PPD).

Current research shows around 33% of mothers and 17% of fathers report anxiety symptoms and 16% mothers and 10% of dads report symptoms of depression. Take into account that these are *reported* experiences; the real figures are probably much higher.

And when we think about life changes, it makes sense that one study found women who'd had successful careers prior to motherhood had higher risk for PPD. Perhaps they had more losses to grieve?

**STEPS:**

**Talk about it**—with your partner and with other mothers. Share what you miss and ask what they miss too. Just sharing at this honest level can be comforting.

**Work out what you can change and what you can't.** There's no point wasting energy on what you can't change, you'll just be more exhausted. Grieve the losses you can't change and then turn your focus to what you can.

**Make a plan.** Think of ways you can realistically include things that you miss into your new life. Is it catching up with old friends? A night out occasionally? A hobby or interest? Your old job part-time from home? Make them a priority again.

## Feeling Guilty

*Sometimes not everything gets done, sometimes the baby doesn't get bathed and the dishes sit there for days. Most of the time I'm OK, but I have those moments when I'm in bed and I can see the baby next to me and hear my son in the other room and I think they deserve more.*

Not living up to a birth plan. Breastfeeding didn't come naturally. Bonding didn't happen right away. Wanting to spend time away from your baby. Knowing you're neglecting your partner, but not having the energy to do anything about it. Missing life-before, spending money you may not think you've earned. The competing demands of work and children leave you feeling like you're failing in both areas—the pile of things to feel guilty about is endless.

**CHECK YOUR COMPASS:**

**Are you beating yourself up?** We lost the shared wisdom and support for parents when we lost the village. Books and parenting courses can only take you so far. Hospitals send mothers home far too early, before you're fully recovered and confident about breastfeeding and baby care and most people severely underestimate the need for postpartum support.

**There is healthy guilt.** Healthy guilt is a sign that you've done something that doesn't feel right to you and an emotional energy that motivates you to make amends and modify your behavior so you can respond differently in the future.

**"Mother guilt" is not healthy guilt.** The guilt many mothers feel is the result of totally unreasonable cultural and social expectations that you can allow to seep in and infect how you feel about yourself. Guilt is also closely linked with self-esteem. Inoculate yourself from expectations that unfairly weigh you down.

**Guilt will continue if you don't address it.** There will be a lifetime of things to feel guilty about if you let them. Shop-bought birthday cakes, recycled Halloween costumes, letting someone else's child eat too much candy. Buying food that's not organic. I'm happy to put my hand up and say I've done it all. Heck, on a bad week I gave my kids 2-minute noodles three nights in a row—microwaved. And I'm OK with all that. It doesn't make me a bad parent; it means there were times I was completely exhausted and needed more help. You will be too. You can only do the best you can do at the time. Keep expectations of yourself in line with the reality—of this particular week. Next week may be different.

**Where's your boundary?** Decide what to let in and what to let bounce off. Who you are going to let define you—others, or yourself? Whoever you let define you also has sway over your self-esteem. Trust me, you don't want anyone else to be in charge of this.

**STEPS:**

**Think about what you really want.** Do you want to be perfect or real? Have a tidy home or a good day? Don't put pressure on yourself to be perfect. Repeat after me: *happy and relaxed, happy and relaxed, happy and relaxed*.... Your whole family will benefit.

**Value what you do.** If you were working *any* other job 24/7, you would deserve time off. You wouldn't be expected to do more than one thing at a time and you would feel completely justified in rewarding yourself and being rewarded. In so many ways, mothers (and stay-at-home-partners) are devalued, which can leave you feeling guilty about things you used to think were your right to have. Don't buy into it.

**Value you.** If you're sick, get your partner or someone else to stay home so you can rest. Take time out, even if you don't think you deserve it. You do! You'll soon see the benefits of having regular "me time"—for yourself and your family. After a particularly harrowing day, or yucky week, treat yourself. I'm a big believer in self-compensation. The next time you have an all-nighter, plan for time off pampering ASAP.

**Don't be a martyr.** Continually sacrificing your needs for the sake of others breeds anger and resentment—you towards yourself, you towards your family, and later them towards you. Regularly saving time and energy for you brings balance.

**Let your partner know if you're not getting the support you expect.** If the unreasonable expectations are coming from your partner, it's time for a healthy discussion—maybe more than one.

**Build self-esteem from the inside out**. Healthy self-esteem protects you from unwarranted expectations and judgments of others, and also the unrealistic cultural and social pressures to be a people pleaser and emotional caretaker. Rather than listening to outside voices, tune in and listen to your own inner voice and turn up the volume instead.

## Feeling Jealous

*I hate how he can just come and go as he pleases, and I'm just stuck here all day and all night.*

*You'd think I'd just fallen off the face of the planet since our son came along.*

Feelings of jealousy are normal for both partners. Mothers can feel jealous of her partner's opportunities to "escape," to more freely spend money, to be impulsive or spontaneous or to make decisions that don't have to consider the needs of a baby. Fathers can feel left out of the planning, excitement and support leading up to the birth. They can feel ignored during it and excluded from bonding afterwards.

At a time when you expected to be more in love than ever, twinges of jealousy can be surprising. Both parents can feel like the baby has somehow replaced them in their partner's affections and this needs to be addressed.

### CHECK YOUR COMPASS:

**What needs work**? Which family relationship needs more TLC? Your partner may need more bonding time with baby or it might be the bond between the two of you that needs some extra attention.

**Build trust.** Nurturing your relationship is the antidote for jealousy.

### STEPS:

**Ask for what you need**—attention, reassurance, one-on-one time or the opportunity to hash out what's bothering you. Parents who are preoccupied with the baby simply may not be aware of losing touch with each other.

## Not Feeling Much at All

*I've been through a roller coaster of emotions since becoming a mother, but my husband just is not on the same ride. He doesn't seem to feel much at all.*

Becoming a father is likely to have impacted your partner more than anything he's ever experienced up until now. That being said, his life simply hasn't changed *as fast or as far* as yours, and this will be reflected in your emotions. While he's getting used to life on a merry-go-round, you're probably white-knuckled on the big dipper.

It's also a common misconception that men don't have feelings like women do. This is only partly true. Of course, men have feelings, but they might not experience or express them in the same *ways.* This difference can cause problems in relationships, especially when a woman interprets her partner's *not revealing* his emotions as *not caring.* He may experience her distress at this as criticism—causing him to clam up even more.

**CHECK YOUR COMPASS:**

**A new perspective.** Think about your partner's role-models. They may have grown up in a family where they didn't see male role-models expressing many emotions. This can send a powerful message to boys: don't feel, and if you do, *don't show it.*

**Understand and respect the ways your partner is different.** Women tend to talk to other women. We get more practice and become comfortable revealing our vulnerabilities and expressing ourselves. Men may have far fewer opportunities to bring their inside stuff outside with other men. If they had more practice, they might have more confidence.

**Move towards each other and meet halfway.** Problems begin when couples turn away from each other to cope with the gap between them, but this just widens the gap farther. Your emotion may overwhelm him; his lack of emotion will leave you underwhelmed. Pull yourself up into your head and speak from your thoughts initially to give him time to gradually settle into his feelings. Then you can connect on both your thought and feeling levels. Relationship counseling can help facilitate this.

**STEPS:**

**Don't wait for your partner to initiate conversations.** They probably won't feel the same urgency to share what's going on inside, because for them it may not be that big a deal. But be sure you do initiate a conversation, especially if your partner has been turning away from you by working harder, escaping into alcohol or drugs, losing themselves online or gaming, or spending more time with friends—all common coping mechanisms. Even in happy relationships, most of the time it's the woman who will bring up relationship issues.

**Give your partner opportunities to find out what your day is like.** Let them take the reins on the weekends. Not as punishment (although it may feel like it), but so they can actually experience, rather than just listen to, life as you know it. Spending time with their child is good for both of them—to develop confidence in his parenting abilities. And it's good for you to have a break.

## Feeling More Sensitive

*Since becoming a mother, I feel more sensitive to the plight of other mothers, even if they live on the other side of the world*

*When my wife passed over our baby, I held him in my arms for the first time. It filled a big void in my life I didn't even know existed.*

*I can't believe it, I cry in movies now that I'm a dad.*

One of the most amazing, but often unexpected and sometimes painful things that can happen when you become a family is that you can feel more sensitive to other's joys, fears and sorrows. Empathy means you sense and understand the felt-experience of another person. You don't just try on their shoes; you walk in them long enough for them to pinch.

**CHECK YOUR COMPASS:**

**Honor this.** The ability to feel empathy is a *significant* developmental milestone in your life. It signals a huge leap in psychological and emotional growth.

**It has impact.** It can be tricky if only one parent suddenly develops a significant capacity for empathy. The good news is empathy can be cultivated.

**Empathy is a gift.** Where both partners experience a new or deepened sense of empathy, it can lead to wonderful things in our families, our communities—and in our world.

**STEPS:**

**Support your partner in developing empathy**. Empathy is a learned skill. First, you need to develop self-awareness; you can't identify and be sensitive to what another person feels unless you are familiar with that feeling inside you first. The second step is self-acceptance; you can only accept the full spectrum of another's range of feelings when you are first comfortable with your own. With awareness and acceptance, it's only a short distance to understanding and then to empathy.

**Create safety**. Unless they first feel it's safe to do this, your partner won't be able to go inwards and explore, or have the confidence to say, what's happening inside.

**Model empathy**. Respond to your partner in the way you want to be responded to.

## Feeling Contentment, Joy, Gratitude, Hope and Love Like You've Never Felt Before

*IVF was absolute hell.*
*Finally deciding to adopt brought hope back into our lives.*

*Teething was pretty ordinary, and controlled crying was gut-wrenching, we won't be doing that again! The transition from breastfeeding to solids was downright painful; toilet training has been frustrating; and the first morning at pre-school was depressing. Other than that—I'm really enjoying it!*

*Seeing my partner's love for our baby, well….*

In this stage, we've spoken about what people often refer to as "negative" emotions. But as you've learned, *all* your emotions are important; they're all signals to pay attention to, listen to and learn from. They guide you to what you need to thrive.

And besides, once you're prepared for surviving the challenges in the different stages, as you're working through them now, you'll have more left over for all the joys, delights and wonders of parenthood. And there are so many of them. Parents generally describe themselves as happier and more fulfilled and their life as having more meaning than non-parents. And nothing can compare to the love of a child.

Now, if you're also doing a good job of self-care and couple-care, and embracing your new emotions, you'll be at least a little ahead of the curve for the next stage, and you're likely to find it easier to navigate than if you hadn't been doing the work in each stage up until now.

Speaking of self-care, now might be a good time to take a break. What do you need to do? I ask because the next stage is also challenging—we're about to go even deeper.

# Stage Six: Nurturing Your Parent-Selves

## (Your Family's First Few Years and Beyond)

Up to now, although the landscape you have traveled through may be different for each of you, you have been going through the stages pretty much as a couple. In this next stage of the journey however, you may find yourselves travelling large parts of it alone. And feeling lost.

Because, while most of us expect having a baby will, in some ways, change our life, what most of us don't expect is that having a baby also will, in some ways, change our *selves.* Parenthood is as much a deep inner journey of the self as it is something you take with your partner. For them too.

Your sense of who you are as a parent, your level of vulnerability, your self-esteem, and how you feel about yourself, your partner, your own parents and even your friends (especially the ones who are still going out partying) and even how you feel about the world you are bringing your child into can shift. Your relationships can change when you change, and *vice versa.* That's a lot of change.

As aspects of your life shift, you may find you change aspects of yourself in order to adapt. You might feel expanded in some ways and reduced in others. Both take some adjustment. For some people, parenthood can feel like a midlife crisis—a time when you re-evaluate yourself, or even discover who you really are for the first time.

And, as challenging as this might be for a woman becoming a mother, or a man becoming a father, imagine what it might be like for your LGBTQ friends.

Parenthood is an invitation to look deeper. Parenthood invites you to the innermost core of yourself—to ask the questions: "What's important to me?" "What do I think, feel and want for myself—for my partner, my family?" And while the asking of these questions can leave you a bit dazed and confused, discovering the answers is where the adventure of discovery on the inside really begins.

But it's challenging. Especially when nobody's talking about this stuff, or if they are, telling you how you should be doing it, or even worse, pretending everything is fine when it's not. It can be hard to find understanding for what you're going through.

And yet, being validated, especially by those closest to us, is a fundamental relationship need. When your inner self is not seen, recognized, acknowledged or appreciated, it can become a quest. You might find you try to meet your need for validation in other ways, like buying the right "thing" or trying too hard to be good at something else. Your partner can do the same.

But the transformation of your identity, probably more than any other change, can lead to being more bonded with your partner. Because the closer you get to the core of yourself, and the more comfortable you are there, the more you can let them in.

## New Aspects of Yourself

*I've been feeling out of sorts since I became a mother. I feel "different" but I can't even put it into words.*

*I experienced immediate growth in becoming a mom. It was a very honest, raw and intense hit of reality and insight. While this helped me in becoming a loving mother, it put a divide in my relationship with my partner. A sudden feeling of responsibility and a newfound depth presented itself to me, but my partner didn't experience it. We grew apart and were operating on entirely different levels, in fact, like strangers.*

*My toddler is out of control. The other day she had a full-scale tantrum in the supermarket. And then I just lost it. I don't know what happened—I was so incredibly humiliated.*

Your sense of identity is based on a number of things, including your appearance, your job, hobbies and interests, your goals and ambitions. All these can change after you become a parent.

Partners often aren't aware of the huge impact having a baby can have on a mother's sense of herself and it can be hard for mothers to put words to. A shifting sense of self is hard to pin down and explain. You might just feel "different" or "not yourself."

It's frustrating trying to explain something that's not clear to you, let alone your partner, especially when you're preoccupied with a baby or toddler and sleep deprived too. What you may be more aware of (and your partner as well) is being snappy, frustrated or confused for no apparent reason, or feeling resentful towards your partner because they didn't have to change as much you do.

When one partner goes through a period of change, it can create a sense of disconnection for both of you. The further you get from your pre-baby self, the further away you can also feel from your partner. It can be lonely when you're experiencing something but can't share it, or your partner doesn't understand when you do.

And then your partner may interpret any difficulty communicating as frustration, criticism or judgment, take it personally and react in ways that leave you both feeling cut off from each other. By understanding what's going on, you can stay connected with yourself—and each other.

**CHECK YOUR COMPASS:**

**New awareness.** Parenthood extends your boundaries. Any new aspects outside the old boundary will challenge your sense of who you thought you were. Sometimes the "old" you can feel at odds with the new-parent part. Maybe you were an artist, but you don't have time for art now—does that mean you're still an artist? This can be very disorienting.

**Where did the guides go?** If you had crossed the threshold into parenthood in a different culture or at an earlier time, rituals and traditions would have guided you. Extended family and community would have provided you with practical and emotional support as you found your feet.

For example, when a new baby arrives in a small town in southern Italy, church bells ring at ten o'clock every morning to remind everyone of the new family's needs. In Bali, a new addition is not just for the immediate family: the whole village comes together to feast, celebrate and make offerings for the baby's future—which is considered a community responsibility.

**Be mindful of your expectations (again).** If you didn't expect becoming a mother would affect you as a person, and it has, you might be feeling some surprise or distress around that.

And if you expect your partner to understand, how might they? Only someone else in the same situation can really, fully understand what it's like. Which is why it's so important to connect honestly with other mothers who may well be struggling with similar issues. That way you'll feel less alone and more "normal" again.

**Your parenting self, and your partner's, will continue to evolve**. Even when you've had children for some time, you're likely to find that as they grow, or a new child arrives (especially if they're a different gender), it can continue to bring out new aspects of you to navigate in your relationship.

I'll give you a personal example. I hated sports as a child. Hated them. But when our children started playing soccer and netball, going to their games was the highlight of my weekend, and of course I was keen for my husband to come too. Him, not so much.

**Your future**. Some of the biggest arguments can arise when children become adolescents. Negotiating appropriate activities or curfews can bring out new aspects of your parent personality, like over-protection (more often mothers) or risk-taking (more often dads) that can then lead to conflict. This can be a big shock if things have run smoothly up until then—but also normal.

**A window for more meaningful connection.** Being able to resolve tricky parenting issues can lead to feeling more bonded than ever with your partner. Be proud of yourselves and each other every time you attempt it, even if you don't get it right.

**STEPS:**

**Don't panic.** What you're experiencing is a natural part of becoming a parent. Find ways to self-soothe and calm yourself so you can develop the deeper voice of your intuition. This is the voice that can guide you through.

**Be transparent.** Let your partner know what's going on, even if you don't fully understand it yourself, and keep talking. Saying something like "I know I've been a bit touchy lately and I'm not really sure why" starts a conversation with your partner that can last as long as the changing does. Chances are, they're going through their own journey of transformation and are also struggling to find the words to describe it. Help each other out.

**Catch your self-talk.** Being self-critical can contribute to anxiety or depression, so it's important you're aware of any negative mind-chatter: "I should know how to do this," "I shouldn't feel this way," or "I'm doing a lousy job." Catch negative statements and replace them with more user-friendly ones like, "it's OK, I'm still learning," "I can do it differently next time" or "I did well." Using positive self-talk goes a long way to increasing your self-esteem.

**Spend time doing things that help you feel like** *you.* Make it a priority ASAP to make (even small) pockets of time to spend indulging your passions, pampering yourself or rekindling your interests—the better you are at loving yourself, the more you'll have left over for loving everyone else. Promise.

**Spend time with friends.** Old friends are your link to the old you, the you that you were before life and love got complicated and messy. Basking in the warmth of good friends nurtures your soul and leaves you feeling renewed again. Do it regularly.

## New Aspects of Your Partner

*I never realized my husband could be so impatient. I ignored it when it was directed at me, but it's a shock to see him getting so frustrated with our son.*

*We disagree on how to manage a tantrum. My husband thinks we should punish our child. I was shocked.*

It's particularly unsettling to see your partner react negatively towards your children, especially if you feel things more keenly on their behalf. And the incredibly powerful protective instinct that comes with parenting makes you want to pounce on anybody that threatens your offspring.

But just as there are times when you will feel impatient, annoyed or angry, so will your partner. Have you ever notice that you're more aware of when your partner is doing the "wrong" thing than when you are?

Whether it's trying to dress a toddler who can't stand still, or refereeing playground disputes, it's important not to make the mistake of jumping in (unless you're asked). It's good for all of you for your partner to experience parenting in all its fullness—the good, the bad and the ugly.

**CHECK YOUR COMPASS:**

**You're both adjusting.** That looks really awkward sometimes.

**There are a lot of annoying but normal behaviors** that come with each stage of childhood. Prepare for them as you're doing with the stages of parenthood now, so your expectations of your child going forward are realistic. This takes the pressure off your little one and gives them room to grow in their own ways, rather than your imposed ones. Knowledge also reduces frustration for all and prepares you to both to deal with your little critter calmly and confidently.

If you or your partner react in a way you regret, use it as a teaching opportunity to model for your child the healing power of a good apology.

**STEPS:**

**Have release valves**. As you've learned, anger and frustration build up, so we need to find release valves to alleviate them. Talking is one way of avoiding an emotion explosion. Have ongoing conversations around the hopes and expectations you each have for your child, so you can then move towards navigating them.

**Talk about the situation away from your child.** Find agreement about parenting strategies. It's not good for a child to think that they're the cause of their parents' arguments—at any age.

**Encourage your partner to have time off.** Just as you need time to yourself and time out from your responsibilities, so do they.

**Encourage your partner to talk to friends**—over a coffee or a beer, or during golf or after tennis. If he doesn't have any dad-friends, but you do, invite them over to share daddy war stories. Spending time with other parents normalizes and validates your experiences and opens extra lines of communication and support for you both. And you never know when you'll need it.

**Recognize the flipside**. Seeing your child bring out the best in your partner is like tapping into a wellspring of love. It's so great when they step in and handle a crisis that you're not coping with—when they tenderly attend to cuts and scrapes, fix a broken toy or spend an hour playing on the floor when you've given up long ago. One of the things that many mothers are most appreciative of is the softer, more sensitive side of their partner that parenthood brings out. *I*t's like falling in love all over again.

## Body Image

*I used to be a skinny sun-bleached blonde and now, over a year after giving birth, I'm still an overweight, housebound brunette. I look in the mirror and I don't recognize myself. I can't imagine what my husband thinks.*

While you may have been prepared for body changes during pregnancy, thanks to another myth of motherhood, you may also have expected that your post-baby body would just bounce back. It can be shocking and depressing when you're left with a baby belly, stretch marks or varicose veins. This can affect your self-esteem.

**CHECK YOUR COMPASS:**

**It takes time to adjust.** Transform the basis for how you feel about yourself. The first step is to recognize that your body's journey is a personal thing. Pregnancy brings about changes that are common to all, but also unique to you. The battle scars you carry are a mark of motherhood from carrying the baby you cherish.

**Have you set a trap for yourself?** Don't compare yourself with other mothers, and certainly not with the dietician-and-personal-trained, and-probably-photo-shopped post-baby bodies of celebrities. They're not really "real." It must be terrible to live a life of starvation diets and manic exercise, living in fear of a photographer leaping from bushes the moment you let your stomach muscles relax. Feel compassion for them—and don't do that to yourself.

**Sharpening focus.** Now's the time to center yourself around what's really important. When you focus too much on your appearance rather than more important issues like health, fitness and wellbeing, you can miss opportunities for deeper personal growth. It's fine to want to look your best, but if your self-esteem depends on it, it can leave you feeling insecure.

Prioritizing health and wellbeing gets you closer to the core of who you are, not just who you are on the surface—and its good preparation for aging gracefully.

**Your body serves you.** Appreciate your body more for what it does than for what it looks like. Your body is a wondrous thing that enables you to do what you want—to live a full life, to express and receive love, to share experiences. Your body has performed the miracle of growing, bearing and nourishing a baby. Notice how it moves and what it's able to achieve and give thanks to it.

**Who is your judge?** What negative judgments are you whispering in your own ear? Use the "Best Friend Rule." If your best friend was looking a bit rough around the edges, would you judge her, or would you give her a hug and help? Would it be more important that she looked good, or that she was well?

**Your partner has a different view.** Partners are usually *much* less concerned about their partner's post-baby body than mothers. While dads may notice the physical changes, it's more often with a sense of wonder and appreciation.

**It *is* important for your partner to be aware** that you may be very sensitive about body issues and that you may need a lot of reassurance about your attractiveness and desirability. You need to be told that you're beautiful, not just in words, but actions too.

**STEPS:**

**Share how you want your partner to respond.** When you open up to your partner, you invite them in. If you don't get the response you were hoping for, let them know in a non-judgmental way what you want to hear instead.

For example, you might complain about your weight to your partner. They might see this as an invitation to problem solve and suggest you join a gym. This can sound like a criticism to you because what you actually wanted to hear is that you're still gorgeous. Once you have been reassured that you are, maybe the next conversation could be that your partner is happy to mind the baby if you want to go for a walk.

**Keep it simple.** What your body needs to feel at its best is simple—well fueled, well exercised and well rested. When you have a small child, the physical toll involved in their care requires you to do a better job of these three things. The better you are at meeting these basic needs, the quicker your body will recover.

**Make yourself a priority.** Parenthood is the perfect time to ask for help, and get others used to the idea that you need it. If being fit wasn't important before, having a child can be a great motivator. You'll cope much better with the rigors of parenthood—surviving fatigue, managing stress and reveling in playground funfests if you're fit. Maybe join a gym with childcare or do evening classes so there's kid-free time too.

When looking after yourself becomes more important than how you look, you know you're on the right track.

## Self-Esteem

*I've gone from a capable career woman, respected for my experience and knowledge, to someone who can feel insecure about menial, day-to-day tasks. WTF?*

When you think of who you are, it's often in terms of qualities you recognize in yourself, or that others might use to describe you: knowledgeable, cheerful or efficient, for example. If I moved you from a situation where you were able to be these things (like on a normal before-baby day) to one where you weren't (like on a normal at-home-with-baby day), you may feel for a while like you've lost yourself.

It's easy, pre-baby, to coordinate a great outfit when nobody's spit up on your shoulder, to be efficient at work where you're in control (as opposed to at home where the baby is), knowledgeable or cheerful after a good night's sleep.

Some mothers are affected by their changes in lifestyle more than others. For example, if you worked long and hard, and invested lots to establish a career before having your baby, you may have a harder time adjusting to motherhood.

When you're used to getting recognition, awards and concrete results for your efforts at work or study, it can be a real challenge to find purpose, fulfillment or a sense of self-worth in the daily grind of motherhood.

Nobody gives you a bottle of champagne for superior diaper changing or an A+ for the quality of packed lunches. Motherhood can feel like it thrusts you into invisibility. Even those of us happy to leave our jobs can miss the dynamic parts of ourselves we may leave behind for a while. It's like taking the leap from *Sex and the City* to *Babes and the 'Burbs.*

A drop in self-esteem is common in new mothers. Not meeting your expectations of yourself, being subjected to other people's judgments and comparisons (even from strangers), dropping in social status if you've left work for a while or completely, feeling isolated and maybe un-sexy too will make even a Goddess Earth Mother Incarnate feel like she's not herself any more.

*I'm more sensitive to my husband's criticism since I became a mother. Is this normal?*

Absolutely. One of the single biggest influences on self-esteem is your partner's attitude towards you. Negative comments from a partner can leave you feeling deflated, devalued and depressed—and is fodder for M-A-J-O-R conflict.

On the other hand, positive feedback supports your self-esteem and increases your confidence in, and enjoyment of, mothering. And while it's important that your partner appreciates and validates your role—it's even more important that *you* do.

**CHECK YOUR COMPASS:**

**You are responsible for your self-esteem.** Healthy self-esteem grows from the inside out. Parenting is the best opportunity you'll have to round out aspects of your own growth.

**A reminder.** This is not a job you were meant to do without support. Your partner has an invested interest in your child being bought up in a warm, loving and secure home—and an equal responsibility to contribute to this.

**STEPS:**

**Be aware of your personal boundaries.** Your partner's attitude towards you doesn't define you—your own does. If he says something negative and you let this affect the way you feel about yourself, it's going to hurt. Let his comments bounce off with a "you don't know what you're talking about" thought of your own. There's a saying that "all criticism is autobiographical."

**Re-evaluate yourself.** Remember I mentioned an identity crisis in Part I? A motherhood identity crisis might mean re-evaluating what gives you a sense of purpose, fulfillment or validation. For me, it was taking my role as a mother as seriously as I had my vocation—researching parenting styles, how to build children's self-esteem and discipline them gently. Be prepared to work these things through with your partner.

**Reconnect with yourself.** If you're taking time off the treadmill of work or academic life, this can be an opportunity to connect with the rich world inside you. You may be surprised at what truly brings you deep satisfaction and joy. If you continue to miss some aspects of your old life, it might be that these things are an important part of who you are. Find ways to integrate them back into your days.

**Grow and heal.** Working on your own personal issues can give parents a real sense of achievement and means you can consciously parent your children instead of being on autopilot. The better you get at parenting, the better you'll feel about yourself.

## Society—The Big Picture

*When I left work to raise our baby, I thought that I was being treated as if I was unemployed, even though I was working much harder than I ever did when I was getting paid.*

*I didn't think women were particularly disadvantaged socially and politically until I became a mother. Suddenly I realized what little importance was given to all the things that were now important to me—like clean local amenities, quality part-time work, affordable childcare or adequate school funding.*

*I was breastfeeding the other day and someone growled at me to "cover up." I was shocked.*

*I want to be a really active dad, but there are so few services that are dad-friendly in our area, it's really discouraged me.*

It's taking a very long time for society to catch up with what parents need and deserve. Both parents can be disadvantaged by the attitudes they bump into in the local and wider community in which they live, work and raise their children. This can be particularly true for mothers and even more so for LGBTQ parents.

**Check Your Compass:**

**Times have changed**. You may remember that in the traditional rite of passage model of parenthood, the third stage was parents emerging after all that hard work with a greater social standing.

Well, it totally sucks that it's almost the opposite for parents today—especially for mothers. Were you aware that there wasn't even *legal protection f*or a woman to breastfeed in public in some states in the U.S. if somebody complained that she was "exposing herself" (and plenty of people were complaining). Ugh!

**Have you notice the double standard yet?** You'll find breasts spilling from billboards or the pages of a magazine if they're there to sell something.

**Have you become invisible?** When women leave paid work to stay at home with their children and do "the most important job in the world," they are somehow reduced by society. One way you may get your sense of identity is from how other people regard you. When you feel invisible, lose your voice or our ability to earn because you want to work part time or in jobs that leave you with enough energy to care for children afterwards, what image of parenthood does our culture reflect back to you?

**Fathers and partners can be undervalued too.** Prenatal classes often exclude fathers' needs and perspectives. There are new mother's groups, but not many new dad's ones. The media often portrays fathers as being incompetent. Employers don't generally honor the importance of parenthood by promoting family/friendly work practices. Fathers are often seen as parenting assistants to mothers, rather than having a direct relationship with their own child. If a mother reinforces this, it has further ramifications for his dad-self-esteem—and their relationship.

**There are effects of this**. Messages about value and worth can affect confidence and self-esteem and fuel feelings of disempowerment or despair. And if you don't see where these messages are coming from, you may find yourself blaming your partner instead.

**STEPS:**

**Don't let outside pressures in.** Establish a boundary around your home to protect what's inside from what's going on in the outside world. You may not get the respect you deserve outside your home, but you're certainly entitled to it inside.

**Listen to your inner voice.** Make sure it is louder and stronger than the messages you may be getting from outside sources. The voice inside you is the most important one. Listen to it, edit it if you have to, and then share it with whoever else needs to hear it.

**Get angry—but not at your partner (you want them on your side).** Much of what mothers (or stay-at-home partners) do is invisible labor—invisible when the partner gets home; invisible to non-parent friends and family and invisible to those who consider a stay-at-home parent to not be working.

**Speak up.** Use your frustration to champion the parenthood cause. Get involved in issues that light your fire—online, with other parents, right up the food chain. The more voices we have, the more we will be heard. Have a word with the people responsible for meeting your needs as a parent, like your manager, local politician or community group leader.

## Bored but No Direction

*I'm bored at home, but I don't know what to do,*
*I don't want my old job back.*

As babies grow, the balance between looking after the baby and looking after the home can tip. Those of us who carved an ambitious arc in the world before them can feel deflated that our role in life has been reduced to keeping a house clean.

So, while you may revel in the role of mother, you may not feel the same about homemaker (or that derogatory term "housewife"—who the heck wants to be married to their house?). So you might find yourself becoming increasingly irritated, or even depressed.

If this is the case, it might be a good time to think about going back to work, doing a course or taking up a new interest. Your discontent may be that you're craving additional challenges or stimulation—and, if you're planning to go back into the workforce, a perfect time to finish studies or retrain for a new career.

Parenthood can challenge you to think about what you really want to do in the world.

**CHECK YOUR COMPASS:**

**Have your values changed?** I know parents who left behind careers in real estate, law and the airlines to do teaching, youth advocacy and social work. Parenthood can connect you more with your core values and that can lead to more meaningful, purposeful or personally fulfilling work roles.

**Employers favor parents.** Parents returning to the workforce are reliable, have great skills and are eager to put them to good use. The vocational world has changed, and it is now not unusual for people to retrain for a new career in midlife. There's still a long way to go, but employers of choice are aware of the work-life juggling, along with the childcare crisis, that new parents face, and are making moves to retain existing parent employees and attract new ones. Family-friendly policies are also increasingly on the political agenda.

**Sometimes the best way to find what you want** is through knowing what you *don't* want. I didn't want to be bored. The lack of mental stimulation that came with the baby stage propelled me into finally writing this guidebook.

**What's your passion?** The most contented workers are those who would do their job even if they weren't paid for it. Use this time to investigate opportunities and perhaps turn a passion or creative ability into a viable vocation. Being happy in your job makes you happier generally, so your whole family benefits.

**STEPS:**

**Hold on to what you enjoyed doing pre-baby**—that makes it easier to go back later. You may have to scale down activities or interests for a while, but you don't need to sacrifice them completely.

**Take advantage of educational opportunities.** Luckily, there's more scope now than ever before. Most colleges and universities have on-site day care and flexible, part-time or correspondence options.

**Consider part-time work.** Working outside the home can be good for your self-esteem and time away from your child can make you appreciate the time with them even more.

**Be prepared to readjust your expectations—again.** You may have an easy newborn and plan to return to work early, only to find you later regret it because your little one has become like Velcro (separation anxiety peaks for them between 10 and 18 months and eases up around 2 years).

Babies also get a lot more interesting and fun, and develop so quickly, it gets harder to miss out on all that yummy stuff.

**Let your partner know what's going on**. When you're feeling frustrated or bored with life and you don't communicate this to our partner, they may feel like you're frustrated or bored with *them.*

## Lost in the Family

*Since having children, I have no real hobbies of my own—all my interests and activities seem to be an extension of someone else's.*

For the stay-at-home parent, days are largely made up of tasks and responsibilities that revolve around children's needs. Giving up Friday night drinks, afternoons shopping and weekends away are a big adjustment. You might not even realize what you miss: I remember my son's first school dance when he was five. I spent days planning what to wear and then kept bugging him to dance with me.

**CHECK YOUR COMPASS:**

**It takes time** to adjust to letting go of things you enjoy, and even more time before you find new ones. In the meantime, you might feel like you're in limbo. But limbo can be a time to gather yourself together and be more prepared for the next stage.

**Is there room for growth?** The first step is to make time for you. Mothers can feel guilty (or that there is something wrong with them) for wanting to spend time away from their children. It doesn't mean you don't love them or aren't cut out to be a mother—quite the opposite—it means you know you need to recharge your batteries and have balance in your life to be the best parent you can be.

**Some perspective:** What's the absolutely best job in the world you could think of? Now imagine you had to do that job day and night, seven days a week with no meal breaks, no sick leave, no annual leave and no end in sight. That's parenthood. It's OK to want and need a break, and it's both physically, mentally, emotionally and spiritually healthy for you to do so.

**STEPS:**

**Guard your precious time.** You may feel so bad about leaving your child(ren) that you try to justify the time away by doing "important" things like grocery shopping or running errands. Do things that re-charge your battery instead.

**Find activities that create balance.** Activities can be relaxing or stimulating. What kind relax you? Which ones get your blood pumping? Reading, going to the gym, watching a movie, doing handcrafts, dancing, listening to music, having a night out with friends? On days that you're bored, plan to do something stimulating and on days you're stressed, plan to do something relaxing. Balance helps you and your family—both in the short-term and in the long run. And parenthood is the longest run I know.

**Grow yourself.** Remember in the section on Growing, that different interests and activities from your partner's are also good for your relationship to grow. If you haven't had much opportunity before having children to develop your own individual pursuits, now's your time.

**Look around for resources.** More and more businesses are catering to parents who also want to have a life. Indoor play centers and outdoor cafes have some of the best coffee around. Some shops stock a basket of toys so customers can browse in peace. If your favorite doesn't, suggest they add one. Your local movie theater may have "Baby's Day Out" screenings where you can watch a movie without being embarrassed by a grumpy baby or kamikaze toddler. If your local one doesn't, suggest it.

## Dad's Roles

*I want my husband to be more involved with our family. He's very caught up in his career and when he gets home, he goes straight on the computer. I'm really annoyed.*

*My wife and I argue a lot about the hours I work. I have a demanding job and she likes our lifestyle, but she wants more help with our children. I can't do both.*

It may not just be the time you spend at work that's causing conflict. Work time and work worries can seep in and take away from family life. Dads who live in the study or garage—who are preoccupied with work issues, even on weekends or family holidays, are making work their priority and therefore distancing themselves from their family.

*As a dad, I want to be at home and help out, but I also feel the financial responsibility. I don't know how to do it all.*

*Sometimes I feel like all I am is a paycheck and a plumber.*

Dad's roles have changed considerably over the past generation, dads these days can understandably feel stretched. Most fathers are there for the birth, take paternity leave and want to be involved in their family's day-to-day life.

Dads have their own identity issues to grapple with too. A big chunk of a man's sense of identity and self-esteem is often their vocation, and this can be even truer after baby; when your sense of accomplishment is tied to providing for your family. Trying to be at home for your family, and also work for them, is a huge juggle. This is where quality time really comes in.

**CHECK YOUR COMPASS:**

**What does your pie look like?** New fathers can have a shaky dad-self-esteem and feel more secure at work. But riding this through has huge benefits. Cowan and Cowan's Becoming a Family Project asked each member of a couple to divide a pie chart up into Parent, Worker/Student, Partner pieces. The more equal mothers' and fathers' "parent" slices, the happier both were in their relationship. Men with larger "parent" parts also had higher self-esteem.

**STEPS:**

**Make the time you have with them count.** There are two ways you can do this: The first is to be involved as much as possible in the everyday routine of your child, even if it only means supervising teeth cleaning, and reading a bedtime story. The second is to participate in the things that create memories of you—attending to a scrape, kicking a ball or building a cubbyhouse under the table. Get your partner to take photos so your children have a lifelong sense of how you were with them.

**Bring your struggles to the surface**. As well as trying to find a balance between work and family, most fathers also have to cope with a loss of downtime. Some might even feel the need to let go of some aspects of their lives that aren't family friendly. Saying goodbye to daytrips of hiking or playing golf, or extreme sports, because you or your partner considers them unsuitable, can cause frustration and resentment.

**Talk it out**. Let your partner know (don't blame!) what's going on for you. She's probably unaware of the impact, but chances are she's struggling with her own version of this issue. If you're feeling overwhelmed by all the expectations, let her know that too. Work with what's important right now and leave the rest for later. Just being heard might be enough.

*My own dad was very strict and also very remote; it was mainly mom and us kids. I don't really know where I fit in as a father.*

I feel sad when I think of the hundreds of fathers over the years who have shared with me their feelings of bitterness, anger, fear or loss towards their own father—men who tried to mold them through criticism and control rather than through encouragement and guidance.

Reflecting on how you were fathered—what you appreciated and how you want to be with your child, and also on what you would have liked and needed from your dad—can be motivation for you to create a great relationship with your children, a better one with yourself, your partner—and maybe even with your own dad too.

**CHECK YOUR COMPASS:**

**You matter forever.** According to research, children whose dads read to them have better language skills. Age-appropriate dad-type "rough and tumble" play develops confidence. A father's relationship with his daughter provides a model for all her future relationships with men. If you're involved in her life, she's likely to have more grounded (and less romantic) expectations of future partners and is also more likely to be trusting of them. Adolescent girls who have a good relationship with their father are less likely to get pregnant, and if that's not enough to convince you, this one surely will—research says they're also less likely to attempt suicide.

There's good news for boys too. Boys who have an involved dad have a clearer sense of identity and higher self-esteem. They're also better able to form and sustain healthy adult relationships, with both women and other men. They're also less likely to suicide or have trouble with the law. All of this is massive for kids.

**You may be a first generation dad** to: a) model for your child what it means to be both a man and a nurturer as well; b) know how important close relationships are and how to protect and tend to them; c) know what a parenting team is and how to keep up your side; and d) share power in an intimate relationship.

It's exciting to think what a difference *this* generation of fathers will make in our homes, our communities and our world.

**STEPS:**

**Don't compare.** Your dad was bought up in a very different time where dad roles and responsibilities were confined and restrictive, and despite his probably doing the best job he could, it will feel like he fell short compared to your own expectations of yourself. You might need to grieve and come to peace with some aspects of this (see Part III).

**Decide** ***how*** **you want to** ***be*** **different,** and what you will need to *do* differently. If you have a clear picture of what prevented you from feeling close to your dad (e.g., he yelled, was critical or was at the bar instead of home), then you know what you *don't* want to copy.

**Be involved forever**. Get on the floor and play with your baby, read your toddler stories, play games with older ones. Kick a soccer ball. Attend doctor's appointments so you can be the one to dry the tears. Take time off work to attend those boring school events; you'll be in the photos forever. Get in the kitchen and teach your kids how to make your favorite breakfast. Volunteer at school occasionally; other mothers will love you as well. Be a taxi driver for your teenager and give them your wise advice while they're a captive audience. Even if they don't want to hear it at the time, they'll remember it. Your partner will be grateful for all this too.

*I don't understand my partner. She wants help with our kids, but just gets annoyed with me when I do, and then I get frustrated.*

Mothers can be so involved with our children that we lose touch with ourselves. We may not even realize we're hungry, or need to go to the bathroom, until hours later. It's frustrating for us and sometimes we take this frustration out on our partner.

**CHECK YOUR COMPASS:**

**She might not admit it, but she needs you.** Lots of moms try so hard to prove themselves good at mothering that they inadvertently leave their partner out. Others cope with overwhelming demands by going on automatic pilot. In this the case, your offers of help might feel like they will send her off course.

**Realize you play a huge role.** Your partner looks to you to give her positive feedback—reassurance that you will be there for her and sometimes a shoulder to cry on. And this benefits your children. Research by Wendy le Blanc found when a partner is supportive, 75% of mothers enjoy childcare and 85% find a strong sense of purpose in it.

I'm going to stop you here because there's something important I want to point out.

**Your attitude to your partner affects your children.** The same le Blanc research found that when a partner is unsupportive, 80% of women are irritated by the duties of motherhood and 87% derive little meaning or purpose in that role. Especially in the absence of things that used to define her sense of identity—work, friendships, interests, etc.—a big part of her self-esteem now is how she feels about herself as a mother. So, be mindful of how you regard her.

**STEPS:**

**Raise her awareness.** Gently let her know what you've noticed. If she's on autopilot, she may be shocked to hear what that looks like from your point of view. Let her know you understand but reiterate that you want to be involved.

**Keep talking about your needs and desires** as they unfold, because they can change a lot in the first few years of parenthood. Sharing openly and honestly about this stuff prevents issues from building up, reduces tension and creates more harmony in your home.

**Share all the different experiences of parenthood**—the insecurity, frustration and relentlessness of it—so you can sympathize with each other and also share the joyful moments and milestones. It also means you can avoid the "who works harder" competition that many parents get caught in.

Now might be a good time in your journey to take stock of where we are. We started with your skills for loving, learning and growing. You probably learned more than you were prepared for to there. You learned how to combine them and put them into action in Thriving.

Then we talked about what you needed to prepare for giving your baby the best possible start. You leaped, and you landed in the nest you built, and then when you came down from the tree, you checked your map, only to find it didn't quite match the territory you found yourself in, and you had to wade through all those expectations.

But despite all these challenges, you did such a great job of looking after your baby, it finally came time to turn your attention to yourself and your partner. We looked at self-care and couple-care in Setting Up Base Camp. Now you know that this is where you can go back to any time life swerves in a different direction and becomes extra challenging.

From there, we started to get really deep into the woods—and then the lake. We looked at the deeper emotions of parenthood and how they can shape you and your relationship. And then, in the last stage, we looked at how the changes of parenthood can change you too and why it's so important to support each other to grow into our parent-selves.

And here we are, back at going forward again.

Remember in the beginning, when I told you that you were going to roll up your Thriving skills and stick them in your backpack so they would be there for you to pull out and use whenever you needed them?

Pull them out now.

# Stage Seven: Growing Together Through Differences

## (Your Family's First Few Years and Forever)

It's possible that you've discovered this guidebook, or someone has recommended it to you, at this stage in your parenthood journey. If that's the case, go ahead, let's walk together. But I encourage you to go back at some stage and start at the beginning, even if you have older children. This will help you make a lot more sense of how you got here in the first place.

And where we're going now.

See that mountain over there? The one with the snow on top? That's where we're headed. I'll warn you, there's one particular peak that might just be the biggest challenge you have faced so far. But we'll get to that soon.

When you become parents, exhaustion, lost sleep, reduced freedoms, new responsibilities, more intense emotions and steep learning curves are a recipe for conflict. New differences are introduced into your partnership. Conflict arises from saying, "You're different from me and I don't like it."

Most of us weren't taught how to deal with differences in our close relationships, so we tend to react to them in one of two ways. We fight or we don't talk about them. But here's the thing. Knowing how to manage conflict brings you closer instead of pushing you apart.

And while this can make a dramatic difference to your partnership, the real winner is your child. Unresolved conflict, or competition between parents, will reduce your capacity to be the best parent you can be and undermine your ability to work as a parenting team.

In this stage, you'll be putting everything you've learned so far about parenthood and relationships into practice. Parenthood sends parents into a different relationship stage. It grows you up again. It's stressful. Each stage of the journey can bring new conflicts that you may never have had to deal with as a couple before. Parenthood is a time of considerable changes inside you, and the adjustments you're negotiating inside yourself also need to be shared with your partner.

And yet, all this can bring you closer, rather than sending you apart, when you know how.

On the way up the mountain we'll be going through some thick wooded areas that are hard to find your way through. There are forest paths that you're not likely to see at first. In fact, you may not even see a path until you're actually on it. And at times you'll have to trust and take steps even when you can't see what lies ahead.

The ability for you and your partner to find your way through conflict is a true indication of the maturity of a relationship—and a *real* practice of parenthood. Like emotional awareness and assertiveness, this is a life-skill you will want to pass on to your children.

This stage of the journey shows you ways to grow up—together.

## No Time to Talk

*We're both so busy with the kids and working, there's no time to sit down and have a proper conversation.*

With the gazillion tasks that go with caring for children, everything else can feel like less of a priority. But fifteen minutes a day with your partner now may mean avoiding fifteen *years* of unnecessary gripes.

**CHECK YOUR COMPASS:**

**Commitment to your relationship is a commitment to your children.** The tone of your relationship is the background music for your children, so a daily couple's break, at least for a coffee or a short walk, to connect with your partner is important.

**Issues don't have to be resolved all in one shot**. Uninterrupted time is rare, so discussions might have to be in smaller chunks over several days.

This also gives you time to calm down if needed and digest what's been said. It's better to call one or more time-outs if things get heated than to push for hasty but ineffective resolutions that one or both of you aren't happy with.

**STEPS:**

**Find ways to stay in touch**. If you can't be at home for a face-to-face talk, call, text or email just to check in and see how your partner's day is. Five minutes of focused caring is worth more than an hour of half-hearted attention.

## Partner Doesn't Listen

*When I talk about my issues with the kids, my husband doesn't want to listen. I end up following him around the house, yelling to get his attention. It's very frustrating.*

It *is* frustrating if you share your worries with your partner because you hope that by doing so, they will help you to resolve them. When your attempts are ignored or blocked, not only are you left with the original problem, but also with a relationship problem too. You'll both want to avoid this.

**CHECK YOUR COMPASS:**

**How are you saying your words?** It's not only *what* you say but also *how* you say it that can make it hard for your partner to listen. Tone of voice, body language, gestures and facial expressions communicate even more than your words.

**What are you saying?** Absolutes (must, always, never, etc.), blaming, criticizing and nagging are likely to cause your partner to switch off, shut down or become defensive. You can't get your message across. You're also likely to find your partner is less willing to discuss issues in the future.

**Remember that your feelings are like the layers of an onion.** Blaming, criticizing and nagging come from the outer layer of annoyance or frustration. Believe it or not, they can be attempts to connect with your partner, but in ways that don't leave you feeling exposed or vulnerable.

**What's below?** Underneath the frustration are likely to be feelings of hurt or disappointment, but you may not want to communicate these feelings directly to your partner for fear they might respond in a way that just hurts more.

You may be blaming, criticizing or nagging to try to change your partner and avoid the hurt. But here's the problem, you may actually create new hurt for yourself—by pushing them away.

**Know what you want.** At the heart of criticism, blame or nagging is a request for changed behavior. Ask for what you want instead.

**STEPS:**

**Absolutely avoid absolutes.** "You never," "you always" or "you should" sound judgmental, controlling or domineering. Use your Thriving skills instead.

**Be slow to blame.** You blame when you judge another to be responsible for a problem. If there's to be any blame, it's best left to when all the facts have become clear to *both* parties, and the other person *chooses* to take responsibility. Premature blame will just cause your partner to become defensive.

**Be aware that criticism can be both constructive and destructive.** Unless it's constructive (accurate, sensitive and agreed to by the other person), criticism can slay self-esteem. If you criticize your partner, they will probably shut down to protect themselves, or get angry with you. And this doesn't just affect your relationship—research shows that fathers who regularly feel criticized find it harder to bond with their children.

**Know your partner can feel blamed or criticized, even if that wasn't your intention.** Shame, blame, criticism and control were used to discipline children in previous generations. So if your partner's parents did this, they're likely to get defensive and react as if you're blaming or criticizing them, *even when you're not.* You can break this negative parenting pattern for your own children.

**Realize your attempts to be heard may sound like nagging to your partner.** It's easy to repeat yourself at the times you're frustrated or impatient. You may be sleep deprived and have forgotten you've already told your partner something. True nagging is a way of attempting to control, and often shame, someone. That's not good.

**Shift from criticism to request.** Use your Thriving skills for this.

**Look into the future.** Recounting the last 27 times your partner did something wrong is not going to inspire them to do it right next time.

## Nagging

*My wife nags me constantly about helping her more with the kids. I know she's got a point, but I'm sick of hearing it, and all I want to do is walk away.*

It's annoying and frustrating for you to be nagged, and also annoying for her to be shut out, so now's the time to find a different way to talk that work for both of you.

### CHECK YOUR COMPASS:

**Men and women can communicate in different ways.** There's a theory that men tend to think linearly (working towards a goal or solution), whereas women tend to think globally (examine a situation from different angles). What might sound like nagging to you might be her attempt to help you see a different side of things.

**How do you process information?** Some people are "external processors." Thinking out loud helps them to make sense of things. Others are internal processors and have this conversation on the inside. When external processors interpret or interrupt their internal processing partner, you both end up getting frustrated.

**Are you contributing?** Ways to shut your partner down include ignoring, continually interrupting or walking away. If its understanding or connection she's after, she's going to feel frustrated—and will have *even more* resolve to let you know it.

**Is it a habit?** You may not listen for some reason—lack of sleep, a child's interruption, and the conversation gets heated, so it may be better to walk away than stay and fight. If these are infrequent and due to external circumstances, they may have little effect. But if they become a habit, they will cause your partner to feel shut down. After a while, this can mean they're less likely to open up, unable to trust that they'll be responded to appropriately. You might like that idea, but ultimately it will negatively affect both of you.

**What's going on inside?** Ignoring, daydreaming, interrupting and walking out can be ways of regulating anxiety, avoiding arguments or because you're feeling overwhelmed. If you stop the conversation, you keep some control in the moment, but risk creating long-term problems. Or are you doing these things because you're not interested in the topic? If this is the case, ask yourself why.

### STEPS:

**Challenge yourself.** Do you consider yourself and your partner equals? Do you consider their concerns as important as your own? Do you want to be supported and are you willing to be supportive in return? Are you and your partner individuals? Do you both have a right to your own thoughts, feelings, values and beliefs? Not just in theory—but what does this look like in real life? Live these values.

**Manage your feelings**. If your partner is making a genuine effort to speak appropriately, you owe it them to listen. Manage whatever feelings come up so they don't block your hearing your partner. If you can't let your partner know you're having trouble, take a break and try again until you can. Managing your feelings gets easier with practice.

**Manage your responses.** Say what you've heard them say. Repeat back what you can remember so they know you got it the first time. Plan a time to do what they've asked and let them know when this will be or say why you can't. Walking away is like turbocharging your partner—not what you want.

**Be honest**. If you can't listen at that moment for whatever reason, share why. Saying, "I can't listen to you right now because I…." is better than your partner thinking that you just don't care.

## Not Talking

*I have some issues with the way my husband parents our children, but I don't want to argue so I don't say anything.*

Not talking about issues doesn't solve them—in fact, according to Gottman, the number one predictor of divorce is the *habitual avoidance* of conflict.

*There are issues simmering below the surface, but when I try to raise them, my husband says, "I don't want to talk about it."*

This may be because he is uncomfortable with facing issues directly. Maybe his experience of talking in the past (either with you, a previous relationship or in his own family) has been negative, and he's understandably hesitant to go down that road again (unless it's on a motorcycle so he can escape when he needs to).

How you react and respond to each other is partly determined by your attachment style. Go back and read that section again so you're not taking your partner's natural responses personally.

There's something else I need to mention here. "I don't want to talk about it," combined with frequent irritability or withdrawal, could be an early sign of depression. That's around the corner in Part III.

But for now, I want to point something out. See that part of the mountain over there where there are no trees? Well, actually that's a very slippery slope. I have seen parents go down it before and I want to share with you what happened to them.

At first it starts with small irritations, things you can't really put your finger on, so you ignore them. If they keep happening though, tension rises, and you may find yourselves snapping at each other. If you don't clear these "snaps" up, tension will increase. When it does, you're more likely to start negatively interpreting your partner's intentions, making assumptions and having more misunderstandings—and have less motivation to resolve them.

At this point you might start to feel more distant from your partner. If this continues, feelings of disconnection and pessimism about your relationship can become *fixed.* I have seen this happen in relationships, when one partner is ready to walk out—and the other one may not even be aware that a problem existed.

I don't want this to happen to you, so let's avoid that slope completely and go another way.

**CHECK YOUR COMPASS:**

**You affect each other.** How you act causes a reaction in your partner and *vice versa.* If you habitually avoid discussions, you will compel your partner to try to engage you. The more you resist, the harder they will try, causing you to resist even more. You both have more control over this dance than you realize.

**Parenthood is a level playing field.** Your child has two parents. You are both important to them. This means the thoughts, ideas, opinions, hopes, dreams and fears you each have for your family are equally important. Your child wants you to be their team.

**Are you afraid of differences?** You don't need to be. Just make sure navigating them is safe and productive. Do your part in this and call out your partner (gently) when they don't.

**STEPS:**

**Wonder what's underneath**. "Don't worry about it" might mean "I don't have the energy to argue and I'm afraid to talk because I don't have the self-control or the skills for this right now."

**Talk regularly**. A release valve prevents things from building up and discharges tension that can rupture your relationship.

## Doing Conflict Differently

*Whenever things got heated, we would go our separate ways until we calmed down; he would go for a drive and I would go for a run. With a small child now, we can't do that anymore.*

By the time you started your family, you may have had several years' of managing differences between you effectively enough. Afterwards though, many pre-baby strategies may not work. Some couples can argue enthusiastically to discharge the tension and then fall happily into each other's arms. But babies—and children—don't like yelling. If your main issue before baby was keeping the house clean, on a double income you could hire a cleaner. Before baby you could avoid having difficult discussions or just agree to disagree. You can't do that about circumcision or vaccination, or how to discipline your child or which school to send them to, because these need to be joint decisions.

You can't make big decisions that one of you is unhappy with either (like naming a child). The bitterness of the losing partner is likely to affect the relationship for a long time to come—and your child.

**CHECK YOUR COMPASS:**

Doing conflict well *binds* you as a couple. Knowing your partner loves, accepts, respects and values you, even when you can't agree on an issue, builds trust and security.

**Where's your stuff?** Your stuff is your stuff; your partner's stuff is their stuff. But where you can find compromise, agreement or at the very least, maintain goodwill despite your differences, you build "us" stuff.

Oh, perfect timing, here's our campground for the night. Let's say you start off in the same tent and then you have a disagreement and decide to move into two separate ones. You could put them at opposite ends of the campsite facing away from each other, but where would your child go? If you pitch them facing each other with a picnic blanket in between, your child can at least play on it while you're both figuring out the sleeping arrangements.

**STEPS:**

**Commit to equality.** Major decisions you made as a couple before baby may have required one of you to step up more than the other, depending on your strengths, experience or interest level. One of you may have taken more responsibility planning your wedding or buying your home for instance. Parenthood, however, is the ultimate equalizer: you are *both* important to your baby.

**Find middle ground for parenting issues.** You will be confronted with sensitive and difficult topics way, waaaay, into the future, that you'll need to work through—especially when it comes to your child's behavior. Contradictory messages from both parents cause anxiety in children of all ages—from infants to teens. Because it doesn't matter which parent's directions they follow, the other parent will be angry or disappointed with them. You really need to find middle ground to support your child here.

## Frequent Conflict

*My husband and I seem to be arguing so much more since we had our baby; is this normal?*

*I hate to say it, but at the times my partner and I have differences I tend to take it out on the kids.*

More frequent conflict is normal, yes. Cowan and Cowan's landmark study found a whopping 92% percent of couples experienced increased conflict and disagreement in their baby's first year. And if you argue about the following, you're even more normal: housework, finances, in-laws, parenting styles and which one of you is causing all the problems.

**CHECK YOUR COMPASS:**

**How do you feel about differences?** You may be scared of them because your own parents didn't handle them well.

**How you "do" conflict is a strong predictor for your future**. Couples who react to differences with stonewalling, criticism, contempt, or defensiveness are the most likely to develop serious relationship problems. Contempt, being disrespectful or treating another as less-than, is the biggest predictor of relationship breakdown according to Gottman. Couples who are able to embrace differences will thrive. It's not what you disagree about; it's how you disagree that matters.

**What's underneath?** Withdrawal and avoidance can be ways of managing anxiety or feelings of hurt.

**STEPS:**

**Accept your partner as an individual**, who has their own point of view, and is entitled to it. Respecting your partner, your child's other parent, shows self-respect and teaches your child respect too.

**Let your partner influence you.** This is one of the most important ingredients in managing conflict. Gottman's research found that if one partner did not accept the other's influence (particularly a male partner), it was a high predictor of divorce.

**Feel your initial reaction.** What you will first be aware of is your reaction of fight, flight, freeze or fix. Remember, this automatic defensive reaction that you would have used in childhood prompts you to see your partner as an enemy to attack, avoid, or retreat from, or a problem to be solved.

**Respond instead:** "Hold" your childlike part of you that's primed to react long enough to gather yourself, feel your deeper feelings and find your assertive voice.

**Make time to talk**, begin gently, use "I" language and be hard on the issue, but soft on the person.

**Recognize signs of overwhelm.** When you feel flooded emotionally, can't think straight or start to feel agitated, stop and take time-out for at least 20 minutes until your body calms and you can think clearly again. Then come back and have another attempt, so the issue doesn't remain unmanaged—again. The best way to prevent flooding is to keep practicing safe Thriving skills.

**Self-soothe.** Rising levels of anxiety and desperation escalate arguments. You may throw unhelpful words out in an attempt to say, "This is important, you need to listen to me." Or, "I want to stop now, I'm not coping with this." Self-soothing, like slowing your breathing, reassuring yourself that you're OK, or calling time-out, prevent you from saying or doing things you may regret.

**Debrief arguments after you've both cooled down.** Saying something like, "I got angry because I thought you didn't care," helps your partner understand your triggers and avoid them.

**Express appreciation for each other often throughout the day**. This prevents negative feelings from building up. It's easy for both parents to start taking each other for granted. When your partner does something you appreciate, tell them.

**Know how to repair your relationship**. Good friends are careful not to say things that may hurt the other. The relationship is more important to them than the issue they may disagree about. When couples continually fail to repair the damage from arguments, there is a greater than 90% prediction for divorce, according to Gottman's research. When you cause a rupture, the bond between you is affected and you need to restore it before you try to discuss the same issue again.

## Warning Signs

In their book, *Becoming Parents: How to Strengthen Your Marriage as Your Family Grows,* the authors describe four patterns that can mean real trouble for a relationship

**Escalation**: This is when partners lose control and "up the ante," like a poker game. You might initiate a discussion by making a $5 criticism and your partner responds with a $20 defensive reply. You might throw out a $50 negative retort and your partner might have a $75 comeback, which you trump with a $100 threat of walking out. As well as being destructive to your relationship, the actual issue remains unresolved. The next time you try to broach the problem (and there *will b*e a next time), you already have $255 worth of frustration and resentment between you before you even get started.

**Invalidation:** This can range from subtle criticism to obvious contempt, including ignoring someone's concerns, minimizing their experience or negatively judging them. Invalidation puts the other person down, attacks their self-esteem and, especially when subtle, is hard to defend against. Invalidation causes people to shut down and become resentful. Whenever someone is "one down," it undermines equality and the stability of a family structure.

**Negative interpretations**: This includes mind reading your partner's intentions, making assumptions about them and not sharing responsibility for clearing up misunderstandings. People who regularly make negative interpretations often won't listen to their partner's explanations or point of view. They can use their own false truths to justify their over-reactions of becoming defensive or attacking. This leaves the other partner feeling constantly misunderstood, powerless, without a voice and can lead to depression.

**Withdrawal/avoidance**. Conflict is uncomfortable for most people. When you're already depleted, distracted or tired, it's even more exhausting, so no wonder you'll want to avoid it. Sometimes it makes sense to shelve an issue for a better time. But constant withdrawal/avoidance—a person's continued unwillingness to address issues—is likely to undermine the foundations of a family.

## Conflict into the Future

*We have been fighting about the kids for years. There are so many issues. I'm just so sick and tired of it.*

I'm going to give you a pair of binoculars here so you can see way ahead to what might be in your future. Remember that snow-capped peak I pointed out to your earlier? There's some tricky territory there that you'll want to avoid. Can you see it? I'll show you where it is.

CHECK YOUR COMPASS:

**It's more important to be real than to be right.** "Being right" is a one up/one down position. If you've been fighting for years, it may be because you've been aiming for the wrong thing. If you stubbornly cling to your own version of reality, and fight for supremacy over your partner's, they will always be wrong. Resentment will rise and you'll teach your children that thinking independently is a bad thing because it causes arguments. Your whole family loses.

**Look forwards and backwards.** Unless you can start to find areas of agreement, *especially* about the issues of raising your children, you will be forcing them to choose one parent over another. This is a no-win situation that causes great tension for them. Anxiety is passed down in families this way—sometimes for generations. Maybe that's how it was in your family and why you're having this problem now. Read that again. You will need to be the ones to break this cycle. And you can.

**You'll need courage**. Being real means opening up, risking becoming vulnerable and inviting your partner in. This takes more courage and strength than clinging desperately to an opinion and a lot less time and energy than fighting for years.

**The issue is not the problem**. Most distress comes from not being able to navigate the issue well. When you don't allow your partner to have different perceptions, points of view, or interpretations—when you assume your way is the only way, when you take their perception as a personal rejection or become defensive—you are likely to escalate even simple and easily resolved issues.

**Beware of self-intoxication.** Unresolved conflict is fuelled when you "talk yourself up." A mental play list of your partner's faults can breed frustration over and over, clouding your view of them. You can think of vicious insults for your partner that only happen in your head. Have you ever noticed that if you partner talks to you when you're in the middle of an "inside" argument, you may snap at them and cause a "real" one? You will now. The more unresolved issues that sit between you, the more likely you are to have stuff stored in your head and your heart—more fuel for the next one.

**Check your perception**. The way you interpret your partner's words will stir up an emotion in you. You will then direct that emotion to your partner in words that will then be interpreted by them, and so on. Check your perceptions with your partner *before* you respond.

**STEPS:**

**Respond—don't react.** Override the fight/flight/freeze reaction. Responding is like a muscle you need to exercise until it becomes stronger than your default automatic reactivity.

**See disagreements as opportunities** to get to know yourself better, your partner better, and to understand and accept the gap between you as an opportunity to reach across it.

**Embrace your inner strength and let your partner have theirs**. Too often we blame our partner when it takes two to fight. In a normal, healthy relationship your partner is reacting to you as much as you are to them: a defense can look like an attack to someone else. If you're going to stick around for the more challenging parts of parenthood, we'll explore unhealthy relationship dynamics in Part III.

Here's the good news: while it takes two to fight, it only takes one to stop. *Respond* and you can avoid triggering your partner's defenses—and elicit a more positive response from them that won't trigger you. Staying stuck in your own negative reactions will pretty much guarantee no change in your partner.

**Accept what you can't change and work with what you can.** You can't change your partner's personality. But your partner can change their behavior, communication patterns, beliefs or parenting styles. Let your partner know that you appreciate who they are, their role as your child's other parent or what they mean to you first. This helps them to be open to specific requests for change.

**Know when to get professional help**. Some circumstances need additional support before conflict can be addressed. They are an undiagnosed or unmanaged mental health condition or an addiction, if you or your partner is abusive. For conflict to be managed safely and healthily, these issues need to be addressed with the help of a counselor. Attempting it on your own is frustrating, heartbreaking and potentially very risky. (For more see Part III.)

**Accept your partner's reality.** Just as your thoughts and feelings about a situation are the sum result of *your* life up until now, so are your partner's. They will be unique, different and equally valid.

*We have a number of petty issues that keep coming up. They're not a big deal but they don't get resolved.*

So often we can find ourselves arguing heatedly over things that really aren't important. Silly things like whether the bookshelf should be on the left or the right, or whose turn it is to empty the trash. Maybe it's making simple decisions about the kids. Looking back on those impassioned moments, you may of wonder why on earth you were so upset.

**CHECK YOUR COMPASS:**

**Do you need more information**? If you can't come to a decision, it may be that you don't have enough information to sway you one way or the other. Research, dig deeper and find information that changes your mind or resonates with your own good sense.

Are your big arguments triggered by small things? Can't put your finger on an issue? Going round in circles? Ever feel like you or your partner are overreacting? This may be because there are triggers to hidden concerns underneath. If you've been arguing for weeks about the trash, it's time for a wholly different type of talk. Exploring what's really going on can save you *years* of petty arguments.

**STEPS:**

**Have an intentional talk about hidden concerns**. In the book, *Becoming Parents: How to Strengthen Your Marriage as Your Family Grows, t*he authors identify the following:

**Power and control**. Who makes the decisions? Who influences whom? Who has the final say? This issue is common for parents where it's more important to be right than to be in a partnership. This hidden concern is also more likely to be triggered after you become parents with new decisions, stresses, vulnerabilities and triggers from your own childhood coming up. Again.

**Needing and caring.** How much do you love me? Am I a priority for you? For example, when one person harps on at the other (like about things not being done around the house), are there feelings of righteous indignation attached to thoughts like "if he/she doesn't do ____, then it means they don't really care about me." This hidden concern is more likely to be triggered if you have anxiety about the baby replacing you in your partner's affections.

**Recognition.** Do you appreciate me? Do you see what I have done? Does your partner recognize the value of who you are or acknowledge things you do? These hidden concerns can be triggered when you become parents with the added responsibilities and rapid shifts in your new roles—and the invisible nature of the work of parenting. You can spend a whole day tidying a house that only takes five minutes to get trashed.

**Commitment.** Will you support me? Can I count on your interest and energy? Are you in this for the long haul? After baby, commitment stakes are higher and arguments can be triggered that mask underlying anxieties, particularly if you experienced some type of abandonment in childhood.

**Integrity.** Do you think I'm lying? Or making things up? Do you think I would do such a thing? Who do you think I am? This hidden issue can be activated by invalidation. When your partner questions your attitude, values, beliefs, thoughts, feelings or motives, it can feel like they are questioning the validity of *you* as a person. That's insulting and painful.

**Acceptance** is the hidden issue at the bottom of all others. At our very core, we are likely to most desire acceptance, and fear rejection—especially from our partner. The irony of this is that we can be so afraid of our partner seeing the real us—the ways we keep them out and our real selves hidden—that we can cause *them* to feel rejected.

**Don't problem solve**. Hidden concerns are not problems to be solved, which is why problem solving doesn't work when these issues are triggered, but not acknowledged, during conflicts. Deal with hidden concerns by safely and respectfully having conversations with the intent of understanding each other's hopes and worries. These are lovely conversations to have.

## Ready to Give Up

*Our kids are older now. We used to fight a lot, but we just don't bother any more. I feel bored and I don't really know what I'm doing here.*

Remember the onion? You relate to people at different levels—strangers will only see what's on the surface, but as you build trust, you allow people to see more, and relate to them in a more intimate way. The reverse is also true. Where trust has been eroded over time or broken (even if it was a long time ago), you'll start to protect yourself and reveal less SEE NOTE layers of yourself. A relationship in which only surface layers are revealed will feel shallow—and boring.

*I don't have problems with anyone else—what's wrong with my partner? Maybe we're not right for each other after all.*

Your relationship with your partner is like no other. You won't speak to anyone else the way you speak to them. You can be more passionate, and more derogatory. Either way, what you're trying to communicate is important—it's how you feel. Communicating on this intimate level takes great skill.

The goal of intimate communication is not to find compromise, or even agreement—although this may be the end result—it's to gain an understanding and acceptance of your separate realities (in-to-me-see, remember?)

When you can't get understanding, you're likely to both get frustrated. This tension fuels arguments. Once you can see your partner's point of view, you can both relax.

**CHECK YOUR COMPASS:**

**Discover the layers.** Because you tend to share your outer layers with the most people, and they with you, you may naturally think that everybody is pretty much alike—that everybody thinks, feels and responds the same way you do. But the deeper you go, the more distinctions you'll find. Eventually, you may even get to specific memories, sometimes buried very deep, that shape your surface attitudes and behaviors.

In conflict, your individual responses to a situation are the end result of a process in your brain that is as unique to you as your fingerprints. It's like a pinball bouncing through your layers of awareness. It may start with a feeling that goes to a thought that jumps to another feeling that sends you to an older memory that, without you even realizing it, is linked to a belief or a value you have. All of this can happen in less than a minute. No wonder we confuse our partner.

**STEPS:**

**Delve into your deeper self** to find a new level of relating. Honesty and openness grow trust. Strip away the falsities and pretenses that can cloud a relationship. Get back to the essence of who you are and how you really want to be with a partner.

**Stop what's not working.** Take responsibility for yourself and what you bring to your relationship. Ditch the accusations, name-calling, defensiveness, dismissiveness, criticism and/or sarcasm.

**Don't jumble issues.** Your partner forgets to put the trash out, which somehow moves to that day, three years ago, when they forgot to do something else, then to how their mother treats you badly as well, and finally to all the ways they just don't love you enough. That's a lot of ground to cover in one conversation.

**Be real.** If your relationship is polite, but the coolness hides the hostility below, pay attention here, please. Families like this can be brought down by one vicious argument. Children growing up in this environment learn to hide their real selves from their future partner. It's much better to carefully bring the conflicts to the surface and resolve them, with the help of a counselor if needed. Children learn so much more from parents who can do conflict, even half-right, than from those who cover issues up. And with practice, you'll get even more skilled at managing conflict.

**Do things differently for a few months.** OK, so you now know you can't change your partner, but you can change your actions and communication patterns—and these are what tend to cause the most distress in relationships. Professional support helps here too.

**Shift the focus**. If you focus on the negatives of your partner, the positives will go unnoticed.

Oh, did you see that bird that just flew by? They're very rare. You hardly see them. It's called a See-me.

What unites you? What brings you mutual joy? What is working in your relationship? What used to? When are things good? When you're on holidays? What's the difference? All are building blocks.

**Don't dwell on what you're not getting**. Ask yourself what you're putting in. Relationships are reciprocal. For them to thrive, they need to be a joint effort.

**Get away from it all—regularly.** We get bored when we're stuck in a rut. What you both may need are opportunities to be your "best selves" again to remind you why you chose each other in the first place. Take a kid-free holiday to fully relax, energize, rediscover and romance. Bring these important things back with you along with your souvenirs. Remembering the good times can also remind you of your bond when you're in the middle of a bad time.

**Ramp up the adventure.** One study showed that couples who do active, stimulating or adventurous activities together are more likely to appreciate their relationship than couples that just do "nice" things. Maybe do both.

**Make friends with other couples.** Different people bring out different sides of us. Sometimes you can discover more about your partner by listening to them talk with others. Take the "newness" home and enjoy it privately.

**Create shared meaning.** You can be bored with your relationship because the meaningfulness of your partnership gets lost in the day-to-day humdrum of family life. One way of preventing this is to develop either regular or spontaneous rituals that symbolize your connection. Go crazy. Wash your partner's hair. Take turns to create a special dish once a week. Revisit the place where you decided to get married. Give a gift that says, "remember when…." What else can you think of?

## Overwhelmed by Arguments

*When my wife and I argue, I feel bombarded. She keeps saying she wants to resolve the issues. Fair enough, but we never do.*

If you feel attacked during conflict, all your energy is likely to go into defending yourself rather than managing the issue, so it's an impossible situation. You need a new strategy.

**CHECK YOUR COMPASS:**

**Surprise! Most conflicts aren't even resolvable.** Remember that Gottman predicts that 69% of relationship conflicts aren't solvable, they're issues that are likely to come up again and again. Examine the issue for hidden concerns and have that important conversation if you need to.

If there are no hidden concerns, you don't have to actually resolve your major differences in order for your relationship to be great. Don't say this to blow her off, however. It doesn't mean there isn't considerable work to be done—just in a different direction. Let her know you're willing to travel down that road with her.

**Focus on feelings, not issues.** Take time to get in touch with all the emotions you're feeling and ask her to do the same. The feelings that come up front and center are likely to affect the way she communicates—and they're the ones you will tune out. It's the quieter feelings in the back that probably haven't had much of a voice. These are the ones that are most likely to make the difference to how you're able to hear each other.

**STEPS:**

**Teach her how to speak to you.** Ask her to speak in smaller, bite-sized chunks. She may feel that when she's finally got your attention and gathered the courage to get started, there's so much to get out that it's hard to stop. This can feel like verbal battery for you.

People can only absorb the amount of information in four normal sentences before they begin to feel overloaded. Tired parents can manage maybe two. Ask her to pause regularly and check that you're still on her wavelength before she continues. Let her know you got one part before she gives you the next.

**Ask for time out**. If you're still getting overwhelmed, tell her you need to take a break before you can take in any more. Let her know you'll be back to continue the discussion when you're able. Go for a walk or do something else until your head is clear. Then go back.

## Use and Abuse of Power

It's natural to want to feel a sense of power or control in your life and in your relationship. Without it, you can resort to power plays, manipulation or punishment through withdrawal. You can also be passive in your relationship (not actively participating, avoiding discussions or making decisions or making your relationship a low priority). All these things are likely to sabotage your family.

> *My wife announced the other day she's enrolled our daughter in a whole year of very expensive music classes. She's not the one that's working and there was no discussion. Zero.*

Making what should be a joint decision without you may be a way of trying to gain a sense of power or control in your relationship. You need to have a discussion with your partner about how you feel about this decision, and also be open to hearing why she may have made it without your input.

**CHECK YOUR COMPASS:**

**There's a balance of influence**. Remember from earlier, when you're both working, earning money and moving towards the same goals, the balance of power between you can be relatively equal. But a baby brings seismic shifts to your *status quo.*

**In more traditional relationships**, fathers or partners can feel the pressure of being a sole provider, put more energy into work and try to gain a sense of control in that sphere of life. Mothers can preempt or react to this by compensating with extra responsibilities and decision-making power around children and the home. Mothers can also demean a father's parenting efforts, forcing them take a back seat in the parenting role.

**This can set you both up for problems down the road,** as you each try to gain power and control in separate domains. For your family's sake, you both want to be in the front seat of the car.

**STEPS:**

**Have an intentional conversation** around sharing decision making in your relationship. Tell her how you feel about this decision, and also be open to hearing why she may have made it without your input.

**Commit to co-creating more equality** in your relationship for the ongoing stability of your family.

*Some days my husband comes home from work, looks disgustedly around the living room and asks, "what have you been doing all day?" I know I've been busy with the kids and I'm exhausted but I have nothing to show for it. I get nervous now when I know he's on his way home.*

Having children is such a huge life change it can leave you both feeling in over your heads. Feeling inadequate can spur some fathers on to regain a sense of power by putting his partner down. This needs to be addressed or it can leave you feeling hopeless or helpless, which can contribute to feelings of depression and further affect your family.

### CHECK YOUR COMPASS:

**You are more than you may realize**. Feeling competent, capable and/or motivated fuels your self-esteem. In the workplace, you're likely to get tangible results for this: wage raises or promotions, sales figures, a word of thanks from the boss, the admiration of your colleagues, feedback from clients. Building inner strength that supports self-esteem is a lifelong journey—it will change depending on your circumstances. When you're at home, you need to rely on yourself more to build yourself up.

**Check the dynamic**. If you tend to be more passive, and your partner tends to be pushier in most aspects of your relationship, you can find yourselves with an unstable foundation for your family. Aim for assertiveness and expect your partner to do the same.

### STEPS:

**Get strong on the inside.** Get in touch with the range of feelings his attitude stirs up in you and prepare yourself with the skills you need to assertively express them to him.

**Speak up.** Silence implies consent. If you don't speak up and assert yourself, others can take your silence as compliance. It's not—especially if you're yelling at them on the inside. Find your voice.

**Teach him how to treat you**. It's OK for him to come home in a bad mood if he's had a bad day. He has a right to his feelings just as you do. But he also has a responsibility not to take his bad mood out on you and the children.

**Tell him what you want to hear instead**. Something like, "I had a bad day at work today. It's not about you. Give me 15 minutes to take a shower and get over it." That way you give him some personal space and goodwill is preserved. If it's clear it's not personal, you can each debrief your day—and find comfort instead of conflict.

**Be aware of the different aspects of family**: finances, home, leisure time, children and the balance of influence in each. Where there's an area of inequality, discuss this with your partner. Expect that as your child grows, aspects of your relationship will change and need to be navigated (like when they start preschool could be a time to renegotiate work and leisure arrangements).

**Be clear about the line between unawareness and abuse.** If, after you've stated your feelings, your partner becomes more aware and modifies his attitude or behavior, this should be the end of it. If, despite your best attempts to communicate, his behavior continues or escalates, or you suspect he is being deliberately hostile or aggressive (putting you down) or passive aggressive (making decisions without you, withdrawing), you may need more support. We'll get there in Part III.

*It doesn't matter how I put it, my partner seems to take what I'm saying wrong.*

*Every time I try to raise an issue, even though I'm doing my best to keep my cool, stay on track and speak respectfully, my partner reacts badly, twists it and we end up in another fight.*

If this is happening consistently, it may be a result of negative interpretations.

Someone who is uncomfortable with intimacy can use negative interpretations as a smokescreen to protect themself. It's like they're saying "you're making me feel uncomfortable, so I'm hopping on my motorcycle and I'm outta here." If you suspect this is the case, you're best off seeking professional help. A relationship counselor can support your partner to become more comfortable with openness and intimacy and help you co-create a closer, more loving family so you can all relax.

But if you think your partner is deliberately making things harder for you, this needs to be addressed, as it can be an unfair and unhealthy way of them trying to gain power over you, which is stepping into abusive territory. More in Part III.

**CHECK YOUR COMPASS:**

**An opportunity for insight.** People tend to assume their partner thinks the same way they do. If you're coming from a *power-with* approach, you'll assume your partner is coming from a position of power-with, too. You'll state your opinion, *invite* your partner to state theirs, and if different, be willing to negotiate, compromise or resolve.

But if a partner is coming from a position of *power-over,* they will *reject* your efforts because they will assume you are seeking power *over* them. They'll also feel justified in being controlling, manipulative or defensive in return—whatever it takes to win. This means despite one partner's best efforts, issues can't be resolved.

**Aim for mutuality.** This is particularly distressing for a newish mother, as she tends to depend more on her relationship with her partner for her sense of wellbeing. She may want more from her partner than previously and be willing to give more in return. But if her partner views the relationship in terms of power-over, he will likely see her as controlling, or attempting to change him, causing him to become hostile, defensive or withdrawn.

**STEPS:**

**Talk about power.** Using the skills in Thriving, open up the lines of communication around how you share influence in your partnership. You may find your partner is completely unaware of their reactions. Make a joint commitment to share power for the stability of your family. You may need to have these conversations in the presence of a counselor. If you suspect your partner's reactions are deliberate, they have crossed the line into abuse. (See Part III.)

**Aim for inner power.** Share responsibility, be accountable for your actions and apologize when you make mistakes. With power-over, there is no responsibility, no accountability and no apology.

## Power and Intimacy

*Sex has deteriorated over the years. At first, I wanted affection, but all he wanted was sex. Then he wouldn't cuddle me because I didn't want it to lead to anything. But I didn't initiate sex because he wouldn't give me a hug. Is there hope for us?*

**CHECK YOUR COMPASS:**

**Recognize a power struggle.** We've touched on the relationship between power and intimacy, and you've learned that having a baby can cause a couple to find themselves in a power struggle. In a power struggle, you are likely to see each other as rivals, not equals, and so get into competition. You're not likely to desire someone who you see as a threat.

**Power struggles create disconnection.** You'll continue to be starved for the affection that makes you feel loved, and they will be denied the physical connection that makes them feel the same way. Your relationship, and your family, will suffer if you can't turn this around. Thankfully you can. There's lots of middle ground here.

**STEPS:**

**Know what you need.** Remember there are two conditions for intimacy to thrive: equality and mutuality. Where there is no equality, there is no motivation. Where intimacy is one-sided, the giver will eventually give up.

**Look deeper.** At the heart of a power struggle are often hidden concerns. Have a look through them again to see if any may be operating below the surface of your relationship. When you leave deeper issues unaddressed, they start to *drive* your relationship, causing confusion, helplessness and resentment. The first step to turning this around is to look under the hood.

*My husband came home the other day, still with his "boss" hat on, and started ordering us around. He had the nerve to want to make love that night.*

One of the biggest destabilizers of a partnership is an imbalance in power—it directly affects all aspects of your relationship—especially your feelings of closeness. You may want to stick around for Part III.

*I feel like I have three children: Mia who's 3, Will who's 6, and Rodney who's 37.*

I imagine Rodney is also aware of this aspect of your relationship, and from his perspective, may feel like you treat him just like his mother. This has consequences for both of you in terms of intimacy—especially your sex life.

**CHECK YOUR COMPASS:**

**Where is the power?** When one partner overly asserts influence over the other, it causes them to withdraw and be less willing to connect. On the other hand, when one partner shares power with the other, it engages them, creating opportunities for closeness and intimacy.

**STEPS:**

**Speak up.** If either you or your partner is in the "one up" or "one down" position occasionally, it may just need to be pointed out when it occurs. If, however, this is characteristic of your relationship, you will need to address it more intentionally. We'll get to that too just around the corner in Part III.

## Fighting in Front of the Kids

*We have two kids. We fight in front of them, is this OK?*

Whether it's OK or not depends on at least three things: how old they are, how often you argue and how you fight.

**CHECK YOUR COMPASS:**

**Babies and young children are highly sensitive to emotion.** Before they develop their use of language, they depend on tone of voice, facial expression and gestures to communicate, so they are like little sponges when it comes to feelings. Anger is extremely frightening to a young child, and babies born into relationships where there is a lot of conflict tend to be more agitated and harder to settle. So, if your fights involve raised voices, name-calling, threats, or worse, get help for everyone's sake.

**You can turn things around.** If fights are disrespectful, damaging or remain unresolved, there is no benefit for your children to witness them. Doing so will lessen their trust of relationships in general. If, however, arguments are infrequent and you're able to manage conflict using the skills in this guide, then it's a good thing to pass on this ability to children. Also, make sure your kids see you make up, or least let them know you've made up as soon as possible after they witness a disagreement. This way they learn to trust that they, too, can be individuals and still be in a loving relationship.

**What do you want for your family?** You are jointly responsible for the tone of your home. If you're fighting all the time, it will be tense and glum for all. If you want your kids to grow up in a warm and loving home, you need to create this environment for them.

**STEPS:**

**Work out what's not working.** If you're continually fighting, there must be reasons why.

**Learn to fight "well."** Re-read Thriving or see a counselor if something seems to be blocking you from using the skills.

**Show them the good stuff.** Let your kids see how much you love each other too. This will balance out their view of your relationship.

## Extended Family

*My mother-in-law is very intrusive—more so since we had a baby. I want my partner to tell her to back off.*

The way to handle this situation depends on a number of things: your relationship with your husband, his relationship with his mother, and your relationship with her.

If either you or your partner have difficulty with your partner's mother, you'll both want to minimize this because it's beneficial for you to have positive relationships with all the potential caregivers in your children's lives. And it's good for your children to grow up with a good relationship with their grandparents.

**CHECK YOUR COMPASS:**

**Beware of triangulation**. Triangulation occurs when a third party (usually another family member or friend) is drawn in to conflict between the original two people. It happens when, instead of Person 1 sorting things out directly with Person 2, they complain instead to Person 3 who then lets Person 1 know that Person 2 is not happy with them and why. This causes a great deal of strife in families, and, as you can imagine, makes things more complicated—and yet people do it all the time—especially with in-laws.

Expecting your partner to be the meat in this particular sandwich is a no-win situation. It is likely to create distress and resentment—for all of you. It's much better that the two with the problem find ways to work it out without contaminating other relationships. Of course, you need to do this sensitively, using all your skills.

**Draw a circle.** Becoming a parent brings a new set of responsibilities, including the responsibility for drawing a boundary around your family and communicating how you want your family to be.

**STEPS:**

**Communicate with kindness**. What looks like intrusiveness to you, may be your mother-in-law's good intentions to help, and it's likely you will need help, and lots of it, well into the future. You won't want to alienate her.

**Use the feedback sandwich: positive, negative, positive.** For example, "Thanks for wanting to be involved, but we'd prefer not to have visitors today. We're all exhausted, but we'd love to see you on Sunday. If you think you can squeeze it in, would you mind bringing your great chicken casserole?"

## Housework and Baby Care

*We argue constantly over who should do what. I want more help, but my husband says he's doing more than he's ever done, and can't do more.*

Arguments over the division of labor in the home is hands down the biggest issue for most couples after children—for years.

**CHECK YOUR COMPASS:**

**Why it's such a big issue.** We've talked about hidden concerns before, and there are lots of them sitting under this particular rock. A partner who is involved in looking after the baby and the home gives a mother a much-needed sense of equality and fairness in her relationship that underpins other elements of it (including intimacy). A mother who's not completely preoccupied with the house and baby, so she can spend much-needed quality time with her mate, makes her partner feel appreciated, valued and loved.

**Problem solving is a skill you'll need.** There are myriad of parenting problems that will crop up throughout your lives together, so the sooner you develop this skill, the better—and it's another great one to pass on to your children. Problem solving is covered back in Thriving.

**STEPS:**

**Plan for it.** The housework issue tends to peak at baby's three- to six-month mark, so if you haven't gotten there yet, you have a heads up. If you're there now, schedule time to talk. If you're past this stage and have struggled through it without benefit, know that you're normal and it's not the fault of either of you. Have conversations instead to process and heal the damage done to your relationship at that time.

**Know the facts.** Australian research found men tend to have an average of three hours more per day of leisure or sleep time than women do. A typical man's combined paid work/caring for children/household chores totals 9 hours, whereas for women it totals 14. I'm not including this as a reason to blame, but to be aware of, and be more realistic about the imbalance.

**Don't look for solutions straight away.** Premature solutions don't last, and then will cause further frustration. Voicing concerns and hopes leads to more sensitive and creative options. Sharing at this more real level binds you and becomes motivation to find solutions that maintain your bond.

**If problem solving isn't working, question why.** Are hidden concerns getting in the way again? Is it your attachment style—or your filters?

**Manage it**. Reassess expectations, downsize clutter (the less stuff you have the less there is to look after), outsource what you can afford, make a list of the chores left over and divide them fairly.

## Finding Your Feet as They Find Theirs: Toddlers

There are two childhood stages that are particularly challenging for a family—the toddler years and teens. This is because toddlers and adolescents are both grappling with important developmental issues of independence, identity and sexuality that, if you haven't already addressed within yourself and in your relationship, can knock you off-balance once again. Any of your own attachment insecurities, can be re-activated at these times.

So just as your toddler is finding their feet, occasionally (or often) falling down and getting up again to give it another try, you may be faced with two steps forwards and one step backwards in your parenting partnership. The good news is all the new awareness and skills you've gained up until now (like becoming *interd*ependent—knowing who you are and allowing your partner to be themselves—and relating in ways that bring you closer together), you get to finally start practicing on your kids.

*My husband can get quite rough with our toddler when they're playing. I don't know if it's good for him. I suggested he do puzzles instead.*

It depends on what you mean by "rough." How is your son reacting to the play? If he's screaming with delight, leave them to it. If it ends in tears, or he's screaming in fear, dad will need to tone it down. But don't discourage him entirely; a safe level of rough and tumble is great for them both.

**CHECK YOUR COMPASS:**

**There are benefits.** Rough and tumble play helps toddlers and children to safely move outside their comfort zones, take measured risks, learn to trust themselves and build confidence to cope with the unknown.

**Your partner's parenting is important.** Your child gets different qualities from both their parents. Rather than being in competition, support each other so they get the best of both worlds.

**STEPS:**

**Share your concerns.** While it may not change the eventual outcome, as your child's other parent, you do have a right to be listened to respectfully and taken seriously.

**Go with it.** Parenthood stretches your learning edge. Whenever you step outside your comfort zone, rather than try to direct or control what comes inside, you get the opportunity to expand it.

*Our toddler "holds" his genitals all the time. My wife slaps his hand away, but I tell her to leave him alone. What's the right thing to do?*

It's normal and natural for toddlers to want to explore—everything. You don't want to make them ashamed of this natural inclination, and it will soon pass. Best to ignore it.

*My partner and I have different ideas about appropriate ways of managing a tantrum. Can you give us any direction?*

The single best piece of advice I can give you to improve your parenting in any situation is this: increase your emotional intelligence. Most of us were disciplined with a focus on limiting our behavior. But behavior is a natural extension of emotion (tantrums are an expression of frustration, and toddlers are doing a lot of learning and can understandably get very frustrated).

Minimize circumstances that give rise to frustration-like hunger, over-stimulation or over-tiredness, and as, you've learned for yourself through this this guide, if not before, work out what the underlying need is.

## Discipline

*I get home late and don't have time for my kids. I miss out on enjoying them, instead I'm the "just you wait until your dad gets home…." guy.*

If the time you spend with your family isn't much fun, you may find you want to spend less time with them. This, in turn, will affect their responsiveness to you—children express displeasure through their behavior—which will just reinforce your feelings of not wanting to spend time with them. On the other hand, the more you enjoy your time with your kids, the more positively your children will respond to you and the more you'll want to hang out with them. Mom will appreciate it too. Definitely a win/win/win for all of you.

*What's hard for me as a dad is the ongoing discipline. I hate having to be continually negative about things. I get frustrated and edgy, especially when I can't clear my head between work and getting home—ready to face the onslaught.*

*My partner and I constantly seem to have a different opinion on how to discipline. He says I'm too soft, I think he's too hard. It's what we argue about the most.*

After the thorny issue of housework, discipline is the next one that causes considerable friction between parents. And while this is uncomfortable for you, it may be more distressing for your child. In relationships where parents argue about appropriate discipline, the child is the biggest loser. Failing to come to agreements about their behavior puts a child in a no-win situation where they'll always have one parent disappointed or irritated with them.

**CHECK YOUR COMPASS:**

**Attention is a legitimate need for a child.** Kids thrive on positive attention—focused one-on-one time where they know they matter. When kids feel connected and important, they naturally want to please and are less likely to act up. It's when kids don't get their needs for positive attention met that they seek other ways to get noticed. For a child, it's better to be in trouble than to be ignored.

**How you were disciplined?** The rules have changed about what's considered appropriate discipline—thanks to knowing more about the negative effects the old "control and criticize" style of parenting had on children's self-development. Shame and fear erode a budding self-esteem.

**Discipline is *not* the same as punishment.** Discipline literally means to "teach a better way." Parents can jump too quickly into punishment without first modeling or instructing children how to do things the way they'd like. As parents, teaching is part of our responsibility. If you haven't done a good job of showing them, it's unfair to punish them for what was actually your own oversight. Oh, and you may have to show them over and over again.

**Want more for your children than just good behavior.** Positive discipline does so much more than just guide behavior—it raises self-esteem, teaches self-regulation, self-reliance and self-responsibility. Positive discipline provides a foundation for the development of children's self-awareness, empathy and capability: good for them and good for their future relationships.

**Stretch yourselves and share the responsibilities.** It's just as important for moms to be involved in giving structure, routine and discipline as it is for dads to be nurturing and empathetic. It's not fair for anyone, if one parent always has to be the "bad cop." Comments like "just wait until your dad gets home" reinforce this. It's also not fair for moms to shoulder the emotional burdens of the family.

**Work together.** If there is one single issue you need to work together on, this is it. Conflicting messages about how a child should behave, especially at the vulnerable times of toddlerhood, when they're starting to form their sense of identity, can leave them anxious and without a framework to build their personality on. Ditto for teens.

**STEPS:**

**Research**. There are lots of great resources about how to positively discipline children. Discuss them so you can jointly make decisions that lay the foundation for the formation of your child's character.

**Aim to be fair but firm**. One parent being hard puts pressure on the other to be soft and *vice versa.* In both cases, it causes resentment. Children need to see that both women and men can be strong and soft as well—and everything in between. The more fully developed we are as individuals, the more capacity we pass on to our children to be their own, complete, selves.

**Find middle ground.** If you stay stuck on discipline issues, you'll leave your child in anxiety limbo, or when they're older, trying to divide and conquer or manipulate you into getting what they want. They can't do this if you're a united front.

**Work toward consistency**. The books all talk about how important it is to be consistent, but this is impossible when your discipline philosophy clashes with your partner's. You can't expect your partner to support you if you are consistently throwing out unconsidered threats of punishment or make bribes you have no intention to follow through. And your child will mistrust you.

To be consistent, you need to first agree that your guidelines are age appropriate and will have a positive effect on your child. Then you can be confident enough to follow through and make them stick.

Agreed-upon strategies also mean you can trust your partner to take over from you when you're too tired to continue on your own. I love it when my resolve is crumbling and my partner steps in with backup and says, "You heard what mom said…."

In these last few stages, you've waded through the waters of strong emotions, delved into the depths of yourself and climbed a mountain of differences. You've finally made it to the last stage of your parenthood adventure—and *the* most transformative one of them all.

# Stage Eight: Bonding Through Intimacy

## (Forever)

Here we are on the top of the mountain you've just climbed, so let's relax and enjoy the view. From here, you can see in every direction. I'm going to share with you what I know can be your future. It doesn't matter which way you look, you only need to know one thing to thrive as a family as you continue on in any direction from here.

It's how to stay connected to one another. And how to re-connect after the times you've walked separate paths for a while. And it's likely you will. As you've now discovered, parenthood will take you in different directions at times. And there are times in life when you'll each have new opportunities for your own personal growth. That's OK. Come together again, grow together again and your whole family can flourish.

The stages of parenthood are complex and intertwined. Navigating them isn't easy, but in one way it *is* surprisingly simple: when you know how to stay bonded with your partner you'll get through **all** of them. Through connection, many of the challenges in each stage of parenthood are *preventable*—or at least more easily managed. The better you get at staying connected through the chaos, the more you'll find that challenges become less of a threat and more of an opportunity to build an even stronger foundation for your family. Even in the midst of wild weather and savage terrain, your bond with your partner grounds you and shelters you against the storms.

You bond with your partner through intimacy. Intimacy occurs on all levels of your being. Intellectual intimacy is sharing your thoughts, ideas, questions and plans; physical intimacy is spending time hanging out with your partner, being affectionate and doing fun stuff together. Emotional bonds grow as you share your deeper feelings, hopes, dreams and fears. Spiritual intimacy comes with the wonder of a waterfall, the peace of meditation, or the reverence of prayer. Bonding also comes through sharing the bliss of parenthood and walking through the fire together when times are tough. Sexual intimacy sets your partnership apart from all other relationships. Intimacy gives you your sense of fit—of belonging together. What feels like the "right" fit may well be different for each of you, especially if one of you feels more comfortable on a motorcycle and the other on a tandem bike.

And so, here's one final challenge of the normal parenthood journey that I need to share with to you. If you have a baby or young child, you're likely to have discovered this for yourself: intimacy is the aspect of your relationship that's probably suffered the most. This is especially true if one of you was at work all day and the other was at home with the baby. It's easy to lead parallel lives and become disconnected. This can go on for years, and for couples who don't know how to navigate the stages of parenthood, it can leave them feeling like they have nothing in common any more—except the children, of course.

In this final stage of your adventure, you'll find more ways to keep your relationship stable, even as your lives and roles continue to change. You'll also discover how to travel together even though, at times, you may feel worlds apart.

## Feeling Disconnected

*Before we became parents, my partner and I both had high-powered jobs. Now that I'm at home with our children, I don't feel connected to his world anymore.*

The time you spend connecting or re-connecting with someone at the end of your separate days carries the tone for the whole evening. Look into each other's eyes, hug and be fully present with them. Five minutes of good quality care for each other is all you need to keep connected, even if your lives are very different now.

*I really threw myself into being a mother and I feel very bonded with my son, but at the same time I feel very distant from my husband.*

With parenthood, time, energy and focus are limited, and if it all goes in one direction, there's not much left over for anything else. The challenge is to find a balance between giving to yourself, your child and also having enough left over for your partner.

The big benefit here though, is that you *get* from your partner too. A loving partner is a power source; your connection sustains you. When you feel emotionally connected, you're not alone. Whatever you're dealing with, you do it together. When you understand how you can become disconnected, you can turn it around.

**CHECK YOUR COMPASS:**

**What are you asking for?** The intense connection you have with your child may pale the connection with your partner. What does "distant" mean to you? What do you want more of?

**This might be difficult for him.** Men in previous generations, and even now, can deny or hide their emotions. Opening up at a time when they may be feeling their most vulnerable is a big ask.

**Prepare to ask anyway**—in a sensitive, respectful way. Parenthood is the very best time for a man to embrace the fullness of his humanity and become familiar with the more vulnerable parts of him that may have been shut down earlier. If done safely, this is healing for him, rich for his relationship with you, and means he passes on the gift of "fully being" to your children.

**What does connection look like?** It could be a look, an affectionate gesture, a kind word. Sometimes your partner may recognize a fleeting offer of emotional connection, sometimes not. They can miss it, or turn away and ignore your attempt, or be preoccupied with other things.

**What signals do you send out?** What do you do? Say? Are you clear about what you want or need? Do you disguise this? If so, why?

**STEPS:**

**Make offers clear.** You may disguise your attempts for connection for fear they may not be responded to in the way you hope. Maybe you make a joke about something that you really mean. A camouflaged signal, "Do you want to take a walk?" may really mean, "I want to be with you now." Leave room for a "no" because your partner may be tired, but he may have be more than happy to snuggle on the couch instead.

**Notice your partner's signals.** Do they ask directly? If no, wonder why not. Signals can be very subtle—a joke, a fleeting touch, catching your eye or a text message.

**Respond positively to their attempts**. In whatever way feels right at the time, a smile of recognition, a wink or a thoughtful word—anything that means "I got it" or "I got you."

**Make more offers.** Mothers can become so consumed connecting with little ones that they can easily become submerged in them. Come up for air, take a breath, look around; see your partner too.

**An exercise.** Have an intentional conversation about each other's signals and the ways you each like to be responded to. Think about your closeness or distance on a scale of one to ten.

For example, "When you say _____, I feel three steps closer," or "When you made that joke, I felt six steps (or six blocks) farther away." You might be surprised by each other's interpretation of intentions.

## Emotional Connection

*My husband has always been a bit reserved. I really expected that when we had children, he would soften and open up more. I'm disappointed.*

*I wanted reassurance from him. I wanted someone adult to talk to at the end of the day. I wanted to share what I was going through with him, and I was going through a lot, but he's not a very good listener.*

### CHECK YOUR COMPASS:

**Intimacy is important for all.** Creating intimacy in your partnership builds trust, understanding, compassion and a strong, loving bond. Once you've established this with your partner, you'll be modeling the same for your children. They'll grow up seeking a similarly nurturing relationship of their own.

**Intimacy can be nurtured**. Remember, there are two conditions for intimacy to thrive: equality and reciprocity. Equality involves trust (that you won't take advantage of me if I am vulnerable with you) and independence (it's OK for us to be different from each other), which, if you'll remember are the first two stages of growth.

Reciprocity requires taking initiative and building competence, which are the next two stages. If you or your partner's personal growth have been sidetracked in any of these stages, you may both need to do some more work for the intimacy between you to grow.

**Be careful what you wish for**. A desire for increased intimacy from you demands increased vulnerability from him because vulnerability and intimacy go hand in hand. Your partner may be uncomfortable with this, so you need to be very sensitive when initiating something. Take your time.

And then *you* may feel some awkwardness if he does open up because it's a new aspect for both of you, even if it's something you've wanted for years.

**Press on regardless**. Anxiety and discomfort are part of growing and adapting. As you both get used to sharing at this deeper level, you'll feel less awkward—and more in love.

**How are you asking?** We tend to open up only if we feel very safe. We can often underestimate how scary we can be to our partner. Examine the ways you've been trying to draw them out. What would it look and feel like to them? You may need a different approach.

**STEPS:**

**Make it safe.** Agree on openness and honesty in your relationship. Expect transparency from each other and a joint responsibility to create comfort for this.

**Model how you want the conversation to go.** If you want your partner to respond to you in a warm, gentle tone, this how you need to speak to them.

**Give them the words to use**. Don't be afraid of being too obvious. They might be grateful for this. Let them know exactly what you want to hear. There's a saying that we teach people how to treat us by how we treat them. This is true with everyone and on all levels of communication.

**Keep trying**. Intimate communication is scary—until it isn't anymore. Go gently—persevere. Your efforts will pay off—forever.

**Appreciate intention, regardless of outcome**. Good intentions may be there, but something like exhaustion, or distraction, can be in the way. Forgive sidetracking and keep coming back to each other.

## Spending Time Together

*I find it difficult to spend quality time with my wife. We used to go out to dinner, just the two of us, and less responsibility, it was easier to talk. Without the baby, we had more energy, time and enthusiasm just to be together.*

*I really enjoy just hanging with my wife and son, but whenever I suggest family outings, she doesn't seem very keen and often makes an excuse to stay home. I usually end up taking our son out on my own.*

*I feel bad, but I just can't wait for him to take the kids out and have time on my own.*

### CHECK YOUR COMPASS:

**You affect each other**. At the same time, you might be looking to your partner for the intimacy needs that are becoming important to you, your partner may be having to adjust to reduced opportunities for the types of intimacy that are important to *them.* It is hard for someone to keep *giving* when they're not *getting* in return.

**Beware of mindreading**. The dilemma for mothers is that they *are* giving… and giving… and giving…. They just don't have much left over. Which is why they're grateful when their partner takes the kids out to give them a much-needed break to recharge. Mothers be mistaken, though, when they expect their partner always recognizes this need.

### STEPS:

**Talk about it.** When you don't understand why your intimacy needs aren't being met, you feel rejected, which can be the beginning of a major rift.

**Be honest.** Tell them you miss them. Tell them you miss spending time with them. Request some quality time, not in a demanding way (they may have more than enough demands already) but in a way that shows that you understand the challenges for them and are willing to work with them so you can make it happen—for the benefit of both of you.

**Use the time you have together mindfully**. Don't talk about the kids unless you need to. Make eye contact and hold your partner's gaze. Hold her hand too. Smile at each other from across the room. Wink. Intimate connection only takes a moment and little effort.

## Desire for Affection—Only

*It's been months. I want to have sex, but all my wife wants from me is to talk and cuddle. It's like a standoff. And I guess I'm feeling pretty rejected.*

***CHECK YOUR COMPASS:***

**You can have** *both, eventually.* Remember, parenthood is not either/or, but both/and. That really pays off here. You've learned that you exist in layers; there are outer and inner layers of intimacy and vulnerability and one leads to the other, closer and closer to the core of you, and of your partner. Sharing thoughts leads to sharing feelings, which leads to affection, which leads to sexual intimacy. Your sexual relationship is an extension of, and is influenced by, how you relate on the other levels. Women generally need a meeting of the minds, a sense of emotional connection and affection in order to feel close to their partner.

**Your partner wears a new hat now**. Conversation, affection and romance are your partner's way of taking her mother-hat off and putting her partner-hat on. At the end of a mother hat day, she needs your help to take it off and switch roles.

If you aren't sensitive to this (or she doesn't make you aware), and you don't spend time just noticing, appreciating or sharing with her, she can feel unsupported and turn down or not initiate sex. Then it's your turn to feel rejected.

**What does sex mean to you?** Women can easily underestimate or dismiss their partner's needs for sex as unimportant. But for many men, a loss of sex is a loss of love. Sex is a primary way to fully relax, connect and be vulnerable with their partner. This is also deeply connected to self-esteem. When a woman rejects her partner sexually, he can feel not wanted or not important as a man (just as she would if she were the one being rejected). He may also feel like you exist just to fix the leaks and pay the bills.

**What's your love language?** In Gary Chapman's book *The Five Love Languages,* he describes different ways we tend to give love:

**Acts of service**: doing the dishes, fixing things, picking up the dry-cleaning. **Physical touch**: cuddles, kisses, holding hands, making love. **Words of affirmation**: "You look great in that," "You mean so much to me," "Thanks for doing a great job with…." **Quality time**: coming home early from work, making time for appointments, organizing a babysitter for kid-free evenings, a weekend away, a coffee date. **Gifts:** a flower on the pillow, a chocolate with the paper, a thoughtful present for a special occasion.

You will tend to give love to your partner in your love language. But here's the thing: if it's not your partner's love language, even though you're giving and giving, it can leave them feeling unloved. The trick is to learn to speak to your partner in *their* love language.

The other thing about knowing your partner's love language is that you won't inadvertently hurt them. If acts of service are your partner's love language, then they're more likely to be upset about those dirty dishes in the sink.

Knowing your partner's love language also helps with a really good apology. For some, the words, "I'm really sorry" mean far more than a bunch of flowers.

**STEPS:**

**Open up.** She needs to know that you're feeling unloved or unimportant. Knowing this makes her feel closer to you. That's the first step to doing something about it right there.

**Talk about your love languages.** Let her know what your love language. Ask her what hers is if you don't know.

**Sidestep further problems.** When you can't share your thoughts and feelings, other types of intimacy are likely to suffer. If this goes on, it can lead to other issues down the track.

*We've been parents for almost a year, and while we have sex occasionally, to be honest, all I want is hugs. Is this normal?*

In a word, yes. For many reasons, your need for non-sexual intimacy is more important after you have a baby. How you negotiate this with your partner is equally important.

**CHECK YOUR COMPASS:**

**It makes sense.** If you're depleted, feeling like you've lost yourself to the baby, or that your body just exists to meet everyone else's demands, saying no to sex for a while can prevent you from feeling even more used up. Find ways to reclaim yourself (see Stage Six) so you have enough "you" for you, and more left over to share.

**Affection is important.** You might find the more nurturing that you give out to a child, the more nurturing you need for yourself (hugs, massages, holding hands) to recharge. You need to be clear to your partner, though, that this comes with no strings attached. If there are, it can feel like another demand on you and you may stop seeking affection. This isn't good for either of you.

**Desire for affection is connected to emotional intimacy**. It's helpful to talk about all the feelings of motherhood with a partner, so you can make sense of them, have your partner understand what's going on for you, include them and share your experiences of parenthood. When you share your emotions, affection closely follows.

**Feelings can be confronting**, it may be new for your partner to experience you like this. If it is, instead of affection flowing as it once did, it might actually be harder for him to be affectionate because he's feeling awkward or uncomfortable. If this is the case, sex will be even more important for him, because that's how he does feel bonded with you.

**STEPS:**

**Be clear about what you want.** Men and women can have very different approaches to how they relate to each other. Where a mother may try to engage her partner—to share with him her understanding of herself and her experiences of the world—her partner may think she is handing him a problem to be solved. He can't understand why she gets frustrated when he has given her solid, practical suggestions. She can't understand why, even after a fairly decent job of explaining herself, he just doesn't get it. Instead of bringing you together—the spirit in which the conversation was begun—you can feel farther apart.

**Talk about it**. It may be uncomfortable for you, but probably not as uncomfortable as it is for him. Make it clear that it's about you, not about him. Let him know what's good for you by using your Thriving skills.

**Find other ways to connect**. Become familiar with each of your love languages and practice using them until you get your mojo back.

## No Time or Energy for Sex

*With three children, we just can't find the time.*

With three kids, finding time and energy for *anything* is a challenge. But if you want something badly enough, it's not about *finding* time; it's about *making* it. It's also about harnessing the energy.

**CHECK YOUR COMPASS:**

**Don't focus on sex.** There're three things essential for a loving relationship: a secure connection, mutual caring, and sexuality. They're all connected. If you work on the first two, the third will follow.

**It only takes a moment.** Tease each other, do something thoughtful, share a joke, make eye contact, wink or smile. Surprise each other. It may take only a moment, but it's a beautiful celebration of your bond.

**STEPS:**

**Make little pockets of time to bond.** Make uninterrupted conversation a priority—however you can.

**Get your kids' cooperation**. Young children can begin to understand the concept of "mommy and daddy time." Older children benefit from helping around the house and you can take more of a break together. Teens can babysit so you can have a coffee date. Seeing their parents care about each other provides children with a sense of security.

**Synchronize bedtimes.** Go to bed together at the same time and talk, snuggle and re-connect. Read each other a paragraph from a book or share a funny story from your day. Having great other types of love life, and the sex—well, you'll find a way. Try waking up together, locking the door and spending a slow Sunday morning in bed while the kids are busy with cartoons.

*I just don't have any energy for sex at the end of the day. Actually, I just don't have the energy for it—period.*

Sometimes "not having time or energy" can be a polite way of saying, "I don't really want to."

**CHECK YOUR COMPASS:**

**Be honest with yourself.** Is sex low on your list of priorities? Sometimes a lack of interest is due to plain tiredness. Or, it could be something else—unspoken anger or resentment, or a way of reclaiming power.

**Reassess your love life.** What makes you feel loved, cherished, appreciated? What makes your partner feel those things? If you're putting time and energy into this, your sex life will eventually recover.

**Be creative.** Fifteen minutes expressing love in your partner's love language is worth more to them than hours in your own language. Request your love needs in ways that are meaningful for you.

**Know why sex is good for a relationship.** Making love is one of the few things we can do that's *just for us*—it's reclaiming relationship territory from the baby invasion.

**STEPS:**

**Take a big breath and be (very gently) honest with your partner.** You need to talk about any underlying unresolved issues. Anger, resentment and contempt are the most effective contraceptives I know—they block positive energy and erode desire. If you don't address this, your sex life will continue to suffer.

**Find ways to re-connect.** What do you appreciate most about your partner? What's special about them? Their quirky sense of humor? A deft hand with a wrench? The way they can still get down on the floor and play a game with your little one, even though they're exhausted? Think about what's special to you and let them know. Don't lose sight of each other over the washing pile. Appreciation and gratitude are great aphrodisiacs.

## Mismatched Libidos

*My wife and I have always had different libidos, but the difference is even worse now that we have kids. Is this normal?*

Absolutely! Research tells us the majority of new mothers, and around half of new dads are not as interested in sex post-baby. While a father's sex drive will return earlier, it's not uncommon for mothers to still be less interested a year or so later, especially if she's breastfeeding. Your desire for intimacy, both physical and non-physical, naturally goes up and down, particularly when you're stressed, preoccupied, sick or tired. So knowing how to navigate this now will help you through all the years of this ahead.

Because your desire to be intimate can fluctuate, it won't always be in sync with your partner's. With infants, a mother's need for intimacy will usually go down because she's busy and preoccupied with the care of the baby. This period may leave you feeling excluded from the growing bond between them. You might seek physical intimacy from her to compensate for this, but if she feels pressured by this, it can lead to greater distance, not closeness. You will want to address it at some point though—the mismatch of sexual appetites can cause tension between couples for *decades.*

There's a saying that women need to feel loved to have sex and men need to have sex to feel loved. The good news is there's a *lot* of fertile middle ground here for both of you.

**CHECK YOUR COMPASS:**

**Understanding**. A new mom's decreased desire for sex is absolutely normal, due to hormones, stress, fatigue, and, thanks to being knee-deep in bodily fluids all day, sensory overload.

**Libido is an extension of how you feel**. So, it changes depending on your circumstances. If you dress in your suit, go out to a stimulating job, get some admiring glances and sparkling adult conversation you'll come home at the end of the day feeling your fabulous self, and of course, want to share that with your partner.

Her day may be the complete opposite—with no time to shower along with feeling stressed or bored or frustrated from her Groundhog Day *déjà vu.* She has nothing left to give. It's likely she'll just feel envious of you.

**Don't take it personally.** Physical fatigue is a major reason sexual appetite is mismatched after baby. While in the beginning, both of you may be exhausted from sharing the night duty, it's usually the mother or stay-at-home parent that takes over the role and does it for longer.

**What's going on inside her?** A mother's fatigue isn't always obvious. She may be experiencing a kind of mental fatigue—an overdose of carrying too much information in her head and responsibility on her shoulders—when is the next feed due? What time is the appointment? What's for dinner? When to book the babysitter? What did the doctor said about treating a fever? What's on the grocery list? When she's in her head-needs mode, it's easy for her to be disconnected from what her body needs.

**Sex is a barometer**. There are exceptions, but generally speaking, the better the relationship, the more satisfying the sex. The reverse is also true. Often a woman's lack of desire can be due to dissatisfaction in other areas of the relationship. Clear them up and you might just find her libido has returned.

**STEPS:**

**Accept that sex life after baby is going to be different**. This isn't anybody's fault, or the result of a failing relationship. Where previously you may have gained satisfaction from sex twice a week, all afternoon or on the beach, the fact is, life has changed for now.

**Accept it's a joint responsibility** to make your sex life what you want it to be. Make your relationship safe so you can ask for sex openly and without shame, then you can say "no" when you don't feel like it without your partner taking offense.

**Don't take each other for granted.** You don't want a relationship where she feels like a sex release valve or kitchen slave, and you feel like a fix-it guy or moneymaking machine and there is no mutual sense of connection—no sense of "us." Both of you are responsible for the wellbeing of your relationship.

**Open the sexuality communication lines**. Getting fears, concerns and hopes out into the open will help you navigate the natural ebb and flow of sexuality that's part of a committed long-term relationship. You need to talk about these things. After all, one day it will be part of your parental responsibility to have honest and open conversations with your child(ren) about their sexuality. Best to get through that discomfort with your partner first.

**Be brave and discuss the possibilities**. Now's a good time to mix things up a bit if you don't have the time, energy or even interest to do things the same old way. Do you have the courage to say what is, or isn't, working for you in the bedroom? Talk about your hopes and desires (or anxieties) around foreplay, masturbation, fantasies and oral sex. Even quickies, as long as they're satisfying for you both, may be an easier option—and for longer than you think.

**Again, beware of mindreading**. If you aren't comfortable talking openly, you're more likely to have expectations of your partner that you haven't expressed. This is unfair to both of you.

**Make dates for sex**. Organize your day so it's achievable. Be nice to each other so no one gets turned off at the last minute. Think loving thoughts about your partner during the day and send a text that says "if you come home with dinner I'll have dessert for you."

## Skin Overdose

*This may sound strange, but when I started breastfeeding, it was like my breasts were for the baby and I didn't want my husband to touch them.*

*After cleaning up the baby and having my two-year-old hanging off me all day, the last thing I want is for my husband to tap me on the shoulder at night.*

Babies are born with what's called skin hunger. They crave body contact, which helps them to thrive. We never outgrow this desire—our urge for physical loving is lifelong. We go from getting it from our parents, to needing it from our partner, and wanting to give it to our children.

A mother whose day is already overfull of being scratched and sucked, covered in bodily fluids and full-body contact, can feel the opposite—a kind of sensory overload or "skin overdose." If a partner is unaware of this, he's likely to feel rejected by a lack of enthusiasm.

**CHECK YOUR COMPASS:**

**Give yourself time.** In the first few months of breastfeeding, especially if they're sore, mothers can feel the need to "protect" their breasts. As you grow more experienced with negotiating everyone's needs (especially your own) and reclaiming your sexual self, this discomfort will resolve.

**Hormones are huge**. If you're breastfeeding, the main reason for reduced sexual desire is hormonal: breastfeeding mothers are infused with oxytocin; a hormone that leaves you feeling relaxed and fulfilled and another called prolactin which can have the effect of reducing sexual desire. And if this wasn't enough, when you're stressed, your body secretes cortisol, a hormone that can also dampen sex drive. All these combine into Mother Nature's natural contraceptive cocktail.

**STEPS:**

**Take the pressure off.** Some couples manage this issue by taking sex off the table, deciding not to even bother for an agreed period of time, and spend that time instead exploring other ways to bond.

**Plan ahead.** What makes a love life exciting and interesting is variety and creativity. Now's a great time to think about what you'd like to do when you both feel ready.

## Body Conscious

*With my saggy boobs and stomach and the extra baby weight I put on, I just don't feel sexy. Goodness knows what my husband thinks.*

Women can be very self-conscious about how their post-baby bodies look and feel, even a long time after childbirth. And it's easy to lose your sensual self under a mountain of laundry and Lego. But reclaiming this aspect of yourself is an important step on the road to motherhood.

**CHECK YOUR COMPASS:**

**Your realities are different.** While you might be thinking negatively about your body, most men are actually in awe of a woman's changing body and the ability to grow and nourish a baby.

**Beware of self-fulfilling prophecies.** If you believe your partner is thinking negatively about your body, you're likely to interpret any hesitancy on their part through your own feelings, rather than for their own reasons (e.g., stress, fatigue) that have nothing to do with you. You could react to your own interpretation by hiding your body, but he may interpret this as *you* not being interested in sex. He may take this personally and react in a way that you will then interpret. Can you see where this is heading?

**Accept yourself.** Remember when we talked about how important it is to have a mutual sense of acceptance in your partnership—about respecting your differences, while at the same time staying connected? Just as this is true of your relationship with your partner, it's also true of your relationship with *your self*. Rejecting aspects of your self, whether it's your body or something on the inside, is likely to sabotage your self-esteem.

**Re-evaluate sexual satisfaction.** You want sex to be so good that you want it *no matter what you look like.* If this isn't the case, it might be time to think about some things. Is there enough romance for you? Do you feel appreciated by your partner? Do you take time to connect as a couple?

**STEPS:**

**Who is the hottest man you can think of?** Would you want a hall pass for them? If a definite "yes" pops into your mind, your libido is still there. If you think about Channing or Idris or Brad (he's still cute!), and you get a spark of desire, your libido hasn't gone missing. Desire isn't the problem—something's blocking it.

**Respect the differences in your post-baby body**—they're the marks of a woman so well loved she was reborn as a mother. Accept, embrace and work with the changes, rather than against them.

**Turn your head off, and your body on**. We get in the way of our own sexuality when our heads speak so loudly that it's all our bodies can hear. Lists of to-dos, shoulds and shouldn'ts and a litany of insecurities that creep into our heads, create feelings that get in the way of what our bodies want instinctively. Bodies like to explore and play—at all ages.

**Discuss lovemaking.** Enlist your partner's help to take your mother-hat off and put your partner-hat on. Affirm what you each like about your sex life first, "I love it when…." and then come up with some ideas about what you both might like try or do differently. You could even get creative and make a game out of it.

**Be bold**. Check out some websites. You might be amazed at what's offered. Saucy games, tasteful books, tantalizing lingerie, explicit how-to movies that leave absolutely nothing to the imagination. You'll need to be selective and sensitive to each other's turn-offs and turn-ons, but there're lots to choose from, and plenty of middle ground if you come from different ends of the sexual spectrum.

**Rediscover your sensuality**. Treat yourself to a massage, a warm scented bath with oils, take up yoga, or dancing or another activity that celebrates how much joy your body can bring. If you can afford it, get a gym membership and cute personal trainer—it's good for your self-esteem and that's good for your sexuality, and that's good for your partner. See the logic here?

> *The other day my husband wanted to buy me some sexy lingerie. I want to feel sexy again. But I look at my potbelly and Caesarean scar, and I just don't.*

There are many physical changes that mothers have to come to terms with: stretch marks, pigmentation, stitches and scars, extra weight, sore nipples and leaking breasts. Need I go on?

Many women find the transition from sexy siren to maternal mother and then into yummy mommy a hard one, but embracing (or re-embracing) your sexuality is healthy for your sense of self, your self-esteem and for your relationship. Letting your hair down at night and getting in touch with your playful, impulsive or adventurous side is a great antidote to boring, repetitive kid-centered times.

### CHECK YOUR COMPASS:

**Sex now can be more satisfying and meaningful than sex before.** It's not honeymoon sex anymore, and it may mean abandoning romantic interludes for the time being, but post-baby sex can be even more exciting when it means dropping defenses and self-consciousness. Accepting and appreciating your body helps you to relax—and relaxation makes for languorous sex.

**Reduce personal insecurities**. Make sex a little about you and a little about your partner, and a *lot* about your partnership. Connecting through understanding, affection and mutual support combats stabs of insecurity that often arise with parenthood.

**Sexy is on the inside.** A woman with an inner confidence, regardless of what she looks like on the outside, is a glorious thing to behold. That you *want* to feel sexy means that you *already* feel desire, but your head is getting in the way by focusing on the outside.

### STEPS:

**Reconnect with your body**. Turn away from the lure of insecurities and ignore the endless to-do lists in your head. Get more familiar with your body language instead.

**Let your body lead the way**. Experiencing yourself being sexually responsive, in spite of your concerns, is empowering. Once you start foreplay (which is even more important post-baby) your attention will be diverted from self-consciousness about how you think your body looks. Instead your attention will be on how good it feels to actually be in it. Reveling in your partner's appreciation and enjoyment, and the bonding between you, are also incentives.

**Share your concerns.** Having your partner affirm what they love about you and that they desire you no less, and probably more than before, is a great aphrodisiac.

**Buy yourself some nice stuff if it helps you feel more confident**. If it makes you feel more comfortable, there are all sorts of outfits that will cover up some parts and leave others exposed. Don't wait for your partner to buy it, their taste may well be different from yours and you're the one who needs to feel sexy—they will appreciate it anyway.

*My wife doesn't want to have sex at the moment, and I understand this, so I've been using porn and masturbating. Is this normal? Is it OK?*

So many things can change through parenthood and this is another one. Some couples who normally use porn may decide it's not right for them at this time, and others who normally don't, do. Some women can be relieved that their partner's use of porn takes the pressure off them; others don't care either way. What's important is that it's a decision made mutually. Because if the porn is furtively stashed and shamefully consumed, it could become a sexual barrier between you.

### CHECK YOUR COMPASS:

**What's normal?** Is your use of porn part of your sexual repertoire? Is it just an "extra"? Or do you rely on it for arousal? The issue with this last one is that regular use of pornography can create an artificial "normal," and with it, an unrealistic expectation of your partner.

What might this mean when you and your partner resume your sexual relationship? If you're conditioned to becoming aroused by nubile leather-clad and stilettoed women, how is this going to affect your level of arousal with your post-baby and just-getting-used-to-the-idea-of-sex-again wife?

**Mothers are often acutely vulnerable in their sexuality**. If she knows that you've been deriving sexual pleasure from looking at women who represent an ideal that she can never live up to, it can leave her feeling deflated—and negatively impact her sex drive, which will, of course, affect you both.

### STEPS:

**Think about the big picture.** Whose needs to consider: hers as well as yours? How are things likely to go if you only consider your own? Honestly answering these questions can help shift focus and guide your decision-making process.

**Talk to her.** Ask for her thoughts and feelings. Is she OK with you masturbating with porn? Does she want to be involved? In what ways? What about quickies? Let her know you don't want to leave her out unless she chooses to be. I have worked with women who felt betrayed by their partner's use of porn, almost as if they'd had an affair. This can be particularly distressing for some at this vulnerable time. Others don't mind at all. Talk to your partner to find out what's OK with her.

*It's been years! Do I just give up trying to initiate sex? Or is there a way to increase my wife's libido?*

These are both good questions. Sex researchers say the biggest turn-on for a woman is her partner's desire for her, but after having a baby, it becomes a fine line to tread. If you're too eager, she may feel pressured or intimidated, but if you're not eager enough, she may take it as a sign you're not interested. That's likely to negatively affect her self-esteem and body image—and in turn, her libido.

**CHECK YOUR COMPASS:**

**Your attitude affects her.** Partners often aren't aware (and women don't always reveal) how very vulnerable she is to your opinions of her, especially now that she's a mother. Be mindful of your influence to help her feel better about herself. She'll be grateful.

**Get it out in the open.** If you don't, you're forced to read (or more often, *mis*read) each other's signals.

**What's her view like?** Ask her what her days are like. Ask her how they affect her. You'll have more insight into why she feels the way she does and why you don't need to take it personally. Libido is affected by depression, so you might want to gently explore this.

**Does she have a sexual history?** Any sexual traumas she may have experienced can be re-activated through motherhood. Tragically, one in five women have been victims of rape and one in five girls have also been child sexual abuse victims. Women who have suffered miscarriages or ectopic pregnancies can also be particularly hesitant about sex. It's important for you to be aware of, and sensitive to, her history before you broach this issue.

**STEPS:**

**Use your positive influence** *liberally*. You love her—let it out! Say it, write it down, send her a text message or an email. Compliment her. Let her know, frequently and in ways that are meaningful to her, how much you love and appreciate her. What ways are meaningful to her? That's a question for her to answer.

**Concentrate on non-sexual intimacy.** Spending time together having fun, relaxing and talking together is just as important to your relationship as a healthy sex life—even more now. That's what you did as you fell in love, and it's what you need to do to stay in love. Studies show that spending time together and being affectionate declines when leading up to your baby's six-month mark, so be aware of this, because it's important—non-sexual intimacy bonds you emotionally.

**Get to know what turns her on.** For some women, it's a deft hand with a vacuum cleaner. Research has found that a father being actively engaged in household responsibilities has a positive effect on sex life (and also the chance of her wanting another baby at some point). Others can watch their partners do the dishes without any hint of a tingle.

Foreplay means different things for different women. Some are seduced with flowers or chocolates, others a massage, and yet for others, the "three A's" are great aphrodisiacs—attention, acknowledgement and appreciation.

**Kiss her**. Many partners stop kissing after kids come. I mean *really* kissing. A peck on the cheek doesn't cut it. For many women, a deep passionate kiss is very arousing. It gives them time to come down out of their heads and reconnect with their bodies. It's also a great invitation. If she pulls away, she doesn't want to go any further, but if she doesn't, and the kiss gets more passionate, well then….

**Don't shut down or shut her out**. Men can shut down emotionally to guard against being triggered by sexual rejection, but women are *less* likely to want to have sex with a cold and non-communicative partner. This can become a vicious cycle that plays out for years.

**Come up with agreed signals.** She could have a signal that says "no"—like turning the light off before you get to bed or wearing her old PJs, which mean "not tonight." You'll know without having to ask what the status is. But red satin could be your green light.

**Get help**. If you've done all you can, now's the time to seek professional advice, rather than let this situation continue. There could be underlying issues getting in the way. Unearthing and talking these through with a counselor (who is well trained and experienced in dealing with what is a very private issue for you) will get you where you'd both probably prefer to be.

## Lust Languages

Getting through "Not tonight, honey, I have a baby" by knowing your partner's Lust Language.

1. **Trust**

Being in the bedroom (living room, kitchen, etc.) with someone who takes you by the hand, is willing to walk with, and support you in sexual adventures, who is mindful of your sexual comfort zone, but willing and patient enough to help you extend beyond it, if you wish, who partners you in sex as a private, shared joy, is sexy.

2. **Desire**

When your partner looks at you like you're drop-dead gorgeous, treats you like the precious love of their life, handles you like you're hot and wants to ravish you when you're ripe for it—you'll be ready.

3. **Humor**

Humor is sexy. Someone who can make you laugh in their own quirky way, and shares private jokes, makes for a great prelude to sex.

4. **A skilled hand**

With the iron, with a mop, with the washing machine—a partner who pulls their weight around the house respects and values you. That's empowering—and sexy.

5. **The knowing of you**

A deep connection with someone who knows you to your core, who celebrates your uniqueness and values you for the person you are, is a big turn-on.

You may not have noticed it, but over our time together as we've been travelling through the stages of parenthood, I have been giving you countless steps to stay bonded through all of them, all along the way. These steps are here for you to go back to again and again as life unfolds ahead of you. Re-trace the ones that have worked for you before and try some new ones if you find that you're not where you want to be.

If you ever start to feel lost in the years ahead, even when your children are teenagers, just skim the bold points in this guide. They will help you to orient yourself, find your feet again and move forward through the stages together.

There's some even more challenging terrain in the next part of the journey that you may or may not want to walk through. I invite you to at least take a look, because even if this isn't on your path, it may be one that someone you know and care about is having to travel down and they won't want to be walking alone. Otherwise, I'll see you on the other side at our final meeting place, where we'll say goodbye.

# PART III:

# EXTRA SUPPORT FOR PARENTHOOD

As hard as the following issues are to raise with you, I have included this section because I want you to be aware of them. If you're being affected by any of these situations, then not understanding them, not talking about them and not being able to seek further support and guidance through them can cause you and your family even more distress.

If these issues apply to your family, I'm hoping reading what follows will be your first step in getting help. While you can go a long way toward avoiding the pitfalls of parenthood that you've discovered up to now by following the advice in this guide, the extreme challenges in this last section of our journey really do require professional help and in-person support from a counselor or doctor—maybe even a managed recovery program and/or a support group of fellow travelers too.

If you're doing such a great job of preparing ahead before your baby joins you, know that most of the issues in this section are *preventable*. The risk for physical injuries and birth trauma can be reduced through prenatal education, awareness of different birth preferences and the roles of interventions.

Depression and anxiety can be minimized and managed. Grief and loss can be worked through and healed. Affairs, addictions and abuse can be avoided through self-awareness, emotional intelligence, courage and loving connection.

So, take a deep breath, be brave and let's begin.

# Coping with Birth Trauma, Grief, Depression and Anxiety

Periods of trauma, grief or depression are severely challenging. Sometimes they can take you and your partner down to rock bottom. This can be a desolate, lonely and frightening place. It can also be a place that brings you together and makes you stronger than you might ever have imagined. I have seen people, couples and families flourish more after hitting the bottom and coming back up compared with those that never got close.

## Birth Trauma

*The simple tasks of eating, sleeping, making phone calls and running errands seem insurmountable. I feel so anxious that I can barely breathe, and any reminder of my pregnancy or birth feels like a giant wave knocking me off my feet and leaving me gasping for air.*

*Birth trauma affects partners too. Women experience it directly; men see and try to deal with its effects. Men have to understand that their woman's experiences have affected them; women have to know that their partner has been affected too.*

*My partner wants us to have another baby, but after what I experienced first time, I don't think I can do it again. At all.*

Trauma happens by degrees. Even if you experienced a "normal" birth, you can feel shocked and overwhelmed by it. When the birth goes "normally," according to your delivery team, it can still feel wrong to you—and then, things can go wrong.

A long and drawn-out labor, a complicated birth, induction, forceps or vacuum extraction, perineal tears, pelvic floor trauma or an emergency Caesarean birth, can all contribute to trauma. If a baby is born prematurely, unwell or with a disability, these are all likely to contribute to trauma too.

CHECK YOUR COMPASS:

**Trauma happens when "normal" becomes not-normal very quickly.** Trauma comes from feeling completely powerless against an overwhelming force. Normally, when you're threatened, fear energizes your body, preparing it to deal with the threat—the fight/flight/freeze response that we've spoken about.

But when you're afraid, and you can't do anything about the situation (like with an emergency Caesarean), the fight/flight/freeze response gets triggered, but there's no way for it to run its course. You may get stuck in panic mode. And then, on top of that, you have a baby. Which is a total spinout. The best way I've heard it described is like having a serious car accident on the way to your wedding. And all anyone wants to talk about, is how beautiful the dress is. Which is enough to make you feel like you're going crazy. You're not—the situation is.

**Partners can be affected by birth trauma, too**. From seeing you in extreme pain or emotional distress, some partners can feel responsible, even guilty, for "putting you through" the ordeal of labor and birth. Others, while witnessing medical intervention, can feel like you are being violated in front of their eyes, but powerless to do anything about it. Witnessing a traumatic birth can send most partners into shock, which means they're unable to function normally and "be there" for a birthing mother. Mothers can experience this as abandonment.

These feelings are all normal and likely to pass, especially when they can be talked through supportively. Getting help sooner, rather than later, is good for several reasons. A traumatic birth increases risk for postpartum anxiety and depression, which we'll talk about soon. It can also lead to Post Traumatic Stress Disorder (PTSD). Here're some of the symptoms of PTSD:

- feeling constantly on edge, startling easily, overreacting and being irritable about small things,
- poor sleep, including nightmares,
- reliving the event, having flashbacks, or memories that are triggered by small reminders,
- feeling powerless, helpless or like you're surrendering in the face of future challenges, feeling numb or constricted,
- feeling detached, like you're leaving your body for a while, shutting down, shutting other people out or using alcohol or drugs to do this.

So, if this sounds like you or your partner, please reach out for professional help now because while trauma is complex—and can affect families for years—some of the most effective treatment options are very simple and may only involve a couple of visits.

**STEPS:**

**Expect to be "not normal."** You're likely to be off-kilter for some time afterwards. You might find that you're unable to cope with small, simple tasks. You may feel physically exhausted, but unable to rest. You might find you're compelled to talk about the birth.

Don't live with physical discomfort. Mention any pain or discomfort to your GP, midwife, OB or other care provider to assess for injuries like third- or fourth-degree perineal tears, pelvic floor muscle trauma or pelvic organ prolapse (POP). These are common injuries of childbirth and require treatment to heal.

**Talk about the birth.** Time does not heal all wounds, especially traumatic ones. Debriefing (talking in detail about the birth and your reactions) to a professional, lessens the impact of the trauma, allows the shock to wear off, the feelings of distress and helplessness to dissipate and enables you to get some much-needed emotional support so you can finally relax and start to enjoy your baby. A counselor, midwife or doula, ideally someone you already like and trust, who is also trained in debriefing, is perfect for this job.

**Talk about the birth again**. You may need to talk about different aspects many times over. Do it with good listeners—someone who is interested in what you need to talk about, validates your experience, doesn't judge you, intrude with their own stories, or try to give advice that may not be right for you (that's just *more* frustrating). Trauma leaves you vulnerable and therefore hypersensitive. Revealing your vulnerabilities to someone you thought would comfort you, but who responds to you inappropriately, is likely to just cause further distress.

**Be aware that your partner might not be the best listener, initially.** They may be struggling with aspects of the birth themselves and may also feel blamed, even though this isn't your intention. Once you're both able to talk and listen freely and comfortably, have mutual conversations about the birth and re-connect as a couple. Get the help of a counselor if needed.

**Anything that gets the experience "out" of you can help**. Write out your birth story—what happened, what you thought, what you felt, what you remember. This helps reprocess the traumatic memories that can otherwise stay hidden in your brain or body for years. Do a drawing or painting. Feel the feelings and dance them out. Get a counselor to guide you if needed.

**Be gentle on you both**. Don't judge yourself, compare yourselves with other couples or put pressure on yourself to do more than the very basics. Trauma takes up *a lot o*f mental and emotional energy. Recovering from it is like recovering from a physical injury—you need to take care of yourself, be taken care of, take things slowly, one thing at a time and get assistance. If you haven't got the support, find a caring postpartum doula.

**Get into a routine**. The mindlessness of routine tasks can be comforting when you can't concentrate or think straight. They can anchor your day.

Don't expect the baby to be in a routine yet, though, and don't rush them. Observe and get to know their natural rhythm. Connecting with your baby will help you too.

**Eat well and do gentle exercise.** Nutritious food is natural medicine. Exercise is a natural anxiety reducer and antidepressant.

**Create your village.** Join a group for new parents in your area. If birth trauma is not one of the discussion topics, request that it be included and invite others to discuss it as well. You could even organize your own informal support group or find one online. Sharing with others who have experienced trauma helps you to realize that you're not alone. Social support has been shown to help coping with trauma.

**Research.** Search online and you'll find some great resources. Sites like <solaceformothers.org> Prevention and Treatment of Traumatic Childbirth, <pattch.org>, The Birth Trauma Association <birthtraumaassociation.org.uk> and The Australian Birth Trauma Association <birthtrauma.org.au> are a good start.

**Repair and reconnect as a couple.** Your trust bond with your partner provides a secure base for your relationship and a safe haven for you. If this bond was ruptured during the birth, if you felt let down by your partner, or abandoned by them, repair this—maybe with the help of a relationship counselor or therapist.

Birth trauma is rough going. But—and this may seem strange—if you can work through it, you'll find it can bring you more together. The intensity of a crisis, when you can walk through that fire together, can bind you in a more powerful way than anything else.

## Loss and Grief

*My mother died of breast cancer a few years before our daughter was born. It was incredibly hard. I needed her more than ever. Not only that, but as a mother now, I have come to understand her more. I wish I could share that with her now.*

*We lost a baby four years ago. As much as I want this one, a part of me is dreading it.*

*Our daughter was born with a disability and I felt so sad about what this might mean for her. I was also afraid about what it might mean for us.*

*Anniversaries get to me.*

Some losses are more obvious than others. And many losses can be traumatic too, particularly if they are sudden and unexpected. If you have a baby who doesn't thrive, you may be faced with the loss of a healthy life or a normal childhood for them—and also what a "normal" life would might be for yourselves. Infertility, IVF attempts, miscarriages and ectopic pregnancies all involve loss—and can be linked with anxiety or depression.

Some parents' journey into *becoming us* involves multiple losses: miscarriages of biological and then donor eggs, failed foster or adoption attempts. The distress of each loss can easily blend into the next.

Parents who have lost a twin in utero or at birth are confronted with the incredibly challenging emotional stretch of saying goodbye to one baby while at the same time welcoming another.

Parents of premature babies can feel the loss of a full-term pregnancy and worry over their babies' health. This can be exacerbated by friends and professionals who don't acknowledge the mixed emotions of having a new baby and being anxious about them at the same time.

Those who had a previous pregnancy termination can revisit this and sometimes mourn it for the first time, bringing up feelings of guilt, anxiety or depression that may not have been fully explored at the time.

For those who have lost a parent, becoming a parent ourselves is likely to be a reminder of this. Old bereavements will resurface, particularly around family celebrations such as birthdays or holidays, and be grieved all over again. There's support for this.

**CHECK YOUR COMPASS:**

**People grieve differently**. You and your partner will have different feelings and different needs at different times. One of you may need to honor your loss; the other may need to forget about it for a while. It's all normal here. Be supportive, even if your partner is experiencing something different from you. If you give them the space they need for their own process, you can still stay connected.

**STEPS:**

**Check in with each other**—in the days, weeks, months, and then on the anniversaries following a loss, to see how your mate is doing.

**Allow and encourage expressing feelings**. People can make the mistake of trying to talk you out of your feelings, thinking that if you don't talk, they will just go away. You're likely to end up with *more* feelings—ignored, invalidated or shut down. Our feelings are what make us human and there is no more human time than these challenges of early parenthood. Explore ways to let feelings flow—through talking, journaling, painting or through movement.

**Find out what your partner needs from you or what comforts them.** Do they want to talk? You to listen? A hug or advice? Or just to give them space to work it out in their own way? Let them know what you need too.

**Connect with people who are emotionally supportive.** Reconnect with people who are emotionally supportive. Let them know you appreciate them.

**Embrace rituals.** Rituals are a way of respecting significance—expressing feelings and valuing the special connection we have with those who share our loss. Do something that comforts you both as much as you need. When you're ready, you might like to create a ceremony that symbolizes the loss. Hold hands, blow out a candle or write significant words and entrust them to a special box—whatever is meaningful for you. Give yourselves permission to let go of rituals when the time is right too.

**Know when to get help.** If sadness or depression continue unabated, if after several weeks appetite is still affected or you can't sleep or "switch off" even though you're exhausted, speak to a trusted health care provider or counselor. These are signs you may need extra support.

## Dad's Grief

The loss (letting go) aspect of parenthood can more negatively affect some men. Because many have been raised to hide their vulnerability, they may try to avoid or shut down their emotional process around this. But blocking one emotion also means cutting off others—including love, pride and joy.

With more challenging losses, men's grief, and their experience and expression of it, is as unique as they are. Some will grieve openly, others in private and some turn tears into sweat. I know of one man who created a beautiful garden.

### CHECK YOUR COMPASS:

**Time and space.** Whenever we grieve for something or someone, we can re-experience other unresolved or unhealed hurts and losses, even those we suffered in our childhood. This is particularly true for those who haven't been "allowed" to grieve along the way. The best time to heal old wounds is to integrate them into a new process of grieving and healing. Parenthood is the perfect time for this.

**Healing.** What you feel, you can heal. Sharing your feelings, all of them, and finding comfort with your partner, a good friend, or a counselor if needed, or finding other ways to work them through, helps ease the pain and loneliness of grief.

**STEPS:**

**Make it safe for them to be open**. Care to ask them what's going on. If they're sad, they may need to give themselves "permission" (and trust that you are OK with them) to express this—especially if they were shamed for crying as a child—and many were.

**Encourage sharing.** If your partner is uncomfortable talking about their feelings, they may need more practice and you need to make it *very* safe for this. Don't push. Your partner will have their own time-frame but let them know that you care and are there for them.

**Crying is cleansing**. We release stress hormones when we cry, which reduces emotional pain, body tension and leaves us feeling lighter and more balanced. Burying grief can lead to increased levels of stress hormone toxicity, reduced immune function, and feelings of hopelessness, helplessness and depression, which add to chronic states of physical and emotional ill-health. Maybe going for a drive and crying in the car can help.

**Know when to get help**. If they continue to be moody, or withdraw into work, hobbies, computer games, etc., or you notice an increased use of drugs or alcohol, it's time to get help—these can all be warning signs of grief turning into depression.

## Perinatal Depression and Anxiety

*I have been feeling flat for months. My partner thinks I might be depressed.*

*My doctor has just diagnosed me with Postpartum Anxiety. I thought I would be a natural at this. I feel like a failure.*

*We've adopted. Is it possible for me to be depressed too?*

It's normal for mothers feel down for a few days following their baby's birth. A combination of hormones, a natural feeling of anticlimax following the anticipation and excitement of birth and few nights of sleep deprivation are a sure-fire formula for the Baby Blues, which is common to around 80 percent of mothers. For most, this will pass after a few weeks.

If you're experiencing the loss (letting go) type of depression, you may be up and down longer as you adjust to your new life and your new self. With enough practical and emotional support, there will be more ups and less downs along the way.

For others, it's not so simple. Around one in three women will experience anxiety in the postpartum period and one in six are likely to develop symptoms of depression. Collectively, mental health issues during pregnancy and the first year or so afterward are known as Perinatal Mood and Anxiety Disorders (PMADs).

Personally, I think *our society* is what has a disorder and needs fixing, so I prefer the term Perinatal Mental Health (PMH) conditions. I think it makes perfect sense that so many parents experience anxiety and depression when you consider unrealistic expectations, financial pressures, not enough support, broken medical systems, etc. I could go on. Frankly, I'm surprised more of us aren't anxious or depressed. And you know what? These figures are what're actually *reported,* so actual rates are higher.

The good news is that PMH conditions are preventable, highly treatable and manageable. Because there're a wide variety of contributing factors, and the combination of these factors will be unique to you, there are also many different options for recovery and healing. Speak to a professional so you can get the best advice for you and your family. If someone doesn't take the time to get to know you and just hands you a prescription, find a different provider.

**CHECK YOUR COMPASS:**

**What's your history?** A history of anxiety or depression in your family, or previous periods of these in your own life, can increase the risk. A traumatic birth experience increases risk. Physical conditions like sleep deprivation, low thyroid hormone levels, anemia or high blood pressure can contribute. All are reasons why it's important to include your doctor in what's going on.

**What's happening around you?** Social conditions, like poverty or financial stress, isolation from family and friends, a teenage pregnancy or lack of practical and emotional support are factors. Relationship problems are a big one. So too are the changes to identity and independence that motherhood brings.

**What's happening inside you?** Low self-esteem, crippling beliefs like, "I have to do everything perfectly," unmet expectations and a need to be in control all pile up—as can the shock of childbirth, the worry of not coping, the loneliness of isolation or the stress of being overwhelmed.

**Some perspective**. A diagnosis is *not* a reflection of who you are. In traditional communities such as Malaysia, reported rates of PPD are as low as 3 percent. It's not your fault. You were never meant to be a mother without adequate preparation and support.

What to notice about Postpartum Anxiety:

- not sleeping well even though you're exhausted,
- feeling lethargic or unmotivated, but also restless and unable to relax,
- loss of appetite and sometimes weight loss or gain,
- constant worry, from feeling on edge to panic attacks,
- racing thoughts that can't be switched off,
- feeling lightheaded, short of breath, hot flushes.

What to notice about Obsessive-Compulsive Disorder:

- constant cleaning,
- constant checking the baby,
- intrusive and shocking scary or ugly thoughts or images (often about the baby's safety or sexual in nature) that can make you think you're a bad mother, or even a monster.

Intrusive thoughts are actually very common. They're like someone with a fear of heights imagining themselves standing on the edge of a cliff. Your mind is confronting you with your worst fears. This doesn't make you a monster, it's more likely to mean you care extra much about your baby. A good book for this is *Good Moms Have Scary Thoughts* by Karen Kleiman.

**What to notice about Postpartum Depression (PPD)**: Sometimes this comes on gradually, sometimes suddenly, but usually within the first month of motherhood. It may last for weeks, months or longer.

Here's how it looks:

- feeling flat, miserable or tearful most of the time, but for no obvious reason,
- unable to enjoy yourself, or the baby,
- feeling hopeless or worthless,
- losing interest in what's going on in the outside world, or in things that used to interest you beforehand,
- avoiding other people or places that feel too challenging, which then can add to your feelings of isolation.

Most PMH conditions are mild, fewer are moderate and even fewer are severe. At the very far end of this spectrum is what's called Postpartum Psychosis (PPP), which is very rare (less than 0.2% of births), but I mention it because it is a very serious condition that needs to be acted on quickly. It's likely that a partner will be the first one to notice the symptoms—a loss of contact with reality, delusions, hallucinations or paranoia. So, if your partner is acting and talking strangely, arrange an immediate visit to a clinic, emergency room or hospital, preferably one with a mother and baby unit, for diagnosis and specialist treatment. The good news, despite the severity of PPP, is that women and families (it's scary for everyone), with help, can recover.

**STEPS:**

**Be friends with your doctor.** Or find a new one. If not already, now's a good time to establish a relationship with someone you can trust to travel the parenthood journey with you. Get a checkup and blood test for vitamin deficiencies or underlying health conditions.

**Talk with your family.** Ask questions and listen to how they coped when you or your siblings were born; it may give some insight into your own experience. Opening the lines of communication with parents can be both enlightening and healing. Hopefully you also end up with more offers of help and babysitting.

**Debrief birth trauma** with a trusted professional.

**Connect with other mothers** who share your experience so you can start to feel normal again. Postpartum Support International (PSI) <postpartum.net>, Postpartum Progress <postpartumprogress.com>, Post and Ante Natal Depression Association (PANDA) <panda.org.au>, and the Centre of Perinatal Excellence (COPE) <Cope.org.au> are great resources.

**Build up your support system**—partner, family, friends, community services and healthcare professionals and counselors. I personally think that anyone being treated for depression or anxiety should have a free weekly massage. Close ties are an inoculation against depression and trained professionals a way out.

**Adjust expectations**—of yourself, your partner, your baby, any siblings and your new life.

## Paternal Perinatal Mental Health Conditions

*My partner hasn't been himself since we had our baby. Actually, when I think back, maybe even during the pregnancy.*

*All I can think of is that this baby is just one big drag.*

As a mother, the changes for your partner may not be as intense as those you've experienced but becoming a father has still tilted his world like never before. He might be stressed about things he's not sharing with you and at the same time grieving his own losses—including maybe the loss of you. If he thinks that he's not "allowed" time, or able to adjust to the shifts, these and other factors can contribute to anxiety or depression in dads.

Like mothers, Postpartum Anxiety is more common, with 17% of dads reporting symptoms very similar to those of mothers." One in ten fathers will experience Paternal Postpartum Depression (PPD) overall, but that figure rises to about 25 percent in the three to six months postpartum. And given men's greater reluctance to admit depression, the numbers could be even higher.

**CHECK YOUR COMPASS:**

**Were there warning signs in pregnancy?** Higher stress levels in expectant dads (often due to financial stresses), are linked to lower levels of relationship satisfaction, which are likely to affect bonding with their unborn baby and increase their risk for depression afterwards.

**Fathers' depression may look different to mothers',** but no less devastating for a family. Depression in dads can be less obvious, with men being more moody, agitated, frustrated, aggressive or withdrawn. Because the depression is less obvious, and men are less inclined to reveal it, it's less likely to be recognized and treated, so the effects can linger longer—for all. Once it's recognized, however, depression can be managed, so dad can get himself back and his family back.

**Your partner may not be coping even if you are.** Fathers are naturally affected by any changes in their partner, but they can also suffer PPD themselves, even if their partner is coping well with motherhood. Big changes to lifestyle, loss of independence, increased financial burden and feeling like they've "lost" their partner to the baby are common contributors.

**Other factors include limited social outlets and friendships.** Unemployed dads are more likely to become depressed, as are those in a high-conflict relationship. Not only that, but also where fathers' roles traditionally involved providing for the family and disciplining children, today's fathers are expected to do so much more, and this can lead to their feeling confused, overwhelmed and powerless.

**Trauma can be re-triggered**. In the book *Why Dad's Leave,* author Meryn Callander describes John Travis, MD's estimate that thirty percent of fathers in the U.S. will leave their family in their baby's first three years and that a much larger percentage leave emotionally. Travis named this phenomenon Male Postpartum Abandonment Syndrome (MPAS). He has discovered that the sudden and unexpected loss of connection with an overwhelmed partner can trigger older unrecognized or unresolved birth and childhood traumas—including psychological injuries from medicalized birth and circumcision—that are likely to be outside everyone's awareness. This can contribute to both PPPD and the largely hidden epidemic of disappearing marriages where a man with unresolved childhood abandonment issues now feels abandoned by his partner. Unless this is recognized, he is likely to abandon her—emotionally, if not physically.

**Signs and symptoms of PPPD.** Men suffering from PPPD report feeling useless, inadequate, ashamed or like a failure, but these feelings are often hidden under the following behaviors:

- irritability, anxiety and anger,
- loss of libido,
- changes in appetite,
- risk-taking behavior,
- withdrawal and isolation from others,
- increased work hours,
- increased drug or alcohol use,
- feelings of resentment or jealousy towards the baby.

**STEPS:**

**Get professional help.** Paternal PPD affects the whole family. Research has shown dads with PPPD are less able to support their partner and this can affect how the mother feels about looking after their baby. Dads who suffer from depression are less likely to engage with their children (like reading, singing songs and telling stories) that later affect a child's verbal skills. One study found that boys are twice as likely to have emotional and behavioral problems if their father suffered from depression when they were babies. Speak to your doctor or see a counselor—these things can be prevented.

**Use self-help strategies.** Fathers need to make time for themselves, increase their social support, talk about the changes of parenthood with their partner, family, friends, trainer or physiotherapist; they will be surprised how common their feelings are. Also important is maintaining hobbies or activities and getting regular exercise. Improve their connection with their partner is the best antidote to stress and depression.

**Get involved with your baby.** Fathers who feel confident (and supported) in finding their own ways of caring for and playing with their baby have a stronger connection with them—and are much less likely to get depressed.

# Recovering from Affairs, Addictions or Abuse

Most parents aren't aware that their relationship is vulnerable at the time of having a child. Issues that existed before baby can escalate. New issues arise. Some parents can try to cope with them in ways that end up being destructive to themselves, their partner and their family—pulling all into deeper, more treacherous waters.

Pregnancy and early parenthood can put a great deal of stress on some, and they can struggle in various ways to get through the challenges. Research shows a number of serious issues can begin or increase during this time. Addictions, abuse and affairs can impact a couple at any stage in their relationship, but are particularly distressing at the sensitive and special time of creating a new family.

When we become a family, we trust our partner with our body, our emotions, our children—and our future. Addictions, abuse and affairs erode (or prevent creating) the trust that is the core of a relationship.

But as devastating as these situations are, there is help and there is hope. Couples who find support for these issues (and are able to do the work they need to do) can end up happier and with healthier relationships than beforehand.

If a relationship is based on unrealistic hopes and assumptions, with poor understanding of the issues and poor communication, couples can be blown apart by infidelity, addiction or abuse. They are then forced to re-evaluate the very foundations of their relationship. The amount of work needed to rebuild them—if this is possible and is what they both want—is huge. If they can commit to rebuilding (or building solidly for the first time), it will be clear-eyed and with the wisdom, skill and the very painful work it takes to forgive and to create trust, intimacy and connection.

## Affairs

*Since my partner and I had our baby, I've found myself becoming attracted to a colleague at work. It's nothing serious….*

*There's no easy way to say it. I cheated on my wife. It just happened and I regret it. I don't know what to do.*

*I can't believe my partner would betray me at a time like this and risk losing everything.*

Affairs can happen for several reasons. A major life transition like pregnancy and the birth of a child is one of them. Infidelity is devastating to any relationship but has even more impact on the vulnerable time of increased dependency when starting a family

An affair doesn't necessarily have to be physical. Intense attention and interest—an emotional affair—can still undermine a relationship and the foundations of a family. It's important to know where the line is, so it's not crossed. More on that soon.

### CHECK YOUR COMPASS:

**Most affairs start harmlessly.** When a partner doesn't recognize that they have underlying feelings of being excluded, unappreciated or not wanted that they don't share with their partner, they can consciously or unconsciously be more grateful for any attention or acknowledgement from someone else. Friendship or flirtation can lead to physical and/or emotional connection. Can you see how "one thing led to another…" can happen? It's a very slippery slope.

**Mothers aren't necessarily aware** of a process of their disconnection either. Exhausted, preoccupied, struggling to meet the baby's needs and manage life in general, they may be so engrossed in their own tsunami of experiences that what a partner is going through, or missing, simply isn't on their radar.

**The consequences.** For a mother whose confidence and self-esteem may already have taken a beating, a partner's affair is likely to be traumatic and even result in PTSD. The aftermath can be like dealing with an unexpected death—the death of your relationship as you knew it, and your family as you hoped it to be.

**The stages of grief apply:** the shock of betrayal; the disbelief and denial ("how could you do this to me—and now?"); the rage and anger; the bargaining of soul-searching; and the pain and depression that come with the realization that things will never, ever be the same again.

**The impacts go beyond relationship losses.** A partner who has been betrayed can feel like they've lost *themselves.* An affair cuts deep emotionally and psychologically: a woman can question her sanity (especially if her partner has been denying it), her sense of reality, her sense of what's right, fair and normal. It's not only her partner she can't trust anymore; it's *everything* and *everybody.* For these reasons an affair is a form of mental and emotional abuse.

**The effects.** An affair shatters lives, relationships and families. The secrecy, deception and denial involved in an affair erode the very core of trust a relationship needs to build on. Without it, a marriage isn't healthy or desirable. If trust cannot be rebuilt, then, sadly, the relationship, and the family as it was, isn't viable. Just like a building, repair work needs to be done before restoration. If a repair isn't successful, anything that comes afterwards won't stick. This work is best done with professional help.

**Where is the line?** Affairs expert, Shirley Glass, talks about walls and windows in relationships. Intimacy occurs when the windows are open and you can be transparent about yourself and your life.

In an affair, the person who is cheating begins to withhold information and keep secrets from their spouse, creating walls in the marriage. But windows are opening up to let a third person in. The wider the window opens to the third person, the more the wall needs to go up with the spouse. The only way to repair the damage is to close the window to the third party and start to rebuild the foundation of the marriage. Part of this means acknowledging any pre-existing wall that may have already been in the relationship and each partner taking responsibility for this.

**STEPS (IF YOU ARE THE ONE AT RISK OF OR WHO HAD AN AFFAIR):**

**Take responsibility.** Despite what your partner may or may not have done, you are the one that chose to take your personal or relationship issues outside the boundary of your relationship, rather than deal with them inside.

**Be aware of the effect** on your partner—it will be more than you realize. They will need a lot longer to heal than you're probably comfortable with.

**Be prepared for the end.** Infidelity is a deal-breaker to most marriage vows, spoken or unspoken, so your partner may well want to end your relationship.

**Be open and honest.** Any dishonesty, denial, defensiveness or withholding of information on your part will cause further injury. The only hope you have of redressing this is to show your partner you're capable of being completely transparent with them.

**Realize that healing is a process.** You will both be on different timeframes to recover. Don't pressure them to "get over it." You will just delay the whole process and frustrate you both even more.

**Expect it can take years.** You cannot control the timeframe of their processing; you can only support their process.

**Learn to be emotionally supportive.** Your partner will be more angry, sad, confused, frustrated and hurt than you have ever seen before. All these feelings will be targeted at you. You need to be prepared to weather these storms for as long as they last.

**Acknowledge** the depth of distress your choices have caused your partner and the potential they have to destroy your family.

**Do whatever it takes** to show your partner you "get" what you've done. Make whatever changes you must to make things as right as they can be again. They may have thought things were OK before, so how will you do things differently to prove you're trustworthy now? Check in with them regularly throughout your day so they know what you're doing. Be prepared to talk—*all the time.*

**Get to the bottom of it.** Underlying an affair are likely hidden concerns about connection, intimacy, trust or feeling valued—on both partner's parts. Or it could be due to your attachment styles. It could be that you used the affair to get a particular need met. To repair the damage of an affair (if you can), look for and address underlying issues.

**Deal with the feelings you have related to these issues—**your partner is not responsible for your feelings. Learn to own your feelings and needs and express them appropriately.

**Get professional help.** Show your commitment by getting outside help to give yourselves the best possible chance for recovery.

**STEPS (IF YOUR PARTNER HAD THE AFFAIR):**

**Let your partner know the impact** on you. Don't hold back. Be angry, be vocal, rage and cry when you need to. Without knowing the full ramifications of what their actions have caused, a partner may have less commitment to doing the work needed.

**See a counselor** if you don't feel safe expressing your feelings directly to your partner. Some can't cope with the distress they've caused, which makes it harder to rebuild. Despite this, and whatever happens with the relationship, you need to process your feelings and heal yourself.

**Expect your partner to be transparent from now on**. Secrecy and denial are damaging—more than ever now. You both need to lay yourselves bare and be open and honest from now on.

**Deal with disturbing images.** Don't let images of your partner with their lover torture you. When they pop into your mind, make them as ridiculous as you can by changing or adding things (pockmarks, a tail, giant noses, an udder, missing teeth). Doing this makes the images lose power. Empower yourself by taking control of them.

**Expect your partner to earn back your trust.** Trust = changed behavior + time. You both need to do the work of re-building. If they are unwilling, you may need to consider ending the relationship—it will never be able to fully recover otherwise.

**Expect your partner to break off all contact with the other party.** If this requires them to change jobs, so be it. If your partner refuses to do this, you may need to consider ending the relationship.

**Rebuild yourself.** An affair rips the rug out from under you and can bring your own foundations down. Look after yourself, rebuild your shattered self-esteem and heal yourself. Some suggestions in the section on Birth Trauma might be helpful for you too.

**Rebuild your relationship if you want to**. When you're ready, explore the circumstances in your lives that led to the affair and each take responsibility for what was within your control. Keep the lines of communication open, or open them for the first time, around all aspects of your relationship, so you can honestly and openly share what you need from each other going forward.

## Addictions

*I've always enjoyed a few drinks after work. I was planning on cutting down once we had the baby, but….*

*I thought having a baby would be a sure reason for my partner to get clean.*

*I suspect my husband has been secretly using porn. I feel betrayed.*

For many parents with an addiction, having a family is a huge incentive to reduce or stop using. For others, the increased and often unexpected stresses that come with parenthood can cause an increased reliance on substances or activities that make them feel better—temporarily anyway.

Addictions have a devastating effect on a relationship, particularly at the vulnerable time of creating a family. Your relationship with your partner is supposed to be a source of comfort, pleasure and strength for both of you, but each time someone turns to an activity or substance to self-medicate, they turn away from their partner.

This prevents you *both* from having feelings of connection, gratitude and appreciation of each other and prevents real intimacy. Worse than this, as far as the addicted partner is concerned, if you stand in the way of their source of gratification, you risk becoming the enemy.

**Intimacy is particularly affected by pornography addiction.** An association can develop between the images of the preferred body types, or positions you're aroused by, and your feelings of pleasure and release. Research shows that due to a natural tendency to become de-sensitized over time, regular porn users may need to progress to more intense images (which are often violent or degrading to women) to get sexually aroused.

In the longer term, the user may have to hold these same images in their head in order to "perform"—maybe one reason that studies have linked habitual porn use with erectile dysfunction. And then who are you actually making love to?

People often rely on addictive substances/activities to cope with stress, but this then increases, rather than decreases, stress. Addictions lead to increased tension in a family, which leads to more stress, which leads to more addiction, which leads to more tension…. This vicious cycle is hard to escape from. Addictions are also linked to increased risk for family violence, which we will talk about next.

You have discovered that having a baby can destabilize the foundations of a relationship. Compulsions and addictions make a relationship even less stable because, for an addict, their most important relationship is with their drug of choice. Everything else comes second. Addiction causes people to be preoccupied, distracted, secretive and defensive. At the time of new parenthood, when you really want to be laying the foundations for a lasting family, addictions just erode them.

**CHECK YOUR COMPASS:**

**Understanding.** Addictions often start as a natural curiosity or desire to experiment. They satisfy a want or a need that we might have at the time—like a boost with drugs, to feel loved through sex or to escape through alcohol.

These initial experiences, over time, evolve into a habit and then into an obsession/compulsion with an activity or an addiction to a substance—resulting in emotional or chemical dependence. Surprisingly, compulsions and addictions have three things in common: they all involve repetitive thinking, they all prevent us from doing other things and they all block true intimacy.

**Reduce stigma.** The ways or means of satisfying a compulsion or addiction may be different: drugs, alcohol, sex, gambling, pornography or over-anything (eating, working, spending, exercising, TV or computer games).

**Some addictions are more severe and destructive** than others, but one of the main purposes they serve is the same for all—the suppression of emotions. Self-medication through compulsions and addictions help to cope with feeling unsure, fearful, angry, bored or generally not OK. And as you have learned so far on this journey, there's plenty of that and more to deal with at this time in your lives.

**Addictions can also be a way of self-medicating** an undiagnosed mental illness such as depression, anxiety or Post Traumatic Stress Disorder—conditions that need to be addressed as early as possible—so they don't get worse over time.

**Parenthood, especially at the beginning, is a state of uncertainty.** A time of experiencing things for the first time, of feeling useless, out of control, incompetent, frustrated, anxious or afraid. If you or our partner haven't learned to tolerate these emotional states, you can be compelled to avoid them by turning to something that makes them go away—at least for the time being.

**Experimenting with drugs, alcohol or sex often begins in teenage years**—a time when you may have struggled with self-esteem and identity issues long before you would have become emotionally mature. Learning to accept and manage your emotions (rather than deny or suppress them) is not something generally taught in childhood.

**Now is the time to learn** that one of the healthiest and most nourishing ways to deal with emotional stress is through personal and relationship growth.

**STEPS:**

**Be honest.** If you get the sense that a habit is turning into something more, stop and ask yourself what the underlying need might be. Are the ways you cope with stress working *for* you and your family, or *against?* Turn this around. Give yourself the chance to find new ways of feeling happy and good about yourself.

**Get professional help**. See your doctor. Underlying anxiety or depression can be treated. Investigate natural therapies, eat well and practice healthy stress relief. Work with a drug, alcohol or gambling counselor to overcome those addiction and a relationship counselor to repair your partnership.

**Enlist your partner's help**. Don't blame your partner for the choices you have made or continue to make. Your partner is not responsible for your behavior and blaming them will just keep you stuck. Make it clear that you're taking responsibility for yourself and that you would appreciate their help. You will probably need to do some relationship repair before this can happen. Share both your struggles and your successes. When you have their cooperation, have discussions about hidden concerns and underlying needs and find mutual ways to get your needs met.

**Learn to tolerate, accept and manage your emotions** and how to manage or express them in appropriate ways. If you can, and you support your partner to do the same, you'll find the feeling of being bonded increases with every struggle. The better you get at navigating your feelings, the more respect and admiration you'll have for yourself and each other. This increases your self-esteem so you can feel good—without the props.

## Abuse

*Since I became pregnant, my partner has started to get rough, he's even pushed me a couple of times.*

*My partner doesn't hit me or anything, but he does put me down and tries to rule my life with our son.*

*This has never happened in our relationship before, but my wife has been exploding and even thrown a few things at me since our daughter's birth.*

Abuse isn't only physical: it can also be mental and emotional as well. Making threats, playing mind games, using manipulation and contemptuous criticism are all forms of abuse. So is name calling, undermining a person's confidence and bullying. Continually attacking, discounting or minimizing someone's experience is also abusive. Defensiveness can be abusive too.

Whether physical, mental, or emotional, abuse is an ugly subject to consider—especially in the same space as parenthood. Sadly however, research tells us that the two go hand-in-hand. Relationship abuse can occur at any stage, but is more common (and more devastating) during pregnancy, especially an unplanned one. At a time when couples really need to pull together, abuse will ruin any chance of building the safety and trust essential for a healthy relationship and a stable family.

Abusive attitudes and behaviors can stem from unacknowledged feelings of stress, jealousy, resentment or panic of being trapped and, combined with a lack of self-control, get extreme. Shame has been particularly linked with rage. Abuse can also be a symptom of a mental health condition such as extreme anxiety or PTSD.

**CHECK YOUR COMPASS:**

**Take a clear-eyed look at your relationship**. You have learned that the balance of power between partners can tip when they start a family. Abuse happens where there is an extreme imbalance of power—where one partner consistently tries to diminish another in order to feel more powerful.

**Ask yourself if this feels familiar**. We are attracted to what we knew "as love" in our family of origin. This unspoken dynamic can play out in adult relationships in the same way that it existed in childhood. And then, if not changed, these dynamics can be passed on to the next generation.

**Look under the hood**. A desire for power can stem from an underlying feeling of powerlessness. Remember that you learned about the concept of the inner child, way back in the "Growing" section. Here strong emotions from childhood are trapped in an adult body According to psychologists, childlike feelings of being unloved or undervalued can trigger regression and acting out. Feelings of abandonment, jealousy or not being loved are often used as justification for what really is a lack of control. It's common for abusers to consider *themselves* the ones who have been wronged. Which it's likely they were as a child—abuse is usually passed on.

**Emotions drive the need for power and control.** An abusive or controlling person has not yet mastered self-regulation and self-soothing. They try to manage their emotions by controlling their environment and their partner instead. Of course, this doesn't work, especially when there are young children involved, so their inner tension continues to build.

**The effects on your relationship.** A solid relationship—and a strong family—rests on the shoulders of two equal and independent individuals who *choose* to be together. Where abuse exists, there is no equality, no independence and little choice.

**The effect on your children.** Children who witness abuse are victims of abuse—even very young children. Before they can communicate through words, babies and small children "read" the people around them through tone of voice, body gestures and facial expressions. This makes them extra sensitive to emotions.

In an abusive relationship there's a constant, underlying sense of tension, anxiety or fear. Children soak this toxicity up like a sponge. They're then more at risk for emotional and behavioral problems, difficulty concentrating and performing at school, low self-esteem and potentially growing up to be just like mom or dad.

**STEPS (IF YOUR PARTNER IS ABUSIVE):**

**Know it's not your fault—or your responsibility.** The only person responsible for your partner is your partner. There may be situations that trigger your partner's negative emotions, but it's their responsibility to manage those emotions and express them in appropriate ways.

**Get help. Immediately.** Especially if things have become physical. After a first incident of physical violence, the risk increases that it will happen again if you don't get help.

**Do *not* stay silent.** Tell your family, a trusted friend, your doctor, nurse, counselor or a domestic violence service. There are resources available. Email or phone for help. In the U.S., there's the National Domestic Violence Hotline <thehotline.org>.

**Build power on the inside.** Do it in stages. First, get strong enough to assertively speak up. If this doesn't change things, gather your resources and start building an independent life for yourself while you decide what's next. If your partner still hasn't changed, get strong enough to think about leaving.

**STEPS (IF YOU ARE ABUSIVE):**

**Be honest with yourself.** Most abusers know at some level they aren't happy with themselves. Honesty takes a great deal of courage. Your family will admire and respect you for it.

**Make the decision for yourself.** As you gain mastery over your reactions, your confidence and self-respect will increase. And, as your confidence and self-respect increase, you'll have more control over yourself. Think about the person you want to be in a year's time and start taking steps and making decisions that reflect that image of you *today*.

**Make the decision for your child.** As a parent, you have a responsibility to build for your child the most secure family they can have. Your family is your child's safety net. If they feel safe at home, it gives them the confidence to go out into the world and be the best they can be.

**Make the decision for your partner.** An imbalance of power creates an unstable relationship that won't last. Love and fear cannot coexist. Be prepared that your partner may have to leave you to feel safe, in order for any chance of relationship repair.

**Know that going deeper comes with many, many more advantages than disadvantages.** Many angry men find that when they let go beyond their anger, other frozen feelings that were trapped underneath finally thaw—the discomfort of disappointment, sadness and hurt and the good ones too: joy, passion, relief, pride and love. Letting go of power-over and control to go deeper might initially cause you anxiety, but it's managing the anxiety that gives you your personal power.

**Get help.** It's hard to change, but it's easier to do with someone who knows the process and can walk through the fire with you. A good counselor will not shame or embarrass you, but respect the courage it takes to seek help. Books, courses and counseling are available for individuals and couples. Anger management programs are good for managing anger but are not enough to change the underlying subversive and embedded abuse or most forms of physical violence. You'll need to go deeper for that.

**Examine your role models**. Did you grow up witnessing abuse in your own family? Parents model for their children how to act in certain situations. Patterns are repeated through generations until someone steps up to change them and break the mold. Be the first person in your family line to build the strong muscles of self-awareness and self-control. As Oprah says, "People do the best they know how, and when they know better, they do better." This is your chance to do better.

**What you learned, you can also *unlearn*.** You can only change your behavior by first becoming aware of it. Through understanding how your behavior evolved through your circumstances, you can see you're your circumstances are different now and why your behavior needs to be different too. You'll need to work with your fight/flight response. Changed behavior over time rebuilds trust.

**Learn to express yourself—safely**. Abuse is an inability to control strong emotional impulses—something you may not have had the opportunity or motivation to learn before having children. You do now. Learn how to comfortably say, "I'm mad," rather than acting it out. Or "I'm sorry." Not just in words, but in loving actions that bring your family close to you and build trust again.

The challenges described in this section can undo a family. If there is any chance of salvaging your relationship, I would like to leave you with this: While the normal stresses and strains of parenthood can push you to the limits of your relationship comfort zone, extreme events, like those explored here, can send you over the edge. But being sent over the edge can also *force* you to learn and change and grow.

Growing and healing go hand-in-hand. When you cut yourself, new skin cells grow across the wound and it is healed. In order to heal your hurts and support your partner in their own healing, regardless of whether you do this together or separately, you can grow through them.

If you aren't able to rebuild your original family, you may be able to use the guidance in this book to eventually create a co-parenting friendship with your child's other parent and a more loving and lasting relationship with your next partner. I wish this for you.

# Goodbye for Now

Now you know all the reasons why parenthood is an adventure into the unknown. You're likely to have become lost at times in the uncharted territory of it all and I hope I have helped you find your way again. You've scaled some peaks, dived to some depths and travelled through some wild terrain. And if you're thinking "it wasn't that hard," then perhaps I have done my Parenthood Tour Guide job well, because maybe it could have been. You've taken baby steps and giant leaps. You've faced some fears, shouldered some tough responsibilities, honored some losses and celebrated many milestones. And hopefully there have also been plenty of times in between where you could just relax and enjoy all the wondrous experiences along the way.

As your *becoming us* journey continues and you're becoming more connected with yourself as a person, more confident as a parent, more bonded as a couple and more resilient as a family, you will find more gentle and joyful fair weather days for you all in the seasons of life to come. And yet I hope you've learned that becoming more "us" is not achieved by avoiding thee changes and challenges in life, but by facing them head on, hand-in-hand, and growing through them.

You might even like to think about doing something to honor yourselves and the work you've both done—and will continue to do. When you get married, or commit to each other as life partners, I think you can only really commit up to the point of becoming parents. This is because it's only after you have become parents that you fully know the life and the future you have committed *to.*

So be proud of yourself and proud of your partner and what you're creating together. And celebrate it! Especially because these days, in our increasingly disconnected world, you're having to swim against the tide to be where you are. Along with the village, we have lost many rituals, but there's one that is still beautifully meaningful. I like the idea of partners having some sort of personal *Becoming Us* blessing or re-commitment ceremony when they have experienced, fully and truly, what this means. If you do have one, send me some pics!

I'd like us to stay in touch. Please visit our website: <becomingusfamily,com>, where you can find resources, including trained Becoming Us Facilitators. If you're a professional who works with expecting or new (or not-so-new) parents, I invite you to consider our

Becoming Us professional development training so you can prepare and support parents in a whole-person, whole-family, whole-community "becoming us" way. You can become a Parenthood Tour Guide yourself.

And please, do me a favor. Start talking about all this stuff. If you're on social media, please look for us and join in the conversations. As you now know, parenthood is both blissful and gritty, awesome and awful, satisfying and stressful *and* everything in between. Some parents share only the good stuff, others only the horror stories. The more we start sharing the *all* of it, the better it is for *all* of us and for parents to come.

You also now know that even just a little preparation can make a big difference. So maybe plant a tiny seed for the expecting parents standing in line in front of you at the grocery store. Maybe tell them that people say you can't prepare for parenthood, but that's *so* not true, there's lots you can do, and see where the conversation takes you. If you found *Becoming Us* helpful for you, maybe mention it to them. You may never know what grows from that, but it might be something beautiful for their family.

And so here we are, finally at the end of our time together. Thank you for letting me into your life and for trusting me to walk by your side and guide you on your way. I'll leave you with these reminders: keep working with the changes instead of against them and where attention goes, energy flows. So, keep loving, learning and growing, cram in as much self-care and couple-care as you can, and you'll all be thriving more than just surviving on your journey ahead.

I'm excited to think of your family's future!

# ACKNOWLEDGEMENTS

I will forever be indebted to my literary agent Jenny Darling and Harper Collins Publishing Australia for the original version of *Becoming Us.* This was the beginning of everything.

A researcher and author is only a researcher and author thanks to those who have researched and authored before her. I am well aware that my work stands on top of some big shoulders. My respectful thanks to those referenced at the end of this book, whose work I have drawn upon here and with my clients. Your wisdom has also saved my own sanity many a time. Particular acknowledgement goes to Sue Johnson and Leslie Greenberg, John and Julie Schwartz Gottman, Philip and Carolyn Pape Cowan, Jay Belsky and John Kelly, Harville Hendrix, Dan Wile, Daniel Siegel, Ellyn Bader and Peter Pearson, Jordan Paul, Margaret Paul, Brene Brown, Susan Campbell and in Australia, Steve and Sharon Biddulph, Robin Grille and Wendy le Blanc.

There have been, and continue to be, many new friends and colleagues along the way, and I am grateful to every one of you. I'm glad this guide has paved the way for us to connect and journey together.

Thank you to Postpartum Support International for the invitation to present *Becoming Us* at your 2014 conference and to everyone that approached me afterwards wanting more. That was the beginning of the next stage for *Becoming Us.* Thank you to Darren Mattock and Sue Hawkins for being there on the rollercoaster journey that's followed.

To Barb Suarez, Diane Speier, Sally Placksin, Kelly Evans, Alyssa Berlin, Carol Peat, Enjonae Anderson, Cheryl Sheriff, Kimberly Bepler, Jessica Cowling, Hillery Lyen-Warren, Michelle Comer, Margaret Welton, Sylvia Mead, Natalie Meade, Tracey Anderson Askew, Mercedes Samudio, Rebecca Wong, Nicole Moore, Brett Darnesh, Theresa Soloma, Rita DiRito and others who took a leap of faith to do our very first online of the Becoming Us Professional Training. I love hearing how you're bringing this vital work alive in your communities and about all the families that are benefitting from this.

Thank you to Denise Beaudoin, former Supervisor of Parenting and Prenatal Education and Carrie West, former Manager of Women's Services at Legacy Hospital in Portland, Oregon, who gave Barb Suarez, our very first graduate of the Becoming Us Facilitator Training, the opportunity to pilot our "Before Baby" class, which was supposed to be for only one year but is now in its third year. And expanded to an "After Baby" class as well.

Thank you Nikki Lively, Erika Lawrence and the team at the Family Institute at Northwestern University in Chicago for conducting research on the Becoming Us "Before Baby" program. I am so grateful to you and excited for the next stage of Becoming Us.

I'm honored that hundreds of professionals have now completed our online or live trainings. I'm excited to think of the thousands of families who will be benefitting from their knowledge well into the future.

Thanks also to CAPPA, the Childbirth and Postpartum Professional Association for making *Becoming Us* mandatory reading for your New Parent Educators and to the many other professional organizations who have this guide on your required or recommended reading list. Your clients will thank you too.

Thank you John Travis, for your knowledge, wisdom, existential challenges, wonderful sense of humor and eagle eyes as applied to this edition of the book. Thank you Jen Dudley, as you continue to see opportunities for *Becoming Us* that aren't yet on my horizon. Thank you Eric Fletcher for your technical expertise and late nights putting it into practice. Thank you Sujeewa Lakmal for your gorgeous cover art.

A book is meaningless without a reader. So thank you! I love hearing how *Becoming Us* is being discovered and used, including couples reading it together in bed at night—with some double underlined or highlighted bits. I'm also delighted to hear how many dads are getting the book to give to their partner. I'm grateful to every single reader for being part of a new pioneering generation of parents who are turning away from the unreasonable and unhealthy way our culture seems to be headed and, instead, towards what you and your family need to thrive.

My biggest gratitude, always and forever, is for my family. To Con, and to Zach, Chloe and Lila. I know this book, and all that has followed, has taken me away from you at times. I hope that it will continue to bring us closer together too. It's been quite a journey for all of us and you each mean more to me than 101,793 words can ever say—thank *you*!

# Bibliography


Arp, D. & C. (1998) *Love Life for Parents: How to Have Kids and a Sex Life Too,* Zondervan Publishing House.

Axness, M. (2012). *Parenting for Peace: Raising the Next Generation of Peacemakers,* Sentient Publications.

Bader, E & Pearson, P. (2001) *Tell Me No Lies, How to Stop Lying to Your Partner—and Yourself—in the 4 stages of Marriage,* Skylight Press

Belsky, J & Kelly, J. (1994). *The Transition to Parenthood: How a First Child Changes a Marriage.* Bantam Doubleday.

Biddulph, S. & Biddulph, S. (1988). *The Making of Love,* Doubleday.

Biddulph, S. (1998). *The Secret of Happy Children,* Bay Books.

Biddulph, S. (2002). *Manhood* (3rd Edition), Finch Publishing Pty Limited.

Brenner, H.G. (2003). *I Know I'm in There Somewhere: A Woman's Guide to Finding her Inner Voice and Living a Life of Authenticity,* Gotham Books.

Brown, B. (2007). *I Thought it was Just Me, Making the Journey from "What Will People Think?" to "I am Enough,"* Gotham Books.

Buckley, S.J. (2007). *Gentle Birth, Gentle Mothering,* Celestial Arts.

Burgess, A. (1997). *Fatherhood Reclaimed, the Making of the Modern Father,* Vermilion.

Buttrose, I. & Adams, P. (2005). *Motherguilt—Australian Women Reveal their True Feelings about Motherhood,* Penguin Books

Callander, M.G. (2012). *Why Dads Leave, Insights and Resources for When Partners Become Parents,* Akasha Publications.

Cameron, J. (2002). *The Artist's Way, A Spiritual Path to Higher Creativity,* Souvenir Press.

Campbell, S. (2015), *The Couple's Journey, Intimacy as a Path to Wholeness,* Kindle edition.

Campbell, S.M. & Grey, J. (2015). *Five-Minute Relationship Repair: Quickly Heal Upsets, Deepen Intimacy, and Use Differences to Strengthen Love,* HJ Kramer/New World Library.

Chamberlain, D (2013). *Windows to the Womb, Revealing the Conscious Baby from Conception to Birth,* North Atlantic Books.

Chapman, G. (2010). *The Five Love Languages*, Northfield Publishing.

Clinton, H.R. (1996). *It Takes a Village and Other Lessons Children Teach Us,* Simon & Schuster.

Cockrell, S., O'Neill, C., & Stone, J. (2007). *Babyproofing Your Marriage—How to Laugh More, Argue Less and Communicate Better as Your Family Grows,* HarperCollins.

Code, D. (2009). *To Raise Happy Kids, Put Your Marriage First,* Crossroad Publishing.

Cornelius, H. & Faire, S. (2006). *Everyone Can Win—Responding to Conflict Constructively* (2nd Edition), Simon & Schuster

Cowan, C.P. & Cowan, P.A., (1992). *When Partners Become Parents: The Big Life Change for Couples,* Basic Books

Di Properzio, J. & Margulis, J. (2008). *The Baby Bonding Book for Dads: Building a Closer Connection with your Baby,* Willow Creek Press

Doidge, N. 2007. *The Brain that Changes Itself,* Penguin.

Engel, B. (2002). *The Emotionally Abusive Relationship: How to Stop Being Abused and How to Stop Abusing,* John Wiley & Sons.

Evans, P. (1992). *The Verbally Abusive Relationship: How to Recognize it and How to Respond,* Adams Media Corporation

Feeney, J.A., Hohaus, L., Noller, P. and Alexander, R.P. (2001). *Becoming Parents: Exploring the Bonds Between Mothers, Fathers and their Infants,* Cambridge University Press.

Fletcher, R. (2011). *The Dad Factor,* Finch Publishing.

Flory, V (2013). *Your Child's Emotional Needs: What they are and how to Meet Them,* Finch Publishing.

Gottman, J.M. & DeClaire, J. (2001). *The Relationship Cure: A Five Step Guide to Strengthening Your Marriage, Family and Friendships,* Three Rivers Press.

Gottman, J.M. & DeClaire, J. (1997). *Raising an Emotionally Intelligent Child,* Simon & Schuster.

Gottman, J.M. & Gottman, J.S. (2007). *And Baby Makes Three: The Six-Step Plan for Preserving Marital Intimacy and Rekindling Romance After Baby Arrives,* Crown Publishers.

Gottman, J.M. & Silver, N. (1999). *The Seven Principles for Making Marriage Work,* Three Rivers Press.

Greenberg, L.S. & Goldman R.N. (2008). *Emotion-Focused Couples Therapy: The Dynamics of Emotion, Love and Power,* American Psychological Association.

Grille, R, (2019), *Inner Child Journeys,* Vox Cordis Press.

Grille, R. (2018). *Parenting for a Peaceful World,* Vox Cordis Press.

Grille, R. (2012). *Heart-to-Heart Parenting,* Vox Cordis Press.

Harley, W.F. (20011). *His Needs, Her Needs: Building an Affair-Proof Marriage,* Revell.

Hendrix, H. (1988). *Getting the Love You Want, A Guide for Couples,* Henry Holt and Company.

Hendrix, H. & Hunt, H.L. (1997). *Giving the Love that Heals: A Guide for Parents,* Atria Books.

Hiatt, J.M. (2006). *ADKAR: A Model for Change in Business, Government and our Community,* Prosci Learning Center Publications.

Johnson, S.M. (1996). *The Practice of Emotionally Focused Marital Therapy,* Brunner.

Johnson, S.M. (2002). *Emotionally Focused Couple Therapy with Trauma Survivors,* The Guilford Press.

Johnson, S.M. (2008). *Hold Me Tight: Seven Conversations for a Lifetime of Love,* Little, Brown and Company.

Jordan, P.L., Stanley, S.M. & Markman, H. J. (2001). *Becoming Parents: How to Strenghten Your Marriage as Your Family Grows,* Jossey-Bass.

Kendall-Tackett, K. (2014). *Handbook of Women, Stress and Trauma,* Routledge.

Kirshenbaum, M. (1997). *Too Good to Leave, Too Bad to Stay—A Step-by-Step Guide to Help You Decide Whether to Stay In or Get Out of Your Relationship,* Plume, New York

Kitzinger, S. (1992). *Ourselves as Mothers: The Universal Experience of Motherhood,* Addison-Wesley Publishing.

Kleiman, K (2019) *Good Moms Have Scary Thoughts: A Healing Guide to the Secret Fears of New Mothers,* Familius.

Kleiman, K. (2000). *The Postpartum Husband: Practical Solutions for living with Postpartum Depression,* Xlibris.

Le Blanc, W. (1999). *Naked Motherhood.* Random House Australia, Sydney

Lerner, H. (2014). *The Dance of Anger: A Woman's Guide to Changing the Patterns of Intimate Relationships,* Willam Morrow.

Levine, A. & Heller, R.S.F. (2010). *Attached: The New Science of Adult Attachment and How It Can Help You Find—and Keep—Love,* Tarcher.

Lynn, V. (2012). *The Mommy Plan: Restoring Your Post-Pregnancy Body Naturally, Using Women's Traditional Wisdom,* Post-Pregnancy Wellness Publishers.

Margulis, J. (2013). *The Business of Baby: What Doctors Don't Tell You, What Corporations Try to Sell You and How to Put Your Pregnancy, Childbirth, and Baby Before Their Bottom Line,* Scribner.

Markman, H.J., Stanley, S.M., and Blumberg S.L. (2001). *Fighting for Your Marriage,* Jossey-Bass.

Martyn, E. (2001). *Babyshock! Your Relationship Survival Guide,* Ebury Press.

Masters, R.A. (2012) *Transformation Through Intimacy: The Journey Toward Awakened Monogamy,* North American Books.

Maushart, S. (2000). *The Mask of Motherhood: How Becoming a Mother Changes Our Lives and Why We Never Talk About It,* Penguin.

Paul J & Paul M (1994). *Do I Have to Give Up Me to be Loved By You?* Hazelden.

Paulson, J.F., Sharnail, D., & Bazemore, M.S. (2010). "Prenatal and postpartum depression in fathers and its association with maternal depression: a meta-analysis," *Journal of the American Medical Association:* 303(19): 1961-1969.

Petre, D. (2000). *Father and Child: Men Talk Honestly About Family Life—In All its Stages,* Pan Macmillan Australia.

Power, J. & von Doussa, H. (2013). *Work, Love, Play: Understanding Resilience in Same-Sex Parented Families: Brief Report,* La Trobe University, Melbourne.

Pudney, W. & Cottrell, J. (1998). *Beginning Fatherhood: A Guide for Expectant Fathers,* Finch.

Ramchandri et. al. quoted in Roberts M & Roberts O 2001, *No Sex Please, We're Parents,* ABC Books, Sydney, p. 190.

Real, T. (2008). *The New Rules of Marriage: What You Need to Know to Make Love Work.* Ballantine Books.

Roberts-Fraser, M. (2001). *No Sex Please, We're Parents: How Your Relationship Can Survive the Children and What to do if it Doesn't,* ABC Books (Australian Broadcasting System).

Rothschild, B. (2000). *The Body Remembers: The Psychophysiology of Trauma and Trauma Treatment,* W. W. Norton & Co.

Sachs, B. (1992). *Things Just Haven't Been the Same: Making the Transition from Marriage into Parenthood,* William Morrow.

Siegel, D.J. & Hartzell, M. (2003). *Parenting from the Inside Out: How a Deeper Self-Understanding Can Help You Raise Children Who Thrive,* Tarcher/Putnam.

Siegel, D.J. & Bryson, T.P. (2011). *The Whole Brain Child: 12 Revolutionary Strategies to Nurture Your Child's Developing Mind,* Delacorte

Solomon, M. & Tatkin, S. (2011). *Love and War in Intimate Relationships: Connection, Disconnection and Mutual Regulation in Couple Therapy,* W.W. Norton & Co.

Speier, D. (2019), *Life After Birth: A Parent's Holistic Guide for Thriving in the Fourth Trimester,* Praeclarus Press.

Tatkin, S (2011). *Wired for Love: How Understanding Your Partner's Brain and Attachment Style can Help You Diffuse Conflict and Build a Secure Relationship,* New Harbinger Publications.

Twomey, T. (2009). *Understanding Postpartum Psychosis: A Temporary Madness,* Praeger Publishing.

Verny, T. (1982). *The Secret Life of the Unborn Child, How You Can Prepare Your Unborn Baby for a Happy, Healthy Life,* Dell Publishing.

Viorst, J. (2010). *Necessary Losses: The Loves, Illusions, Dependencies, and Impossible Expectations That All of Us Have to Give up in Order to Grow,* Simon & Shuster.

Wile, D. (2008). *After the Honeymoon: How Conflict and Improve your Relationship,* Collaborative Couple Therapy Group.

Williams, M. (2018) *Daddy Blues: Postnatal Depression and Fatherhood,* Trigger Publishing.

Wilson, L & Peters, T.W. (2011). *The Greatest Pregnancy Ever: Keys to the MotherBaby Bond,* Lotus Life Press.

Wolf, N. (2002). *Misconceptions,* Vintage.

CPSIA information can be obtained
at www.ICGtesting.com
Printed in the USA
BVHW031242070420
577091BV00001B/59